Learning on Other People's Kids

Becoming a Teach For America Teacher

Learning on Other People's Kids

Becoming a Teach For America Teacher

by

Barbara Torre Veltri

Information Age Publishing, Inc.
Charlotte, North Carolina • www.infoagepub.com

Library of Congress Cataloging-in-Publication Data

Veltri, Barbara Torre.
  Learning on other people's kids : becoming a Teach for America teacher /
by Barbara Torre Veltri.
    p. cm.
  Includes bibliographical references.
    ISBN 978-1-60752-442-7 (paperback) — ISBN 978-1-60752-443-4 (hardcover) —
ISBN 978-1-60752-444-1 (e-book)
    1. First year teachers—In-service training—United States. 2. Teach for
America (Project) 3. Federal aid to education—United States. 4. Children
with social disabilities—Education—United States. I. Title.
    LB2844.1.N4V45 2010
    371.1—dc22

                                                                    2010000951

Photo Credits:
  Front Cover: © Collin Land
  Back Cover: © stevensonphotography.com

Printed in the United States of America

This book is dedicated to the hundreds of Teach For America corps members who shared their lived experiences in Becoming a Teach For America Teacher with me. This book would not have been possible without you.

CONTENTS

PREFACE

In 1994, federal legislation created the Corporation for National Community Service (CNSC), which has come to be known throughout the United States as AmeriCorps. This quasi-public agency funded and continues to financially support nonprofit organizations. Teach For America (TFA) applied for and assumed the role of America's National Teacher Corps. Teach For America's affiliation with AmeriCorps provides ongoing federal funding, through The Higher Education Act of 2008 and The Edward M. Kennedy Serve America Act, signed into law by President Obama in April of 2009 (United States, 2009).

Teach For America projects that by 2010, 10,000 corps members will teach more than 600,000 underserved students, in grades pre-K through high school, in 35 regions across the United States (www.teachforamerica.org).

Teach For America espouses a traditional business model for its organization. *Inc. Magazine* (Anderson, 2003) notes that successful entrepreneurs direct efforts toward "recruiting and training superior personnel (team-building), developing differentiated strategies, instilling a corporate culture, and budget[ing]."

Wendy Kopp, Teach For America's founder and chief executive officer, envisioned this teacher corps over 20 years ago as a Princeton University sociology major. The TFA model recruits, selects, trains, manages, and prepares future TFA leaders from an applicant pool of intelligent, recent college graduates, who, like Ms. Kopp as a college senior, seek postgraduation direction.

Learning on Other People's Kids: Becoming a Teach For America Teacher
pp. xi–xv
Copyright © 2010 by Information Age Publishing

Teach For America provides access to a teaching job with salaries that range from $26,111-$49,000 (depending on the U.S. region), plus medical and dental benefits for a time commitment of 2 years. This appeals to service-oriented college seniors who appreciate a resume-building citation, seek a high-profile social network with opportunities for shared living with peers, desire camaraderie away from home, and want the opportunity to postpone graduate school and/or a career in the private sector.

In 2009, Teach For America recruited members from 471 undergraduate campuses across the country. As *CBS Evening News with Katie Couric* reported on May 18, 2009, "The government is hiring teachers" (Kaplan, 2009). The segment featured recent college graduates who were accepted to teach in districts that contracted with Teach For America. In *Business Week*, Lindsay Gerdes (2007) reported that Teach For America is one of the "best places to launch a career."

> Prestigious public service outfits like the Peace Corps and Teach For America are nonprofits that have a reputation that will look good on a resume. Both organizations offer finite commitments that have traditionally been viewed favorably by graduate program admissions officers and employers. In fact, Teach For America partners with a number of companies that let employees defer employment for two years to work for the nonprofit. (p. 1)

Over the course of 2 decades, Teach For America successfully created its legacy and its brand of TFA teacher, trained by the organization and then supplied annually to school districts (for a fee). Corps members complete "Institute," which is TFA's streamlined version of teacher education training and referred to as "a 5-week crash course in teaching" (Lipka, 2007). Since 1992, the targeted population for TFAers has remained the same: children from lower socioeconomic communities who attend poorly funded urban and rural public schools.

Teach For America operates regional offices around the country. Urban regions include: Atlanta, Baltimore, Bay Area (California), Boston, Charlotte, Chicago, Dallas, Denver, Houston, Jacksonville, Kansas City, Las Vegas, Los Angeles, Miami, Milwaukee, Twin Cities (Minneapolis/ St. Paul), Minnesota, Nashville, New Haven, (Connecticut), Camden and Newark (New Jersey), Philadelphia, Phoenix, St. Louis, Tulsa, and Washington, DC. Rural sites include the Delta (in Arkansas and Mississippi), rural Hawaii, Memphis, New Mexico, Eastern North Carolina, Rio Grande Valley, South Dakota, and South Louisiana.

Each year, the list grows. Teach For America prioritizes expansion and currently operates seven international regions: Teach First Deutschland (Germany), Teach For India, Noored Kooli (Estonia), Enseña Chile, Teach For Lebanon, Teach First (United Kingdom), Iespējamā Misija (Latvia), and Teach For Australia. The Teach For Australia website entices applicants from all degree disciplines to consider teaching as a prelude to a career ladder outside of education. Teach For Australia (n.d.) boasts, "If you can hold 30 kids' attention on a Friday afternoon, you can do anything in business."

Besides the exposure to regions and locales with which Teach For America is affiliated, corps members who complete their 2-year teaching commitment are awarded an AmeriCorps' stipend, worth close to $5,000 per year of service, for use against any past or future educational expense. Corps members receive this financial stipend regardless of grade level/subject matter placement, or personal/family net worth. Often, taxpayer-funded AmeriCorps awards are doubled by prestigious graduate schools. Universities also provide in-state tuition to incoming cohorts of corps members teaching within their region.

Advocates for a complete overhaul of the education school teacher preparation model maintain that a bachelor's degree, mastery of content knowledge, and a school district's "waiver" should bypass unnecessary courses and time requirements for student teaching (Gammill, 2009; Hoff, 2008). Advocates of this quick entrée to the classroom model note that roadblocks to teaching only impede the needs of districts that have historically experienced teacher shortages.

Colleges of education, education policy researchers, and teacher accreditation councils counter with data. Evidence suggests that distinct ways of knowing accompany tacit understanding (Polanyi, 1962), knowing-in-action (Schön, 1983), and the professional knowledge that distinguishes a neophyte from an expert (Berliner, 1986). The skills listed above have long been recognized as the building blocks of understanding in any career path, whether one aspires to become a cosmetologist, farmer, lawyer, or mechanic. Each occupation mandates consistent situated experience or internship under the tutelage of a master in that field to complete the novice practitioner's critical transition to career professional. Should *learning to teach* historically disadvantaged groups of children, while on the job, be viewed differently?

As I wrote this preface in Phoenix, the outdoor thermometer registered 115 degrees. "Scorcher" is a fitting metaphor for the national debate surrounding teacher preparation and teacher quality. Heated court cases (Hausser, 2009; Honawar, 2007) challenge the intent of the "highly qualified" provision of the No Child Left Behind Act (U.S. Congress, 2001) and the inequitable distribution of "intern" teachers in high-poverty classrooms.

The process, particulars, and problematics in *Becoming a Teach For America Teacher* include the socialization of TFA teachers who learn the culture and complexities of schools, site-based realities, and teaching, while on the job, along with the additional responsibilities and expectations of learning the TFA corps culture.

Over the 10-year period, as I came to know of and work with TFA corps members who arrived annually to teach in classrooms of predominately working- and underclass populations, unexamined questions surfaced. While Teach For America appears to be an effective, efficient, and noble pathway to the classroom in the minds of its supporters, and a program worth supporting (Bartiromo, 2006; Koerner, Lynch, & Martin, 2008; Kopp, 2008), much remains obscured from the public, policymakers, corporate sponsors, applicants, and parents of students who are assigned to TFA teachers.

This work, offering a view from the inside-out, began when, as a newly arrived transplant to the Southwest United States which serves as the primary study site, I was assigned to instruct hundreds of TFA corps members over consecutive years. Their narratives, and mine, offer readers a descriptive view of the site-based realities and experiences involved in *Becoming a Teach for America Teacher.*

AUTHOR'S NOTE

This book is divided into three parts. The first examines the process involved in "making" Teach For America's team, the reasons why intelligent, recent college graduates apply, and how the author came to learn about Teach For America from corps members who offered an insider's view over consecutive years. The second part presents the lived experiences of TFA recruits in schools and how the organization socializes Teach For America teachers. The third section presents TFAers views after their corps teaching experiences, analyzes the "master narrative" as it relates to education of poor children, and raises questions for readers, policy makers, and educators.

This study is longitudinal in scope. It examines the process of *Becoming a Teach For America Teacher* over time, from application through completion of the 2-year commitment, as it touches upon nine themes: site-based realities, the culture of the school, the culture of TFA, the content and pedagogy needed to succeed, classroom management, job-related stress, necessary supports, student achievement, and practitioner reflection. Thousands of exemplars provide rare glimpses into the daily lives and routines of those who commit to teach for a finite 2-year period under the auspices of TFA. This work is a collection of temporal narratives and voices, including my own. I have a perspective, as does each person quoted herein. The scenarios, encounters, and realities that I witnessed firsthand are presented in a rich narrative account at the onset of each chapter.

The title, *Learning on Other People's Kids,* comes directly from sources within the data record of multiple TFA corps member participants, and is quoted verbatim. Pseudonyms are used throughout this work to protect the identity of participants. Former Teach For America corps participants are denoted by first names only in parentheses, such as (Rosa).

ACKNOWLEDGMENTS

Support from mentors, colleagues, family, and friends proved invaluable. David C. Berliner's simple reminder, "You have an interesting story to tell, so tell it," and his educational research on the evolution of the novice to expert teacher anchors this work. Likewise, Linda Darling-Hammond, always an e-mail away, offered encouragement, "Stay with it and stay strong." I am grateful for her mentorship and the humility with which she presents her exemplary body of work dedicated to improving teacher quality and educational equity for all children.

This work is the result of my learning from professors who prodded me to ask the questions and write up my years of fieldwork. Nicholas Appleton, Tom Barone, Gene Glass, and Mary Lee Smith provided me with a foundation into research genres that offer platforms for investigating participants' stories. Thank you for guiding me to think beyond the literal and to critically consider aspects of a *master narrative* in education, as well as its influence on the problematics that emerged from the data.

Dr. Ronald Lewis, who coached and advised from his Alexandria (VA) home, often said, "One candle can't light the world; but one candle can challenge the darkness. Be that candle."

I am indebted to John Affeldt, managing attorney of Public Advocates, Inc., a civil rights law firm, who provided invaluable information on the legal implications of the No Child Left Behind (NCLB) legislation that distinguishes between *intern teachers* and those who are "highly qualified."

Larry Krute and James Finger, colleagues at Manhattanville College in New York, noted that alternative pathways to the classroom do exist for

Learning on Other People's Kids: Becoming a Teach For America Teacher
pp. xvii–xviii
Copyright © 2010 by Information Age Publishing

teachers committed to urban, underresourced public schools for a career, and provided information on the college's *Jumpstart* model that combines 6 months of coursework, practicum, and mentoring, prior to placement of career-change teachers into New York City schools. To date, the program boasts an 85% teacher retention rate, over 9 years.

Thank you to my colleagues at Northern Arizona University: Christine Lemley, Ishmael Munene, and Gerald Wood who read drafts of this work and offered invaluable feedback. Dr. Glen Wilson supported this research and retrieved significant documents. Encouragement and generous support was made possible by my department chair, Dr. Sandra Stone, and Dean Daniel Kain, when I presented this research.

I am indebted to countless veteran educators and administrators who coached and taught alongside Teach For America Teachers in high-needs urban schools. I am particularly grateful to Steve Porter, Taylor's mom, Karen Eades, Sandy Humphreys, Lynn, Dr. W., Dr. B., and Dr. G., for sharing your time, talents, experiences, artifacts, stories, documents, and especially, access to district personnel and culture.

This work could not go forward without the editing, proofreading, and transcription services provided by Sharon Button, Annie, Eve Paludan, Cynthia Parker, Helen Torre, and the data and documents procured from Mark Vite, a dedicated career educator, administrator, and special education advocate.

To my parents, and grown children, Scott and Dana, you listened and gathered data to further this project! Your love and support sustain me.

To my teacher education students, thanks for your patience and interest while I was teaching three courses, and preparing this manuscript.

And, finally, I am indebted and so greatly appreciative of the efforts, guidance, and countless hours of face-to-face interviews, phone calls, documents, e-mail messages, and updates provided by the roughly 400 TFA teachers who participated in this study. It was you who encouraged this work, offered perspectives, advice, and access. It was you who entrusted me with telling your collective stories. It was you who believed in me, provided continual personal and professional contact information, offered consent for audiotaped interviews, provided documents that I never expected to receive, and showed up when I asked for support.

I see every face, remember every visit to your classroom, hold your concerns in confidence, and safeguard the photos, thank you cards, notes, family pictures, and personal updates. Your voices are heard and integrated throughout this book, and I thank you.

PART I

BECOMING A TFA CORPS MEMBER

CHAPTER 1

COACHING THE CORPS

A VIEW FROM THE FIELD: ON LOCATION

I secured a "visitor" spot in the faculty parking area of the Jacobson School in South Phoenix's Randolph District. My destination, on that mild January morning, was the classroom of Laurie Brooks, located at the far end of the campus near the junior playground. Dr. Williams, the principal, spotted me walking and, with his voice magnified by a portable sound system, he commanded, "Barbara, get inside! *Now*!"

"What's going on?" I wondered. With my heart racing, I quickened my pace to a jog, even in high-heeled pumps and a business suit. Wide-eyed, I surveyed the unexpected scene ahead: yellow-and-black police tape crisscrossed the school grounds and law enforcement officers surrounded the playground area.

Just minutes earlier, a gun-wielding suspect in a liquor store robbery had jumped the barbed-wire fence encasing the school's perimeter, seeking refuge in the vicinity of the primary playground area. Uninformed of the danger, I served as the perpetrator's lone target by walking into harm's way during a midday lockdown at an inner-city elementary school.

Laurie, my graduate student and first-year Teach For America teacher, was visibly concerned and anxious when I arrived in her classroom. "Are you okay?" she questioned, empathetically. "We all know the code that came through, 'Mr. Locker is in the building.' So, this isn't a drill, right?" she asked rhetorically. "When I signed up for TFA [Teach For America], I

Learning on Other People's Kids: Becoming a Teach For America Teacher
pp. 3–14

never expected this. But, hey, now you're here going through it with the rest of us."

She shook her head, let out a sigh, and comforted a teary-eyed second grader.

THE RESEARCHER'S JOURNEY: SEEING MYSELF IN MY STUDENTS

The principal escorted me to my classroom, handed me a roster with the names of my second graders in the Northeast Bronx, and left me to survey my surroundings, alone. Forty desks were shoved against the radiator. A wall of textbooks rested on the windowsill. I did not yet know the range of challenges that would face me as an untrained "teacher"—I was hired in late August, shortly before school began. I left a banking job on Wall Street a week earlier because I wanted to teach.

I knew that I lacked student teaching experience, as well as pedagogy and education coursework, yet, I took the job anyway, believing that my degree and desire would suffice. My only experience in an elementary classroom had been during my own years as a student and time spent "playing school" with my five younger siblings. I held onto the teacher guidebooks for dear life, assigning workbook pages as both an assessment of students and self—a sort of barometer to assure that the required material was taught.

Although I was enthusiastic, passionate, and determined to make a difference in the lives of my students by arriving early, staying late, and building relationships, I was forever consumed by guilt. I felt that I was masquerading as a trained teacher. At times, I feared that parents and colleagues would soon realize that I was learning how to teach … on *their* kids. I survived with late-night lesson preparation, and I graded papers every evening, all weekend. Then, in the spring of my first year, I began to take courses in pedagogy, methods, and remediation in the content areas of math and literacy. The extra instruction helped to direct me while I was drowning, yet, I was still entirely consumed by my job, in spite of what society considers "teachers' hours." Even though I possessed strong content knowledge and a high GPA, I kept asking myself, "Am I qualified or even effective as an untrained teacher?"

Twenty-eight years later, almost to the exact day, I arrived in Phoenix during the blast-furnace heat of August. I had spent over 18 years as a teacher and teacher educator in New York and Connecticut specializing in preparing career-change adults who desired to enter teaching. Because of my background, I was hired by Arizona State University to teach a graduate-course for beginning teachers. My class was comprised of 20- to 23-year-olds. Some hailed from all over the country and had arrived in the region only a week before me. They trained to be teachers during a five-week summer institute between their college commencement and the beginning of the next (fall) academic year. They were assigned to high-poverty schools and were members of Teach For America.

I had never heard of Teach For America until I met corps members during the fall semester in 1999. I was not aware that emergency-certified teachers were hired in such high numbers by schools in low socioeconomic districts in the metro-Phoenix region and other regions across America. During that first year of exposure to TFA, my work involved teaching bimonthly seminars for 42 beginning Teach For America teachers from three urban districts. The 3-hour instructional sessions, which spanned the entire year, were conducted on-site in one district's governing board conference room. One third of each district's teachers were new hires, and half of them were Teach For America novices.

Over the first few weeks of class, my TFA teachers shared their classroom experiences and their reasons for applying to Teach For America. Since I was new to the Phoenix region, and also began my career in education without education training when I was about their age, I unabashedly expressed an allegiance to the TFAers who were beneath my wing. I saw a rise in their students' self-esteem, which would not have occurred with a continuous stream of substitute teachers. In one corps cohort, 26 members were fluent Spanish speakers, facilitating communication with their students' parents during conferences and during home visits. TFAers wrote wish lists for classroom supplies and spent thousands of dollars of their own money to enrich their students' experiences. TFAers examined the "free and reduced" lunch offerings at their school's cafeteria, exposed health violations (such as expired products and moldy pizza) to the district administration, advocating for healthier foods, and monitored the government's subsidized lunch program's daily menus for an entire year. I observed TFAers building relationships as they coached, cajoled, and encouraged their students with high-fives and incentive gatherings.

And while the presence of TFA seemed preferable to the alternative—a steady stream of substitute teachers—after a few months of observation, I began to notice patterns that illuminated specific and recurrent needs that most of these beginning teachers brought with them to subsequent class sessions. Although Teach For America teachers were working alongside other new teachers in challenging districts, their situation was unique for a number of reasons. In the first cohort I worked with, 99% of TFA beginning teachers were new to both the assigned geographic region *and to teaching*. Second, unlike other beginning teachers whom I taught, the TFAers had undergone specialized training, known as "Corps Training Institute," which served as the only point of reference for almost every

educational theory, practitioner idea, and justification for teacher thinking that found its way into our class discussions and their repertoire of
teaching strategies. Third, TFAers were mostly young, intelligent, recent
graduates; some were alumni from the most competitive 4-year universities, including: Duke, Stanford, Harvard, The University of Michigan,
The University of Pennsylvania, and Cornell. Regardless of one's undergraduate alma mater, the TFA teacher prototype remained constant.
Teach For America wanted high-achievers in academic, leadership, and
professional capacities.

During course seminars for all beginning teachers, I noticed a unique
peer relationship dynamic among TFAers who supported each other by
forming cliques, even when grade-level groups would have been more
effective. Corps members' collective high-intellectual and verbal abilities
did not mask their naiveté and inexperience with school culture or the
other realities that faced teachers who were assigned to poor, urban
schools. During class discussions, I learned that corps members' ideas
were fed through the "TFA grapevine." In other words, if something
worked for one corps member, it was offered as a solution for others.
When problems arose, the group collectively kicked into problem-solving
mode and collaborated to interrupt the issue. Sometimes group support
was appropriate, but in most instances, "rookies were helping rookies."
Action plans were not based on "best practice" research or previous
guided practice with a mentor teacher. I felt concern when I learned that
second-year corps members were routinely mentoring the first-year corps
members. The TFA teachers also noted why the lack of experienced mentors was problematic:

> I was assigned a TFA mentor. She was a second-year corps member who was
> also teaching Special Education. I thought, "Well, she must know what she is
> doing." I listened to her during TFA's Learning Teams. She talked about
> what worked in her classroom. Then at TFA's social gatherings she told me
> that she didn't really know what was going on and I should find someone at
> my school with experience in Special Education. (Sania)

I empathized with my floundering TFA students and continued to
teach early evening classes for beginning teachers. I wondered why some
corps members feigned boredom when I assigned opportunities for practitioner reflection periods, which served to elucidate issues that beginning
teachers experienced. Other TFA students spent too much time discussing pressing events in their own classrooms, which frequently had little
bearing on the academic topic at hand. Moreover, I observed recurring
unprofessional behaviors, from high school pranks, such as throwing
snacks to one another across the room, to sleeping on the conference

tables, sprawled out in front of the group. I thought to myself, "Would this be happening in a graduate business class?"

> Barb, it's Thursday and I'm tired. How long is this class going to be? (Cornelia)

While teaching in the heat of Arizona could exhaust anyone, the TFA Top-10 Beginning Teacher Needs Surveys reflected a deficiency in both training and clinical experience. I was informed that each Teach For America corps member underwent a unique student teaching practicum and teacher training, which differed in length, scope, and field experience from traditionally prepared beginning teachers. The primary difference is that TFAers do not complete the standard 15-week classroom internship, required application, or reflection in essential areas, such as: (a) classroom management; (b) curriculum and pedagogy; (c) time management/stress; (d) accommodating student needs; (e) navigating school culture; (f) legal issues; or (g) planning lessons.

I learned that Teach For America's 5-week Corps Training Institute was held in one of TFA's regional training sites. From Institute, TFA sent corps members to all domestic regions in the United States. My students told me that Institute was systematized, rigorous, and headed by former and current TFAers. Unlike the credentialed beginning teachers in my classes, "Institute" training left corps members without a cooperating teacher or university supervisor "lifeline" to contact when questions arose during their rookie year. Having a "lifeline "is essential in the educational field. The lack of experienced "go-to" educators that Teach For America teachers trusted enough to provide immediate feedback or practitioner-tested solutions was a real concern. My readily-available-teacher-educator self, who was not affiliated with TFA or the district, provided an opening for a barrage of queries, such as this one:

> Can I speak to you privately? I have a question, I need to ask you because you are someone who knows more than other corps members do. I would ask someone on my campus, but I'm only here a month and I get the idea that I'm not supposed to ask questions from non-TFA people, and I don't feel comfortable with my school-site mentor. (Dana)

Corps members were aware of my own entrée into teaching. It became widely known that I held K-12 certification, was approachable, and willing to support any novice TFAer who wanted to tap my base of experience, borrow materials, or request strategies for immediate use with students. The TFA corps members thrived on feedback and suggestions, such as this:

> Barb, that idea you gave me ... it really worked with my kids! (Joe)

When TFAers asked questions related to their own practice in class, I often told stories of my first year teaching to help them see how I, too, struggled with pedagogy and classroom management as an uncertified beginning teacher. However, I learned quickly that what corps members needed, above all, was to know that their discussions and queries would be kept private. Exposing one's difficulties and asking me for help might be construed as going outside TFA's organization. It did not take long for me to realize that the TFAers' spontaneous "appointments" after class or questions via e-mail were occurring with regularity.

In one instance, an athletically built 22-year-old University of Michigan alum helped to transport course materials to my car one evening in exchange for advice on solving some "issues" with his female students who were pushing behavior limits. He clearly felt uncomfortable but was uncertain of the appropriate actions to take to eliminate the problem. He said:

> Barb, I have this group of seventh-grade girls in my English class. They are giving me a hard time. The principal says I'm doing great. She is never around. These girls are always coming into the classroom when I am working and calling out in class. Two of them keep coming up to my desk. What do you suggest I do? I know you said before not to be alone in the room with them. I'm taking that advice. (Michael)

After another class, my student, Marla, who had expected to be placed in a high school setting, instead of the fourth-grade class she was unprepared for, decided that quitting TFA in October was her only option. Providing a pep talk and age-appropriate materials stashed in my closet for a curriculum emergency, I encouraged her to finish what she started. I guided her in completing the school year, but she could not endure her 2-year TFA commitment.

Over the academic year, I noted that these were not isolated instances. With no one to run interference for the TFAers, who found themselves overwhelmed and teaching in high-poverty schools in the region, frustrations surfaced. Similar to my own first-year experiences, the majority of TFAers were surprised by the difficulty of teaching. I noted to myself that teaching in high-poverty communities and teaching without certification were not their only challenges; teaching through TFA presented another set of pressures.

> Last year was a nightmare. I'll admit. I did not reach the 80% achievement gains TFA tells us we are supposed to meet. (Brandon)

The first group of TFA teachers that I instructed insisted that it was not enough for me to hear or read about their teacher landscape during class meetings or assignments. They urged me to visit their classrooms consistently to see for myself the realities to which they referred in our seminar discussions, which often carried over into coffee shop or parking lot meetings. This open invitation from corps members provided me with a *view from the field,* which thickened the collection of my e-mail and journal conversations with the TFA teachers. Later, I decided to use this information to set the stage for each chapter of this book to illustrate examples of our shared experiences. I chronicled my own reflections through field notes about the days spent in TFA classrooms and conversations with mentor teachers and administrators, both within and outside the original study region. My findings led me to suggest to the university's assistant dean that a Teach For America cohort be developed to specifically gear instruction toward TFAers, resulting in a K-8 master's degree in education with teacher certification. My Teach For America teachers spent countless hours preparing lessons to teach the next day and most were juggling professional development courses twice a week during their first year. This tight schedule proved to be both a blessing and a curse, since the learning curve to process the complexities of teaching was steep and time was short. The TFA teachers were bombarded with paperwork from TFA, the district, and their graduate courses.

> I didn't know what anything was about. All of a sudden, TFA was giving me a package of things and then the University was giving me a package of things because we started at the University immediately. I didn't have any time. (Nan)

My conversations with TFAers and their mentors generated questions relating to training, professional development, and support. Some corps members took the initiative to contact TFA's national administration, resulting in visits from Teach For America's New York leadership. Still, TFA novices insisted that I meet with TFA district personnel, so I did during those early years. These meetings expanded access and broadened my view of what the journey to becoming a Teach For America teacher entailed. I was privy to a culture that extended beyond TFA classrooms. This added a personal dimension to my professional relationships with corps members. It became commonplace for me to interact with Teach For America's executive and program directors. I would visit TFA's local offices without prior notice because it was en route to corps members' site schools, and, at one time, TFA's regional offices hosted our weekly university classes. Because of my work, I had an insider's view.

In late August, 2000, one of my university students, a first-year corps member, introduced me to TFA's founder, Wendy Kopp. We spoke briefly during a TFA fund-raising event held at Bank One Ball Park, renamed Chase Field, prior to an Arizona Diamondbacks' game. TFA's executive director invited me to the game and mentioned to Ms. Kopp that I was instructing and supporting corps members as a liaison to both the university and local school districts.

I recall telling Ms. Kopp that TFAers were "trying" but they needed strategies, supplies, and additional support. She thanked me for my efforts on behalf of the corps, but then she responded to my concern in an even tone, explaining that corps members were expected to be proactive in finding what they needed—including help from their on-site school-based mentors.

At the conclusion of the 1999-2000 academic year, I shared concerns from the mentor teachers who worked with TFA, the district administrators who hired TFA, and more importantly, the TFA beginning teachers themselves, with the university administrators. My job description changed from course instructor who met with TFA students weekly, to "the coach of the corps" and TFA/University liaison. This title meant that I would be in TFAers classrooms every day of the week. I had a defined role but no precise format to follow—there was no handbook, course outline, nor curriculum guide for coaching TFA's alternatively certified teachers. Based on the firsthand knowledge and information acquired from TFAers during my first year, I adapted course requirements. I also structured my guidance based on recollections embedded in my psyche, from what I needed to know as an uncertified urban teaching novice decades before. Determined to support the corps members as much as possible, I made myself available to the new cohort before they even set foot in their classrooms. At a meeting held at a second-year corps member's apartment complex, I noticed the faces of TFA newcomers. They sported the now-familiar glazed expression that I noticed on cohort members the year before, which they attributed to the intense TFA Institute Training that the group had recently completed. I learned that their training consisted of 18-plus-hour days that spanned over 5 weeks.

> Training was really intense. Like we were up at 6:00 every morning at the latest, and working until midnight, one o'clock every day. (Curtis)

I met some novice TFA teachers who arrived in their teaching region after a flight or three-day road trip to begin the task of readying their classrooms for students.

> We arrived from TFA training and had to begin teaching the following day. People said, "Don't worry." But, it was a disaster. How could they do that to us? (Gloria)

The sense of nervous anticipation and exhaustion served as a commonality that bonded the new corps with each other. It did not matter if they graduated from Williams or a small mid-western college, novice TFAers who were new to both the region and teaching, did not know what challenge to tackle first. They wondered, "Should I prepare lessons or set up my classroom? Construct bulletin boards or read the district's new teacher handbook? Review each student's cumulative file or set up a management plan?" The new TFA teachers were almost stunned by the overwhelming list of tasks.

> I remember sitting in the middle of my room not knowing where to start because I walked in and all the furniture was literally in a heap in the middle of the room and I had no idea that was going to happen. I thought the first week I could spend figuring out lesson plans and looking at the textbooks and making up things for the walls. (Roberta)

I recognized their need, so I helped them. We worked together on bulletin boards, student assessment files, management plans, and short cuts that encouraged topical curriculum planning by the week. Most were unaware of the extra time necessary for grading papers, homework, and written assignments, in addition to preparation for the next day. Few were confident about creating lessons that accommodated a range of student learners. This proved especially daunting for the majority of corps members assigned to primary, elementary, and special education placements.

I was informed that Teach For America's training and limited clinical summer school involved team teaching experiences, which encouraged corps members to learn the culture of schools and teaching while on the job. However, they were consumed with responsibilities for their own class. I remembered how that felt, and when they requested my time to observe them and offer specific feedback on their practice, I was there. Corps members wanted someone who would listen, make sense of issues related to their students, and offer an action plan. Most balked at the "one-size-fits-all corps member" feedback model that seemed to be a TFA organizational tool, yet, they were not keen on sharing what was not working with their TFA program directors (PDs), who made the rounds visiting several schools in one day with clipboards in hand.

> Barb, this lesson sucked and I suck as a teacher. How can I make this work? (Craig)

For my university work, I met frequently with all the major players: TFA and district administrators, university professors, mentor teachers, colleagues, students, and TFAers. I was questioned by each "stake-holder" as if I had the answers, but, I had questions of my own, and the list grew longer each day. Occasionally, issues were so compelling that I felt obligated by moral conscience to seek answers from my university associate dean, whose contacts within the state department of education, districts, and legal circles, supported my fieldwork.

During on-site observations in hundreds of TFA classrooms, I had opportunities to "take-in" all that TFAers experienced; their struggles kept me immersed in this project. While I did not ever *intend* for TFA to be the focus of my research, shadowing the "insiders" spawned questions that gnawed at me. I wondered who would teach in urban poverty classrooms, if TFAers were not hired, as high-needs districts tended to recruit and rely on TFA teachers.

In my capacity as a teacher-educator working with successive cohorts of TFAers, I observed the day-to-day practices of schooling within corps members' classrooms and provided feedback on their practice. My teacher-as-researcher opportunities deepened my tiered access providing what Cochran-Smith and Lytle (1993) characterize as, "the primary knowledge source for the improvement of practice—namely, classroom phenomena that can be observed" (p. 6).

I also developed what Clandinin and Connelly (2000) describe as "intimacy of relationship" with my participants (p. 78). Depending upon the situation, my assigned duties served to integrate an array of interchangeable roles, from privileged participant and/or participant observer to research instrument. All of the above offer, what Wolcott (2001) describes as, "an ethnographic perspective" to this study.

After years of observations, discussions with corps members, reviews of journals, e-mails, and written reflections, I accumulated a plethora of data. My field notes recorded what narrative researchers, Clandinin and Connelly (2000) term as, "actions, doings, and happenings, the rhythms and cycles, and the narrative threads that are complex and difficult to disentangle" (pp. 78-79). Moreover, as personal conversations and interviews with TFA teachers and site-based staff were chronicled, an understanding of the way that individual TFA teachers experienced their entire first and second year emerged.

Since I was familiar with corps culture to an extent, and privy to TFAers issues and experiences, I developed a base of understanding that few shared. Successive cohorts of corps members suggested that their accounts be the topic of, not only a study, but—eventually, a book. Somehow, I was entrusted with telling the story that integrates hundreds of voices, whose experiences provide a unique vantage point from which readers can learn about the lived realities of Teach For America teachers. This work employs what Clandinin and Connelly (2000) describe as:

four directions in any inquiry: *inward* and *outward*, *backward* and *forward*. By inward, we mean toward the internal conditions, such as feelings, hopes, aesthetic reactions, and moral dispositions. By outward, we mean toward the existential conditions, that is, the environment. By backward and forward, we refer to temporality—past, present, and future. To *experience an experience*—that is, to do research into an experience—is to experience it simultaneously in these four ways and to ask questions pointing each way ... by looking not only to the event but to its past and to its future. (p. 50)

It became my task to weave a tapestry from the narrative threads offered by a larger circle that included, Teach For America alums, corps members, applicants, TFA parents, and administrators who worked with and hired TFA staff, and, do it in such a way that it would (a) inform, (b) invite a wider audience to interact with the text, (c) sequentially chronicle the TFA experience, and d) raise questions. Corps members suggested to me, that a study about their experiences in *Becoming Teach For America Teachers* was interesting and important to the public policy debate that surrounds alternative pathways to teaching in high-poverty urban and rural schools. Many were torn between their desire to do something concrete to fix a system that appeared broken, while reflecting on whether they, as novice TFA teachers, were sufficiently prepared to be teaching in the first place.

Today, 10 years after my initial encounter with my first class of TFA teachers, the archival data continues to grow and includes audio-taped interviews, personal notes, Facebook messages, e-mails, documents, contracts, tax returns, and annual reports.

As I witnessed and experienced aspects of TFAers site-based realities, it did not take long for my teacher educator "antennae" to sense the burning questions that revolved around the construct of the TFA teacher, who looked different at the chalkboard than other beginning teachers. My personal teacher educator "archives" provided a surface understanding of certain aspects of what a TFA affiliation entailed. What I did not know, and came to discover, were answers to five burning questions, that are answered within the chapters of this book:

1. Why do top college graduates apply to Teach For America?
2. How does Teach For America recruit and train its corps?
3. How are recruits socialized into their roles as TFA teachers?
4. How does a TFA teacher learn the complexities of the school, community, and teaching?
5. How do corps members view their work and TFA's mission in poverty schools?

While the voices that offer insight to the questions raised above, are predominantly, those of participants, my narration and questions are also integrated within this work, and best described by Clandinin and Connelly (2000):

> The narrative anthropologist also offers an "I," the "I" that grows out of the ambiguous, shifting participant observation relationships, the "I" who learns by seeing and telling stories along the way, and who writes stories of relationship. There is a temporality and a situatedness to the anthropologist's writing: relationships to the "I" of the inquirer that imply the biases, perspectives, and particular learnings that the inquirer was able to engage in. (p. 9)

CHAPTER 2

WHY BECOME
A TFA TEACHER?

A VIEW FROM THE FIELD: RECRUITING ON CAMPUS

"TEACHFOR solving our nation's greatest injustice," accented in TFA's signature navy blue lettering, announced Teach For America's on-campus visit, as did placards prominently displayed around the Memorial Union, the hub of student activity. I decided to attend the info session on Thursday, October 18th, 2008, at 12:30 PM.

Ryan, currently employed as a program director (PD) with Teach For America, was dressed in a modern cut, navy business suit, sky-blue shirt, sans tie, and black shoes. His dazzling smile captivated his young audience. He was movie-star handsome: dark-eyed, fit, savvy, young, charismatic, clean-shaven, and olive complexioned. His upbeat personality gelled with the 25 undergrads who feasted on a free lunch of pizza and soft drinks. His presentation included slides of his smiling, former fifth graders, whose shades of brown faces were accented by their white uniform shirts. Ryan shared his teaching challenges without dwelling on the details. Instead, he touched the hearts of his audience with a poignant account of how he fulfilled a promise to a student's mother that her son would be successful.

Several statements emblazoned on PowerPoint slides bearing the navy blue TFA logo in the corner, caught my attention. Messages stressed post-

Learning on Other People's Kids: Becoming a Teach For America Teacher
pp. 15–35
Copyright © 2010 by Information Age Publishing

TFA perks. A quote from Yale University's Law School dean encouraged perspective applicants to consider TFA's 2-year commitment, and full beginning teacher salary, prior to applying. One slide noted that prestigious investment banking institutions and companies, such as Google and Morgan Stanley, deferred start dates for new hires that opted to join Teach For America. Another addressed the post-TFA career paths of alums, including a surgeon in California, and policy advisor to former Arizona Governor Janet Napolitano. The focus on postteaching career paths was stressed to the mostly noneducation major audience, then the floor was open for questions.

"Will TFA accept engineering majors?" questioned a confident male in his early twenties.

"Yes to engineering majors!" shouted Ryan.

"I am the first generation to graduate from college, why should I consider TFA?" asked a young Navajo (Diné) woman, seated with her friend.

"Look at the advantages of teaching with TFA and *then* going on to your chosen career path. You will have an insider's view of the issues that need to be addressed," Ryan continued.

"How are we supposed to know how to teach if we haven't had any education courses or student teaching?" challenged a young Latina.

"TFA *will* train you, and you *will* be a teacher!" Ryan countered with a smile.

Ryan concluded his TFA presentation by subtly encouraging the right candidates to apply. He emphasized the generous AmeriCorps stipend that was viewed as a financial perk, and awarded regardless of family income or subject area assignment. The AmeriCorps money would be given in addition to one's beginning teacher salary and benefits. The meeting attendees provided their contact information on clipboards, mindful of TFA's rolling application cut-off dates, competitive selection process, and multitude of regional teaching assignments.

RECRUITMENT, APPLICATION AND SELECTION

Teach For America recruiters arrive on campuses across the country during the fall semester in search of promising senior applicants. In 2007, Teach For America employed more than 130 full-time recruiters (Lipka, 2007). A few years ago, TFA posters, word of mouth, and a dormitory's resident advisor activated TFA's outreach to potential candidates at universities. Recently, however, social networking has taken over. Internet social networks, such as Facebook, Twitter, and My Space, support TFA recruiters who scan online profiles of promising university juniors and seniors, encouraging them to apply, as in the case below:

My daughter never even considered teaching, let alone teaching for 2 years with TFA. She is a political science major and was contacted through her Facebook page. (Mrs. Diamond, telephone conversation)

Teach For America even advertised its organization in high profile women's magazines directed at both college students and their parents (*Vogue*, 2001; *More*, 2005).

I began my senior year of college, as many students do, questioning whether or not I was truly engaged in the path I'd spent four years preparing for. It was in this mindset that a Teach For America magazine ad in *Vogue* positioned near the astrology page caught my eye. Intrigued, I began to research the program. The more I learned about TFA, the more I believed I'd found a perfect fit. (Caroline)

Current corps members and alumni represent TFA's face on campuses and assure reluctant college juniors and seniors that lacking educational course work or teaching experience is not an issue for acceptance into the organization. Nearly 90% of TFA's applicants pursue studies outside the field of education, and many reiterate that they were influenced by the promising message of TFA's recruiters who noted, "Teaching through TFA is a viable option for you."

Yesterday someone from TFA spoke in my psychology class. She had just finished her 2 years in June. She said that graduate schools would accept us and we could defer [attending] until after we finish with TFA. It sounded good. I didn't even think of it [TFA] before she came in, but since I'm applying to graduate school for school counseling, this might be a good thing to consider. Besides, maybe I'm not ready for grad school just yet. (Megan)

Teach For America's Recruitment Guidelines were provided to current corps members and alumni, whose job it was to influence the right candidates to apply to TFA. The 20-page booklet, scripted by the national organization, was followed verbatim, whether TFA's pitch was made in person, through e-mail, or by phone.[1] "You should have this document with you at all times while on campus so that you can give folks answers to the basic questions (application deadlines, number of sites, locations of our summer institutes, etc.). You should refrain from answering more complicated questions, questions you don't know the answer to, and questions that you are just uncomfortable answering" (Teach For America Recruitment Guidelines, n.d.).

Barb, TFA wanted me to recruit at my alma mater. They sent me the script to follow. Take a look. (Gustav)

Each messenger reiterated the promise: Teach For America would place a noneducation major in a public school classroom as the teacher of record, if one applied before the final cut-off date, in mid-February of his or her senior year in college as noted in TFA's Admission Calendar.

My son's girlfriend recapped her phone query in the e-mail below:

> Hey! I just got off the phone with a lady from TFA. She said that they stopped accepting applications in February, but that I can apply in August for the following year. She said that my political science major and GPA (3.75) from [The University of] Maryland were fine and that I didn't need to have education courses on my resume or experience, and that many of their teachers actually never took an education course. (Erica)

College seniors could meet TFA's application deadline in February and be teaching in their own classroom by July! This led me to wonder what the interview and selection process entailed, so I inquired. After applications were received by the national organization, TFA set up interviews at selected campuses across the country, enlisting the help of former and current corps members. Teach For America administrators and human resources directors evaluated potential candidates.

> They did say at the interview that they don't take a certain percent; they don't take a certain number or anything like that. Out of everyone who applies they take everyone that fits. It wasn't competitive. They [TFA interviewers] wanted to stress that at the group interview … we could all be accepted, if we all fit, or none of us, if none of us were really what they were looking for. Which I guess … I respect that.
>
> I think I had a sense, based on researching online and talking to people, of what they [TFA] were looking for. For some people it's hard to figure out what makes a good Teach For America candidate or what makes you successful in the interview. It's not like they [TFA] hand it to you and say, "This is what we want you to be." They just want you to be it. And, you can't really prepare for it. If they want you to act a certain way or have certain characteristics, they don't present them clearly. It's not like they say, "This is what we are looking for."
>
> So, I applied to TFA in August (2008). I tried to answer questions in a way that was appropriate to their [TFA] mission. They had this personal interview and wanted to know how well you handled stress. And I told them that I was a three-sport athlete and I handled stress well. I had my interview in October, was accepted in November, and was assigned to a school and grade level placement shortly afterward. (Arlinda)

> You begin with the application: grades, honors, recommendations, and two essays. Then you have a phone interview. If you make that cut, you are invited to a group in-person interview that's about six hours long. Then the final cuts are made. (Mike)

The interview took place at UNC. The interview for the entire state of North Carolina was at UNC, so other people would have to come to our campus to interview there. It was fairly competitive. The interview process was (scary). It was not just, you know, you walk in nonchalant. I mean, I know several people who did not get in who were on my interview date, who were surprised they didn't get in. They were very good. But I do know they [TFA] are always looking for science and math majors. (Ali)

One thing I'll tell you, most of us who were accepted were young. TFA looked for certain types. You had to be in your early twenties, so you were still with that college mentality. I think it was because they could mold you into what they wanted you to be. (Tony)

It is not easy to make Teach For America's team. Only 11.7% of the 35,178 individuals who applied to TFA were accepted to join the 2009-2011 corps (Shamma, 2009). The process had not changed much over the years, but the candidate pool increased substantially. Even with the addition of six new regions, TFA only accepted 4,100 of its applicants. While 90% of the students of Teach For America corps members are African American, Hispanic, or Native American, and live in high-poverty communities, 70% of the current corps are Caucasian and female (http://www.teachforamerica.org).

Several applicants questioned the criteria for acceptance and rejection. Andres earned a degree in political economics and art from a New York City urban university.

I applied to TFA and had my final interview at the J. P. Morgan Building in Manhattan in January. We were supposed to prepare a lesson. My girlfriend's mother, a veteran teacher, helped me work on it for about five weeks. There were about 15 of us: two guys, me and another Latino. The rest were female. Probably five were non-White. The interviewer was from human resources. She never taught before. The other guy taught for 1 year with TFA and left. I don't think they were really interested in my lesson. They had all of these cases that we had to work out with our groups.

They wanted to see how we'd react and solve problems when issues came up. I began to wonder about what they really wanted. Did they want us to be teachers their way or care about kids? They were pretty strict. I am someone who believes that kids should be treated with kindness, especially male students of color, since I am one. Maybe I was too naive for them, but I figured, I'd get in and teach my way. But I didn't get in. I speak Spanish, French and English. I was born in Colombia. I thought TFA was more about trying to control you. I thought it would help me further my education. But it didn't work out. They gave me information about other alternative teaching programs. (Andres)

Drew, a Rice University grad, was accepted into The London School of Economics and The Peace Corps, but was rejected by TFA. We spoke a month prior to his semester abroad.

I question TFA's acceptance policies. Recruiters said that I was an ideal candidate. But I don't think that TFA's marketing group makes the decisions for hiring. I have traveled to over 50 countries, but somehow the human resource interviewer, who never taught before and was not a TFA alumna, didn't feel that I made the impression that I thought I did. So, I'm not teaching middle school for TFA, which is what I wanted to do. I'm attending The London School of Economics. I know that they [TFA] look for male candidates, but it [the interview] seemed so random and unprofessional. Both of my parents are PhD's and my education was enriched. I just wanted to bring that to the kids. Maybe these two people didn't care for my responses, but we should at least receive a matrix that assesses abilities over personality traits. (Andrew)

Those accepted by TFA had about two weeks to make their final decision and weigh their options. Decisions were met with both concern and elation by parents of applicants who made the cut, as noted below.

I had lunch with two women today in Los Altos, California and one was oozing with excitement. Her daughter, a Georgetown grad, was accepted to TFA [2008-2010 corps]. You would have thought she won the lottery. (E-mail from A. McDonnell)

Dear Dr. Veltri,
We are trying to find information to help support our daughter, concerning accepting a recent offer to become a Teach For America corps member. I do not know how 5 weeks of training before beginning a teaching assignment could be enough to prepare her properly. She has to sign her contract prior to December seventh. She has never taught before, yet already has her assignment to teach math. (Mrs. Diamond)

THE APPLICANTS:
WHY BECOME A TEACH FOR AMERICA TEACHER?

So, I wondered, "What was it about TFA that captured applicants' interests? Why would people like Ali, Drew, Andres, and Mrs. Diamond's daughter apply?" The range of responses, garnered over the years, presents justification regarding one's decision to join the ranks of Teach For America. For the purpose of clarification, participant responses are organized into four categories, which are ranked and presented in the order of their occurrence in the data record.

1. Expediency: Looking for a Quick Entrée Into Teaching

Teach For America provided a quick route into the teaching profession with no extra expense or time spent taking education courses. The possibility of moving from college to the classroom quickly ranked as the overriding reason for applying to Teach For America. Expediency was cited by 95% of the study participants who were not involved in traditional teacher education and did not want to dedicate more schooling or years preparing for their classroom assignment.

> Why TFA? Why not? When I was younger, I always thought about teaching, but I wasn't really sure that it was the right thing for me. And, when I graduated with a degree in psychology and women's studies, the options were not very varied in what I could do, and I tried finding a job and the things that were out there were not appealing to me.
>
> And, then I heard about TFA and I thought, "This is a good way to know if I enjoy teaching, if it is something I could do for the rest of my life, without actually committing to a degree before trying it." To put in the years to get my teaching degree would have meant doing it without knowing [if I would want to continue] and I didn't want to do that. I just wanted to try it. It was something appealing 'cause I didn't have to have more schooling. I could just start right away. (Marta)[2]

Many had not thought about teaching until they heard about TFA from friends and decided to apply.

> I heard about the program from a friend, and my best friend is an education major, so I decided to apply. (Jennifer)

> I decided to become a teacher when I was accepted into the TFA program. I started thinking about being a teacher when I was much younger because I like kids and it seemed like a fun job. (Lyla)

Several respondents indicated that an application was filed just prior to the deadline. Roughly 25% of the respondents admitted flirting with an eleventh hour application to TFA. Some indicated that they pulled all-nighters to get the required paperwork submitted for timely consideration.

> I had been playing around with the idea of teaching and I thought of what I liked to be around—kids; and who were my role models–family and third-grade teacher; so, I decided I wanted to be one through TFA and I remember sending in the application on January 16th (my sister's birthday) to meet the second deadline for TFA. (Max)

Some were intent on being a teacher, but they did not go through a teacher education program. They applied to TFA because it offered a program that could get them into a classroom and provide informational guidance as well.

> When I found out that I was accepted, the next step was really just to decide or to weigh all of my job offers. And, ultimately, I decided that Teach For America was a valuable program that I wanted to be a part of in order to explore education and to get experience teaching because I wasn't in a teacher education program. I really didn't fit the requirements necessary to become a teacher. In terms of figuring out what credentials we needed for the teacher prep program, the student teaching, and all of that stuff, I didn't have that, so I figured if I wanted to go into education, this would really be the only way that I could do it. (Joel)

For others, joining the teaching profession seemed like a logical outcome of "liking kids." Becoming a teacher through TFA also seemed like an acceptable plan for those who felt that tutoring had provided some experience base for teaching.

> I decided [to become a Teacher with TFA] when I realized that I was good at teaching my peers in high school and college. (Brenda)

> I thought about teaching in College. I had no idea what I wanted to do. All I knew was that I loved kids and I loved to learn. I thought teaching might be a good fit and so I applied to TFA. (Heather)

> I began education coursework my sophomore year in college. However, I decided to stop the program and instead pursue a PhD in biology. I wanted to teach at the college level. When I heard about TFA, I knew it was an opportunity for me to combine my love of science and education and my desire to work with children. (Robyn)

2. Pragmatic Considerations: Financial and Personal: A Plan for After Graduation

> It was October of my senior year at Princeton, and I realized I needed a plan. What was I going to do after graduation? (Kopp, 2003a, p. 3).

Along with the organization's founder, 75% of study participants admitted that they, too, applied to Teach For America in preparation for life after college. Pragmatic considerations swayed many corps members toward becoming a teacher through TFA. Coupled with the allure of expediency, these two motivations comprised almost all of the participants' responses. Most graduates needed more than a volunteer stint post college; therefore, financial considerations within a group context surfaced as a significant reason to apply across all cohorts.

Financial Considerations

There were several financial benefits available for one interested in becoming a TFA teacher in addition to a job and benefits. As noted earlier, the AmeriCorps stipend was a draw. The organization's web site advertises a full first-year teacher's salary and health benefits (provided by school districts) as well as what appears to be viewed as a TFA signing bonus, (that does not require payback), in the form of the AmeriCorps stipend. For most applicants, the package was viewed as a tangible incentive that did not involve extra preparation. An opportunity to earn money for the repayment of college loans or graduate school tuition was cited by 80% of study participants as a major reason for their applying to Teach For America. Although the AmeriCorps voucher was viewed as "a draw" for many recent college graduates in their early twenties, it was also sizeable enough to attract those rare individuals who came to TFA having already completed a master's program of study.

> I was going to go back and earn my PhD, but I couldn't afford it. The stipend really helped and was an incentive for me to apply as it helped to pay off some of my college loan. (Tyler)

The AmeriCorps voucher provided extra funds for furthering education. But, I was surprised to learn that select graduate schools promised to double the stipend's yearly face value of roughly $5,000 ($10,000 over a corps member's 2-year commitment), to $20,000, even if one's future field of study was not limited to a graduate degree in education. The doubled stipend incentives were perceived as an "extra signing bonus" to applicants who would receive the award regardless of (a) grade level assigned or (b) personal or family income.

Awardees did not have to submit financial records to qualify.[3] All TFAers received the Americorps stipend and its extra benefits. The post-service funds funneled high numbers of TFA alumni back into university ranks.

> I came from a middle class background and my mom really had to work to afford my college education. I know that when I apply to graduate school for my M.B.A, places like Notre Dame will double my AmeriCorps stipend from teaching with TFA. The nearly $5,000 per year [of the two year commitment] will be $20,000. Let me tell you, that [amount] for graduate school was quite an incentive. I'll be honest with you. That's a major reason why I applied. (Carla)

Why did I join TFA? The stipends for grad school are a major reason why people sign with TFA in the first place. Where else would you get that kind of money to pay back loans for school? Plus, we were getting paid from our districts, so that was a good deal!

I needed the money. I just finished a master's program and had debt from school. (Cece)

That's why I applied to TFA. I'm just being honest with you. (Cornelia)

In the interview they stressed that if you "finished," you'd get the AmeriCorps' money and it would be good for your career and your resume. They also sensed my concern that other teachers who were trained would not be receiving the stipend. (Arlinda)

A Move With Peer Support: TFA's Organizational Umbrella

Some participants cited Teach For America's group prototype as a reason for applying. Yes, they wanted to go into education through an alternative means and desired to give back, yet they also viewed TFA as a safe way to relocate and work among friends they had not met yet. For this group, the decision to apply hinged on the promise of peer support as well as being cloistered under the umbrella of the organization. There was a perceived sense of belonging and safety that came from being part of a larger community in a new location. One respondent said:

I knew that TFA would offer me a group to be with and a way to start in a new area of the country in a short time period. I also knew that I loved kids and was a quick learner. (Sharyn)

In the Meantime: TFA Then Graduate School

The suggestion, advertised on TFA's website, that affiliation with Teach For America would catch the approving eye of corporations and/or graduate schools resonated with those who believed that affiliation with TFA would benefit them professionally. Teach For America looked good on resumes and, combined with all of the factors noted earlier (job deferment with prestige employers; the AmeriCorps stipend for graduate school; and TFA's high standing with Ivy League law and medical schools), some applicants could not pass up the opportunity. Candidates, who voiced this reason for applying, indicated that they planned to complete the two years and then move on to other career choices.

Well, I was thinking about going into medicine, and that's why I chose biology as my major. I took the MCAT and was all ready to go [to medical school] and then 'cause always in the back of my mind I thought "you know, I kind of would like to try teaching." I thought if I don't do it now before I make this. . .decision to enter medical school, it may not happen. Because once I become committed to medicine, and once I get in, that's going to be it. And I just wasn't sure, and so I heard about TFA [Teach For America] through one of my friends, who was an education major, and I figured I'd apply. (Ali)[4]

They felt that teaching poor children was "a good thing to do in the meantime." In fact, many TFAers were not thinking about teaching as much as they were thinking about earning a living, procuring money for graduate school, and relocating to another part of the country for a brief time.

I was so burned out in my senior year, that I needed to take a break before starting grad school. So, I applied to TFA. If I were to say what I'll be doing next fall, I will be applying to graduate school or law school. (Curtis)[5]

You know, there's only one way to get a perfect score on the application for Harvard Medical School or Harvard Law School under the community service category. You can either spend two years in the Peace Corps or two years with TFA, and that's what motivates some of the corps members. (Antonia)

I wondered if the TFAers, who shared honestly with me, expected to learn from their experiences as teachers or whether they were just passing time. They were quite earnest in their career goals, and I appreciated their honesty in admitting that teaching filled a temporary void until they had earned enough hours to transition from life as an undergraduate to one ready to apply to graduate school or advance on a prestigious career path.

Barb, most of us just graduated [from an undergraduate institution] and don't have our "shit" together, so TFA is a good thing to do, where we go in, do our two years, and then buy some time to figure out the rest of our lives. (Maura)

I was an RA (Resident Assistant) at Indiana University and a computer major. I never considered TFA, but had an e-mail flyer that I was asked to post in the dorms. So, I read it and thought to myself, "Maybe this will work for me. I am not really the IT (information technology) type." And, here I am, teaching computers into year six in the same region that I came out to and love teaching. (Bonnie)[6]

I was thinking about teaching, so I tried TFA. (Justine)

Personal State of Affairs: Needing a Change

Other participants admitted that their consideration of becoming a teacher through TFA was, in part, a reaction to their personal state of affairs. Teach For America offered applicants an opportunity for change when personal circumstances—be they familial, relationship-oriented, or financially related—contributed to their reasons for joining the organization.

> I applied to TFA and so did my boyfriend. We thought it would have been great to both be teaching with TFA. But, we broke up during senior year. I was accepted to TFA and he wasn't, which made things awkward. (Amber)

Participants were quick to note that their decision to apply to TFA was intricately tied to timing. They sought options that included expedited relocation, social support, safety, and networking. Participants in this study perceived Teach For America as a personal growth opportunity buffered by membership in an organization that provided an extension of the college community, complete with roommates, social events and former TFA advisors. Many determined that the organization's perceived camaraderie offered opportunities for interaction within a peer group that shared commonalities such as: age, intelligence, academic pedigree, social justice concerns, martial status (single), and leadership.

> I wanted to get out of where I was living for personal reasons (which you know about) and I figured that by joining TFA I might be around others in the same boat who might be in search of a fresh start (relocating to another part of the country) but not doing it alone. (Grace)[7]
>
> I was tired of the business world and my career path. I knew that there was something better out there, so I thought about teaching. I figured that I could do that with TFA and it turned out to be a good idea. (Melanie)[8]
>
> I had to get away from this relationship that I was in and that was one of the reasons why I applied to TFA. (Brittany)
>
> My parents paid for my college, but they told me I was on my own after that and I knew that I wanted to go somewhere else, but not alone, so TFA offered that support system. (Dion)

3. Altruistic Motivation

Two forms of the "mission mentality" emerged as reasons for applying to Teach For America. The first type of motivation emerged in corps members who felt they were giving back to a specific population, to whom they felt indebted, something that they had received. These new TFA teachers came from working-class or even underclass socioeconomic backgrounds and felt compelled to provide services to children whose backgrounds in some ways mirrored their own. Often, this group of TFAers were children of minority parents whose own educational attainment was limited to less than a high school education.

> I came from a working class family background. It was always a struggle for me. I had teachers who cared, supported, encouraged, and directed me. They told me about scholarships. I wanted to give kids that same educational hope. That's why I applied to TFA. (Iris)

> I grew up in an impoverished area in a Hispanic household in Connecticut. My family faced many of the same obstacles Latino families face in communities all over the United States. My parents had very little education, and they don't speak English. I think I felt guilty that somehow I got out. I knew I wanted to give back—and I have never been one to just write a check. A friend told me about TFA and the rest is history.
>
> I have a theory that if you have been raised in the situations that Marta and I were raised, if all you know is the bottom—then you have some type of ingrained sense of guilt and fear. Honestly, I always feel less than my peers. I can be as well read, educated, and ambitious—but I don't feel equal. I believe it stems from not having role models that I could relate to. Anyway, I wanted to give the kids someone who they knew was like them and who made it. I felt it was only fair that they have a chance to relate to me—since I had no one. (Sonia)[9]

The other group consisted of applicants from middle-upper class families who viewed Teach For America like the Peace Corps—as domestic community service. They noted that TFA provided an opportunity, through a 2-year commitment, to serve a domestic population within the borders of the continental United States and rural Hawaii. These applicants saw an opportunity to work with the less fortunate.

> Well, I got an offer from the Peace Corps and I didn't think I would get an offer from TFA. But, when I got accepted I had to sit down and think, "Why do Teach For America versus something like the Peace Corps?" And, what it came down to was I wanted to do two years of service somewhere to really figure out what I wanted to do after (college) … if teaching was what I wanted to do … if I wanted to stay in a nonprofit field … or … if I just wanted to work for ____ consulting and make a lot of money one day. And, TFA seemed like a good fit at that time because, I wanted to stay close enough to home where I could fly home if I needed to, but not be in the middle of Zimbabwe, where that wouldn't be a possibility. I felt that I should do 2 years of service here in the United States because it's as much needed here sometimes, as it is in another country, ironically enough. (Martina)[10]

Both male and female applicants cited that their primary reason for joining the organization was to fulfill a duty to save kids, especially those who were not fortunate to come from a privileged background. Their own personal values related to educational opportunity seemed to parallel the philosophy of TFA Founder, Wendy Kopp (2003a) who noted, "It takes a lot to help children in low-income communities overcome the disadvantages they bring to school" (p. 182).

> My father is a professor and my mother is also a professional. We (my sister and I) had an excellent education, and as a bilingual male, I wanted to give back aspects of what I could offer to kids who didn't have what I had. When TFA recruited at my school, I thought, I could do this. It would be good to do this and then go on to other things. (Mike)[11]

> I never imagined that there were fourth and fifth graders out there who couldn't borrow or carry or regroup as it's now called. (Meg)[12]

Another theme that emerged among the TFA applicants was a strong calling to fulfill a "social mission." These candidates were seeking personal fulfillment as a byproduct of their TFA work.

> Now, I'm using my undergraduate major by empowering my students for social change. (Shelly)[13]

> I was in a career in business. I wasn't getting anything out of it. I knew that if I had a chance to be with kids and teach them, it would make all the difference. I thought that TFA would give me that chance. (Marilyn)[14]

> Last year [in another career path] I was bored, dissatisfied, etc. I knew there had to be something that I could do that was more meaningful for mankind. (Raqy)

4. Lifelong Educational Aspirations

Fewer than 10% of TFA participants ever considered teaching as a career. A small number considered teaching as a field of concentration during their undergraduate program, but they often admitted in private interview sessions that an education major was frowned upon and/or viewed as "limiting" one's career goals by family members and/or peers. These same participants implied that long-term teaching was not supposed to be their outwardly desired career path, yet these same individuals noted that, inwardly, they sincerely aspired to a career in education and applied to TFA to provide that entrée.

> My parents looked at what a teacher earns and dismissed that as any career path that I would be taking long-term. I am the first one in the family to go

to college and my parents have achieved a certain level of financial success. I am committed to kids and wanted to get into teaching, so I applied to TFA. I told them it was only going to be for two years, but I am committed to education in urban settings. (Jared)[15]

I am a teacher for life. Teach For America offered me, a business major, an opportunity to teach and I took it. (Maura)[16]

I wanted to be a teacher from the second grade when my teacher asked what we wanted to be "when we grew up." Still have the drawing I created. (Amara)[17]

Only 5% of corps members admitted to completing any significant field experience, practicum, or internship under the guidance of professional teachers in urban or rural high-poverty schools. A few had taken a course or two as undergraduates and then opted to pursue a different major for their concentration. A handful of new TFAers reported possessing an education minor, but even fewer reported having any experience teaching in a high-needs setting.

In between my sophomore and junior year at Penn, I decided to stay in Philadelphia. Instead of working, I joined AmeriCorps in Philadelphia. That summer, a reading program was conducted in South Philly, right across the street form the MLK [Martin Luther King, Jr.] Projects. I spent 5 weeks of my summer doing that. My boyfriend was in a teacher education program. When I went to observe him, I found that very inspirational, just seeing the kids that were from all over the city come together in a program that was called AMY (Alternative Middle Years). I saw possibilities in education that made me really excited. Then I spent a semester observing in a South Philadelphia high school. (Antonia)[18]

I decided to apply to TFA when I began teaching, tutoring, and being a classroom aide in the Seattle School District for college credit. I fell in love with the kids and saw the importance of a quality education. (Chuck)[19]

POINTS TO CONSIDER:
WHY BECOME A TEACH FOR AMERICA TEACHER?

The time frame between considering teaching and then actually entering the profession through an alternative program is significant to this study for two reasons: (1) Considering the decision "time frame" offers a point of reference from which other data may be presented and analyzed with respect to the effectiveness of teaching after only short-term exposure to schools, culture, and curriculum in high-poverty communities. (2) The statements noted above raise issues that are inherently value-laden, regarding the perceptions surrounding the education of poor children. Is TFA work viewed as some kind of "community service" to work with less privileged youth? And who is creating this spin?

The initial query included two simple but revealing questions: "When did you decide to become a teacher?" and "Why TFA?" When these two questions were posed in survey format, most of the participants indicated that they "thought about teaching" during their senior year of college, or when TFA recruiters arrived on their campuses. In response to the second questions, most survey participants indicated that they believed that TFA would serve their interests. In actuality, more than 85% of participants did not decide to become a career teacher; they were, in fact, thinking of *becoming a TFA teacher*, which entailed a finite time commitment. Corps members who were committed to teaching as a means of educational reform for the long haul, and mentors who worked in schools with kids as career-committed change agents, questioned why recent college graduates interested in other careers would enter the teaching profession in the first place.

> Well, my son, a recent Stanford graduate, loves kids and would be an awesome teacher. But he was honest when he stated, "You just can't go to Stanford and then be a career teacher. There's that expectation that you are supposed to do something really important in the world and teaching is just not it." (Mr. James)

TFA was perceived as an organization that offers a job, benefits, a resume builder, and something to do while planning one's future career. Pragmatic considerations seemed to drive the majority of corps members' decisions to apply, as applicants knew immediately, that TFA condoned a short-term teaching commitment which offered professional, monetary, networking, and personal benefits for the corps members who finished the program. The majority of TFA applicants were schooled in working hard on the task at hand, while setting the stage for tomorrow and their future goals.

Moreover, in the span of about four years, from when I first met TFA teachers to when I transitioned into my full time university work of supporting TFAers on-site in schools, the attention from both the national media and friends in high places, such as politicians and corporate sponsors, heightened the "service" and "achievement" publicity surrounding TFA. This hype resulted in Teach For America appropriating a status symbol and it became identified as community service for poor children.

This reputation was problematic on several levels. Mike Feinberg, an alum of TFA and cofounder of one of TFA's charter school networks stated, "Because of Teach For America's momentum, teaching has become a desirable, sexy profession among our most talented kids in college today" (see Lipka, 2007, p. A31). Recent graduates are entering the field as a trend, but their duration is short-lived, and we need sustainable programs. Matthew Kramer, president of Teach For America noted, "We do not say, you've got to stay in teaching, that's all that matters" (see Lipka, 2007, p. A34). Identifying TFA teaching as transitory may be stating the obvious, but we must investigate the statement that teaching poor children is "sexy and desirable."

One might question federal and state policies that support TFAers as beneficiaries of the AmeriCorps stipend, funded through the Edward M. Kennedy Service America Act of 2009, in the midst of the national economic crisis. Does the notion of service justify paid "volunteers" who receive funds from U.S. government *and* district payrolls? The blur between volunteer service and government employee warrants scrutiny.

Moreover, the panache associated with teaching through TFA appears to result in a widespread "pressure" to comply with the organization's point-of-view regarding the value of participation. The expectation, initiated during the acceptance notification, is extended to prospective TFAers as well as candidates' parents. Teach For America wants everyone on board to protect the mission and the credibility of the organization.

> I was the recipient of phone calls by other TFA parents who were given the job of convincing me that TFA was a good thing for my daughter, Maxine, since it was only two years and all of these benefits were offered. None of which emphasized teaching! (Mrs. Drake, e-mail correspondence)

> They [TFA] are really good. I mean, after I was accepted I received phone calls. One came from Mississippi State. I was really impressed that a TFA alum, from my university, was calling me to encourage me during my decision week. There was definitely pressure to accept. (Arlinda)

Finally, one might consider whether TFA's timetable was a reasonable one, and whether it allowed for the construct of "becoming" a teacher to gel. Imagine thinking about teaching and applying to TFA in February of one's senior year with training commencing in June? How can highly intelligent recent college graduates expect to be adequately prepared and assume full responsibility for a class of students, who require a knowledgeable and professional teacher, two months after graduation from a non-education program?

I also wondered why so many cited that that teaching kids sounds "fun," or "they were playing with the idea" as their reason for applying to TFA, knowing that they would be teaching mostly poor, mostly minority students? Do these comments suggest that teaching is considered "play," or an endeavor that anyone who "tutors peers on campus" is qualified to do? Some of the statements from candidates seem to imply that teaching "poor kids" is considered "a less than" career, or a form of "community service," and not a "serious" profession.

> I feel as though I've really been a teacher throughout my whole life. We are all teachers. I didn't think about becoming an "official" teacher until my senior year in college. (Jake)

And finally, examination is warranted in regard to the question that I kept asking myself, and the corps members whom I interviewed. "Can you become an instant teacher?" Is there a connection between preparation, time frame, and the consequences for kids and corps members in being hired with less than five weeks of summer TFA training?

For many respondents, the notion of "teaching" is viewed as an inherently familiar or generic construct as if the skill to teach is an almost natural trait that could be passed on through DNA and lie dormant until the moment when one decides to activate it. The ill perception that teaching is as innate as breathing appeared so frequently in the data record that it almost warrants its own category for the coding analysis.

I kept asking myself, "Why did so many candidates feel that they had 'always been a teacher?'" When they shared their majors with me: anthropology, biology, women's studies, political science, sociology, and economics, the list did not include pedagogy.

> I've always been a teacher, but I decided to follow it as a profession during my senior year in college. (Jaqui)[20]

The subjects' construct of the "official teacher" inferred a higher level of responsibility and/or accountability; however, the early spring application to an organization like Teach For America, advertises that no prior experience is necessary to assume such an "official" position. I cannot ignore the contradiction.

About half of the respondents describe their initial consideration of teaching (while applying to TFA) as an activity that is non-specialized, or a one-size-fits-all approach to pedagogy. In other words, there was little or no distinction made between "being good at" teaching peers on the college-level and "being good at" teaching first-graders how to read. Coupled with a naiveté, was an underlying assessment that one's skills, as a peer tutor, was equivalent to teaching experience.

But a critical distinction exists between tutoring peers, thinking *of* teaching and thinking *like a teacher*. Thinking *of* a profession is different from the actuality of being immersed or engaged in the specific work of that chosen field. If we substituted a different career path into the TFA formula, could we expect to speak of it in the same manner? Would anyone suggest, for example, that "We are all lawyers, and there is only a slight distinction between being an "official" lawyer and an "assumed" or "natural" lawyer? We never hear that we are born lawyers or doctors, but we always hear that about teaching. Often one seems to be a born educator. For some reason, teaching is assumed to be a natural human act.

There is a sense of totality—a spontaneous, embedded reaction, an all-consuming nature that one acquires when one begins to truly "think like" a professional in a chosen field (Berliner, 1990; Eisner, 1979/1983; Elbaz, 1983). Teaching, not unlike other career paths, is a profession that involves an enculturation process, and true enculturation is not as simple as thinking *of* teaching. Yet, knowing that decisions about joining TFA were often made during the *last semester of college* raises concerns. Barnett Berry's (2001) journal article titled "No shortcuts to preparing good teachers" seems to echo the sentiment of the mentor teacher below.

> Entering teaching through an alternative route that waits until the last minute almost devalues the traditional training, saying that, 'Colleges of Education don't matter and your commitment to the profession is irrelevant.' If you really wanted to be a teacher and if you really went and studied and tried to do the best and wanted to keep on learning, you'd do it! I feel that personally. Not from the kids [TFAers] but from the whole premise of TFA. (Mrs. Lauria, mentor teacher)

PROBLEMATICS AND PERSISTENT QUESTIONS

Applying to Teach For America offers an opportunity for expedient entry into teaching; however, this quick entrée also poses consequences that directly impacts TFAers' own teaching.

Did TFA's intelligent applicants dismiss the in-depth knowledge and experience that their own teachers possessed which encouraged and supported their intellectual curiosity?

Did the applicants really believe the organization's advertisements, which promised they would become TFA teachers and learn the teaching basics during a 5-week summer crash course, which TFA provided?

Did those who applied to TFA earnestly believe that teaching was an inherent genetic trait or did they equate it with a natural ability such as highly developed care giving?

Was it selfish or selfless to attempt teaching before making a real investment in time and preparation to the field?

Were TFA applicants aware upon joining the corps that without adequate training, as noted in the literature, they would be learning to teach on other people's kids?

Did TFAers view getting paid for their learning-on-the-job "internship," that circumvented traditional licensure preparation, as morally acceptable to the kids who they were learning on?

How was it that intelligent applicants believed that entry into teaching through Teach For America would prepare them in 5 weeks for the education profession, when the majority of applicants had been provided with quality certified teachers throughout their own education who were responsible (in part) for their academic success?

Did those who wanted to "try teaching and see how it goes" through TFA, know the group of students with whom they would be working?

Did TFA applicants feel that they could become an *instant teacher* and take shortcuts into the classroom when poor kids were in need of the best teachers from the start? Did TFA corps members consider that in other professions, such as cosmetology, licensure requires a 9-month program of study to be operating legally? Would an unlicensed person with only minimal training legally be allowed to conduct business to the public?

NOTES

1. Teach For America teachers receive both the AmeriCorps stipend and full salary and benefits. Other AmeriCorps recipients that are members of a "volunteer teacher corps" dedicated to teach in urban Catholic Schools are called "Place Corps" members and receive the AmeriCorps education grant and a modest housing voucher, but *are not paid* a beginning teacher salary that TFAers earn, in amounts ranging from $28,000-$44,000, depending on the region of the country assigned. See Welch (2008) reference for study on Place Corps, a Catholic School urban volunteer teacher corps. Note that while some states provide educational vouchers for teachers who teach special education (K-12) or math/science (7-12) and who demonstrate financial need, no stipulation is placed on TFA teachers who receive both salaries and AmeriCorps funds, that are guaranteed through 2014 through The Edward M. Kennedy Service America Act passed by both Houses of Congress and signed into law by President Obama in April, 2009.

2. Marta is currently a lawyer. She completed her 2-year teaching commitment with TFA and entered law school on the West Coast.

3. In Arizona, the Board of Regents provides a grant for math and science teachers who dedicate 5 years of teaching (in Grades 7-12, and/or in special education K-12) to residents who meet criteria including high school or community college grade point average and qualify for federal financial aid. This was not the case with Teach For America teachers who automati-

cally qualify for AmeriCorps' awards, regardless of family income or grade-level assignment.

4. Ali entered the public health field after TFA and earned a master's degree.
5. Curtis is completing law school.
6. Bonnie remains in education and is heading into year 7.
7. Grace continued to teach after her TFA commitment in a charter school in the region.
8. Melanie completed her 2-year TFA commitment, completed her MBA and returned to the business world.
9. Sonia earned a law degree and is practicing law on the West Coast.
10. Martina practices law on the West Coast.
11. Mike is a writer.
12. Meg entered an MBA program at Stanford after her TFA commitment was completed.
13. Shelley works in NYC in journalism.
14. Marilyn completed 3 years of TFA and entered law school.
15. Jared taught for several years and developed his artistic skills into a full-time business.
16. Maura works in a state education department on the East Coast.
17. Amara teaches in the Tucson area after her 2-year TFA commitment.
18. Antonia works with The Gates Foundation on Education issues. She taught in an urban school where she served a 2-year term as a middle school principal in California.
19. Chuck completed his doctorate in educational leadership and is a principal in an urban school district.
20. Jacqui is a director with a tutoring company.

CHAPTER 3

SCHOOL DISTRICTS AND TEACH FOR AMERICA

A VIEW FROM THE FIELD: MENTORS' MEETING

"I've worked alongside several corps members over the last two years; they are dedicated, hard-working, creative, and intelligent. A major plus for our school," commented a fifth-grade teacher. "They are so bright!" gushed a kindergarten mentor.

"They are homesick, overwhelmed, and trying to keep it together as they teach 25 students. They are learning the content as they try to maintain control, and for many, it's a struggle," said a third-grade teacher. "They've never failed at anything before, so this comes as quite a shock to them," a middle-school teacher piped up. [She had three TFA's under her wing on the seventh- and eighth-grade team.] "They're spoiled, wealthy kids from fancy schools who come here and stay for 2 years and leave. The first year they try to figure out what they're doing, and the second year they figure out where they're going," voiced a 20-year veteran.

"You don't even know what you're talking about!" bellowed a male voice from the back of the room. Steve, a second-year TFAer felt obliged to set the record straight. His deeply set gray-blue eyes glared at the group from behind silver-rimmed glasses. He said:

> If certified and trained quality teachers applied for the hundreds of vacant
> positions that go unfilled every year in the most needy districts in the coun-

Learning on Other People's Kids: Becoming a Teach For America Teacher
pp. 37–51

try, there would be no need for Teach For America. These are the facts: TFA corps members come into districts at their own expense; take education courses at their own expense; teach for two consecutive years minimum at their assigned schools, offer their talents to write and procure grants, develop and run after school programs, serve on committees, and handle tough assignments that few, if any candidates with high level math/science backgrounds, apply for. Who else would be in here if TFA teachers weren't? (Steve)

PUBLIC SCHOOL DISTRICTS AND TEACH FOR AMERICA

The success of our program relies on a continuum that begins well before the summer training institute, with the careful selection of candidates who have the clear potential to succeed. Our experience has taught us that whom we select is as important as the training they receive. We have learned that excellent teachers in urban and rural communities are generally those with strong records of leadership, achievement, and personal responsibility. (TFA *Recruitment Manual*, 2004, p. 12)

The Teach For America organization has successfully established a "brand of teacher" and readied a pool of available candidates that are annually supplied to districts (with a finder's fee). Districts perceptions of incoming TFAers are formed by both the organization's reputation and by the perceived track record of former corps members. Teach For America developed a partnership with successive local district administrations. One district administrator boasted a nine-year relationship with Teach For America, virtually guaranteeing that students would have at least one, if not several, Teach For America teachers during their school career. One superintendent lauded the aptitude of the young corps members and spoke highly of TFA teachers whom he perceived as a bonus commodity for his district.

We have one teacher from Yale and two from another ivy-league school. This is good for the district. (Dr. Krauss, superintendent, Malloy District)

A district's relationship with TFA exists prior to, and independent of, corps member selection, hiring, and training. Teach For America values relationships with districts, as noted in the organization's recruitment message to prospective applicants, which emphasizes the collective expectation.

Because we fulfill very pressing needs in the districts we serve, it is critical for corps members to complete the 2 years for which they signed up. Moreover we enjoy strong relationships with school districts, principals, and communities, and those relationships are damaged when we do not fulfill our obligations. (TFA *Recruitment Manual*, 2004, p. 10)

Initially, districts donated nominal amounts from a district's foundation or from Title Two monies to cover the annual finder's fee that ranged from $1,500 for first-time clients (The Denver Public School in 2007), to $5,000 per TFA teacher, for districts who were long-term recipients of TFA teachers (Roosevelt School District in Phoenix, Arizona) (Anchors, 2003; Meyer, 2007). Over several years, however, Teach For America's introductory rate escalated for school districts. As the corps size increased, so did the annual "fees" paid to the national organization, as each region's public school districts entered into multiyear memorandums of understanding with Teach For America.

Teach For America markets its brand—and its brand of teacher. Pools of available candidates are annually supplied to districts (for a fee).

> We are paying TFA about $3,000 per corps member. That's about $90,000 this year. And I'll tell you that some [districts] are just paying outright the $5,000 that the organization asks for (Mr. Carino, principal).

A district's contractual agreement with Teach For America, Inc. is legally binding over several years when signed by a superintendent and TFA's chief executive officer, Wendy Kopp. When superintendents resign their post (as in the case of Denver Public Schools Superintendent Bennett, who serves as the junior U.S. Senator from Colorado), school boards' successors comply with the terms of the multiyear contract and more importantly, the introduction of Teach For America into the district (Figure 3.1; also see Appendix A).

Few district human resource directors opted out of existing contracts with Teach For America. The exception is noted below:

> When I came here [to Lorenz] we still had a few TFA teachers who were in their second year, and so they finished out [their 2-year TFA commitment] based on our contract with TFA. But I didn't hire any other TFA's. I didn't see the value in spending $50,000 per year, for people who don't stay here. In fact, one left after the first year and TFA expected us to pay for her. We had to take that to court.
>
> They [TFA corps members] leave when they finish their two years. It's just not cost effective to pay salaries and benefits to teachers and that "TFA district fee." I was able to get the teachers I needed for our district and save money. (Mr. Corte, human resources director, Lorenz School District, telephone conversation)

Even in tough economic times, districts continue to hold places for and hire TFAers. In one region where the state is experiencing a 2.5 billion dol-

---

MEMORANDUM OF UNDERSTANDING
BETWEEN
THE BOARD OF EDUCATION OF THE CITY OF
AND TEACH FOR AMERICA, INC.
For School Years 2007-8, 2008-9, 2009-10, and 2010-11

The purpose of this Memorandum of Understanding is to memorialize the terms of an agreement between the The Board of Education of the City of ...... ("District") and Teach For America, Inc. for a four-year period beginning with the commencement of the 2007-08 school year.

WHEREAS, the District seeks to recruit qualified new teachers and to equip them with the ongoing support and professional development necessary to ensure that they succeed in the classroom;

WHEREAS, Teach For America has a proven history of successfully recruiting and training high quality teachers who are specifically equipped to positively impact student achievement in under-resourced communities and developing a pipeline of people with the potential to serve as future leaders, exceptional teachers, school principals, staff and community leaders in an array of capacities; and

BOTH PARTIES HEREBY RESOLVE to enter into this Memorandum of Understanding (also referred to as "Agreement") to carry out the goals and activities of the District and Teach For America set out herein.

I.   **Responsibilities of the District:**

A.   <u>Hiring and Placement Process</u>

    1.   Commit to hiring, as provided herein, Teach For America teachers each year of this Memorandum of Understanding. The District, subject to its needs and available resources, hereby commits to hire an incoming corps of at least 50 teachers for the 2007-2008 school year, 50 for the 2008-2009 school year, and 50 for the 2009-2010 school year, and 50 for the 2010-2011 school year with the possibility of increases as determined by District for District growth. This hiring commitment includes the following:

        A.   Teach For America teachers will be hired across the full range of grade levels and subject matters, including non-critical shortage areas. The goal is 25-50 percent elementary and 50-75 percent secondary, including, depending upon District needs and available resources, 20-25 percent Math/Science, 30-35 percent Communication Arts, and 20 percent special education.

        B.   Teach For America teachers will be "clustered" in groups of two or more at individual schools.

Figure 3.1.   School district contract with Teach For America, Inc.

lar budget deficit, Teach For America's finders' fees amount to two million dollars per year, which translates to 4 million dollars over 2 years, as legally binding agreements (see above) specify a multiyear hiring of future cohorts of corps members. What are the long-term economic policy implications of hiring TFAers out-of-field and in noncritical needs assignments?

> I was a teacher in Oakland and was pink-slipped. I scrambled to find a job in a middle school in San Francisco. I found out that TFA teachers were being hired, even when certified staff like myself, who just happened to be a TFA alum, were being cut. So I ask you, why are TFA teachers being hired? This is such a scam. (Antonia)

DISTRICTS AND TFA'S PROTOTYPICAL CORPS MEMBER

Corps members shared that even before they were hired as districts employees, they were presented as a block of Teach For America teachers. That affiliation, I found out, brought with it a sense of pride, duty, competition, camaraderie, loyalty, team spirit, responsibility, and a public persona that manifested in the form of the "prototypical TFA corps member." The image that the Teach For America's corps presented in the Phoenix region appeared to support a brand of "social efficacy." Top college grads were entrusted with carrying out TFA's "mission" in high-needs urban areas for a limited time frame. With the responsibility came perks that seemed, by the participants' admission, to privilege TFAers over their non-TFA teaching counterparts. New corps members arrived in the region as a group who were members of an "elite" organization.

> We were all rubber-stamped: "You're TFA? Come on in!" (Arianna)

Not only did TFAers receive an AmeriCorps Educational Stipend (from the federal government) that non-TFA teachers didn't receive, but, corps members who arrived in the region as a group were aware that school districts paid an extra fee for their services. One applicant noted,

> I asked one of the TFA program directors who interviewed me, and informed me of my acceptance into the organization, "Why would any district pay for us?" I knew I had no teaching experience. She replied, "We're worth it!" Right then, I felt this sinking feeling in my stomach. I would be taking a job away from someone who spent three years training to be a teacher, but TFA charged a fee for me to learn to teach while on the job. I decided to pass on TFA and go back to get my credential to teach. (Angela)

Novice corps members quickly noted how their TFA affiliation offered them privileges as well as extra duties. Rookies realized immediately that they would be treated "differently," which also implied additional responsibility in the district and new community that would be home, for at least 2 years.

Lodging was provided for us when we first got here in a hotel with room-mates. Meals were provided for some of the days. (Jody)

Teach For America's corps members presented an image within in the region. School districts who hired TFA teachers were familiar with the organization's prototypical teachers and relied upon the annual supply of enthusiastic, hard-working corps members who signed on to teach for a minimum of two years. In fact, TFA teachers were hired in blocks, often without an in-person district interview.

I mean I was at Institute [TFA's Training] and I had this cell phone interview with a principal! I was walking and answering her questions and trying to keep an eye on my students. I thought how do you even know anything about me in a five-minute cell call? It was crazy. I don't know what I said, but I never had an interview like that! (Ali)

Study participants questioned how districts could continue to hired Teach For America teachers, knowing full well that TFA first year teachers were new to teaching, had not been trained through university course work, had not yet even completed TFA's training, and would be learning how to teach on their kids.

And, I must have said it three or four times to them! "I have never taught before!" I wasn't going to lie or pretend that I had taught in my lifetime. (Sonia)

I said I would go anywhere, but what did I know? I had no idea. At this point, I had not even been to Institute so … I had no concept. I had no training in teaching. She [the principal] puts me in third grade, which is a benchmark year, one that is a state test grade. Why would she? There were plenty of positions available. She [the principal] puts me in the third grade position because I truly believe that the district administration felt we [as TFA] were totally qualified. But, they knew we were TFA! (Martina)

TFAers shared that decision-making, with regard to each placement in grade level, subject, and school, was determined either by the entering corps members or the regional TFA leaders who were instrumental in allocating novice teachers for partner district schools.

We went to this interview circle. There were six of us and eight or nine prin-cipals, so more principals than [corps] members. And there had to be two of us in each school [per TFA rule]. So, there were principals that weren't going to get TFA's. And, literally, this is what they said to us. 'Well, we've looked at your resumes. We, of course want you. You can ask us questions. You pick where you want to go." But the point is, that *I shouldn't have been the one choosing*! It should have been her choosing and it wasn't. I felt like I had complete control over where I was going and we felt wanted. (Nan)

Districts presented opportunities, usually offered to more experienced Human Resource professionals, to Teach For America's regional directors who acted as liaisons between the first year emergency teacher candidates and the school administration. Executive and program directors (young TFA alums) assumed duties that included screening, interviewing, and placing applicants in grade-level assignments prior to their contact with any school administrator.

This concerned corps members, alums, and mentors who allude to the high number of TFA teachers who are concentrated into a few district schools.

Barb, when I mentioned my feelings earlier about TFA not being assigned to any grade lower than fourth, I meant it. I realized that many of my students have only had TFA teachers for the past four years. That's the drawback of one school supporting TFA to such an extent that most of the staff is TFA. There are major gaps, and my seventh-/eighth-grade kids have been short-changed because of it. (Sara)

At first, I expected that TFA teachers who were hired in schools where student academic needs were high, met certification requirements for the grade-level and subject areas they were placed in, but, many corps members noted that they were "teaching out-of-field" (e.g., an English major teaching eighth-grade math). More serious questions surfaced with respect to the nearly 20% of TFA novices who were assigned to teach special education with no prior training or clinical exposure to special education classrooms.

I was like, "Oh my God! I'm teaching what?" I didn't know anything about Special Education. Now I have 12 students in my classroom and 8 of them are autistic kids. I love them and wouldn't change anything about my placement, but I had to scramble to learn whatever it took to know what I was supposed to do. And then there was the paperwork I was supposed to fill out. (Rhonda)

The issue of personal and legal responsibility/liability surfaced. Teach For America teachers were often unaware of strategies or modifications stipulated by a student's individual educational plan (IEP), what the laws required, or what documentation was necessary.

Imagine learning how to complete the paperwork related to a Special Education placement while you were becoming a first-year TFA teacher? (Mrs. Calderon, mentor teacher)

I know that TFA needs to do some wheeling and dealing with the districts while we are away at training, so I really didn't have an opportunity to decide. Another thing that you should know, Barb, is when you are applying for Teach For America they have this line at the end of the TFA application saying, "Would you ever consider teaching in a special education class?" I remember rereading that thinking, "Would I ever consider it?" Well, yes, I would consider teaching anything, so I checked it. What I did not understand is that if you checked that box, you are definitely placed in [a] special education [classroom]. That is where they want you.

So, if you consider it, you're in! But they [TFA] don't make that clear to you. Last year, those of us who checked the box, well, that was it. And, we didn't know that it was a definite ... that we would be teaching special education. In fact, no one really did. (Sara)

Mark Vite (MEd), special education consultant to a number of charter and public schools in the Phoenix region argues,

How do TFA teachers know how to carry out the plans and make modifications for kids, if they never completed a thorough Special Education internship and coursework? I don't believe that it's even legal to hire TFA novices in Special Education placements.

Novice TFAers were not superstar teachers upon their arrival in the region. They shared that when they were hired, they were under the assumption that districts would provide mentors for them. The news that the budgets for CPT's (Collaborative Peer Teachers) were cut impacted hundreds of TFA teachers who were often told not to worry:

When we walked in to have our meeting with the principal, [in early June] there were two veteran teachers who were supposed to be our mentors for the year. They are teachers who have taught for 20+ years and are assigned to new teachers in general. So, these two people were going to help us throughout the year. I thought that was great, a wonderful idea, you know, guide me, help me through it.

And they said, "Don't worry, you're going to be fine. We'll be here. The first couple of days of school are a breeze. You just do, you know, getting-to-know-you type of things. Don't worry." Well it turned out that when we started, the district cut back funds on these teachers and we were left to fend for ourselves. (Nan)

I learned that many were promised support in their districts, but it did not materialize. TFA expected first-year corps members to be proactive and seek out their own veteran mentor teachers on their campuses to guide them.

They [TFA organization] tell their new teachers, "Don't worry, the district will in-service you; the district will have staff development; the district will help you; your school will help you." And if you remember, your first year of teaching and mine, people are just too busy, even if they have a mentor system in place, those people are teaching school full time. They can't help you like you need them to. So, I think that's really unfair to them. Because I do think that they come expecting help. (Mrs. Schendis, veteran educator)

Teach For America "standouts" were often cited or acknowledged, not only by district administration, but also, by their former students. This contributed additional emotional tension for new TFA teachers, whose confidence level was fragile at the onset of their first year of teaching.

I inherited a class of sixth graders who had presumed that their fifth-grade teacher (who walked on water as far as they were concerned) would be here instead of me. Mr. Dayton was also TFA and left after one year, which is a TFA no-no. But since he left to enter Harvard Medical School, it seems as if all was forgiven. All I heard for the first three months was, "Mr. Dayton did this, why aren't you doing it? He was TFA, too." It made me feel as if I had to compete with him when I was just trying to figure out how I would handle things. TFA corps members seemed to have enough on our plates without competing with each other, but that's how it was and the districts anticipated us coming in and doing what some of our predecessors had done. (Maggie)

Several TFA teachers were not adequately equipped to handle particular placements. When these individuals shared concerns with TFA, they were told to make the best of it. Some who graduated with a degree in English or Business, for example, were placed in elementary school grades. Often, the match was not exactly what either the school administration or the TFA first-year teacher thought it would be. TFA teachers were rarely reassigned unless it was convenient for the school administration.

I witnessed situations where a first-year TFA teacher who had just become comfortable with one grade level was switched to another by the building administrator, who decided that it would be in the best interest of the school for the teacher to be moved. This was a cause of concern for all first-year TFA teachers. Naturally, they hoped their second year would be more familiar in terms of the curriculum, classroom management plan, environment, and collaboration with grade-level team members.

Furthermore, Teach For America alumnae were quick to point out that their professional protection, provided under TFA's partnered arrangement with their district, ended immediately upon the completion of their second year. This seems to suggest an element of convenience because districts routinely tap the continual supply of first-year corps members, who, in some cases, are hired as replacements for (a) their predecessors (former TFA), (b) ambitious TFA teachers who wish to remain in the district, or (c) a district's veteran teachers. While 60% of the corps members leave upon completion of their 2-year teaching commitment, about one third opt to teach in their district for year three, in order to qualify for in-state tuition benefits for law school or other non-education graduate study. Others, who are exceptionally dedicated to their students, district assignment, and school principal, continue teaching into year five and beyond.

But I learned that some districts are not willing to rehire the non-TFA teacher post-TFA service unless all state credentialing standards are met. Districts prefer to hire new-to-the-district TFA teaching novices, as was the case with Deidre.

> I accepted a job offer today at the Desert Sky High School. I honestly cried after my first interview there. It blew me away to see what a world of difference there is in a school like that versus a school like the one I taught in for the last two years with TFA. I struggle in some ways with going there. I know I need experience in a place that is excellent. I am going to miss my kids like crazy, though. Ultimately I guess kids will need me here too, in a different way.
>
> It seems so ironic that The Smithdale District, of all places, is thrilled to hire me, and the Randolph District [in an urban center] couldn't care less about keeping me around. And, while I'm thankful that things have worked out so well, what about my kids? School started there, today; it's July. Brenda and another teacher are the only people left from our Junior High Team, and there are two new TFA's and a vacancy. If I had my way, none of this would have happened and I would still be at Jackson [School] this year. I'm gaining a new perspective and maybe it will help me to better understand the path I need to take in affecting change. Thank you again for writing to the superintendent [Dr. Williams]. Addressing inequity helps me to stay hopeful. (Deidre)

Deidre completed 2 years in her urban school district as a member of TFA. She was an emergency-certified teacher when she began her first year of teaching. She wanted to remain in her urban school, for year three, but was six credits shy of certification, according to her district, which maintained a long-standing partnership with TFA. District personnel informed Deidre that they would bring her back, but only at substitute pay. The superintendent, who happened to be the principal who saved my life when I walked onto his school campus in the middle of a lockdown (as noted in chapter 1), reiterated the substitute offer to me when I approached him about Deidre's position. With a heavy heart, Deidre left her Randolph District job only to be hired as a biology teacher in an affluent district, with a salary increase. After all, she had two years of experience teaching science and thirty master's-level credits in addition to a content-based undergraduate major, all of which earned a "highly quali-fied" teacher label under the No Child Left Behind Law (U.S. Congress, 2001). Not surprisingly, a first-year TFAer was hired to replace her, prior to any clinical experience or training at TFA Institute.

What did districts gain from their partnership with the TFA organiza-tion? Well, for one thing, districts had an available pool of TFA first-year teachers delivered to them, each fall who they could hire under an "intern" teacher certificate.

> Barb, my HR [human resources] director told me to get as many TFAers as I could. Districts are willing to pay for them, because they don't have to go to recruiting fairs or interview college graduates. TFA does all of that for us. Many of the districts have been asking for TFAers to be trained here in the community. But that suggestion has been presented to TFA for years. TFA is a national program and they have their way of doing things. TFA has its own brand and everyone follows and all alums know what the most recent corps went through. Yeah and it's sort of tied to control. But then the dis-tricts "know" what they are getting. (Mr. Carino, principal)

Teach For America's emergency certified teachers earn a first year teacher's salary and benefits, but they are not entitled to pay increases from university course work or district staff development [from most dis-tricts] until they attain certification, usually at the completion of two years of classes at an accredited institution. This saves the district money, as cer-tified beginning teachers are entitled to an incremental pay increase based on how many additional credits are attained during each calendar year. In other districts, TFA receives raises for coursework, as well.

> In my district we were told that TFAers would get pay raises at the end of the year, when they complete master's level courses. Why should they be getting raises for taking master's level courses? Do they know how to teach in the first place? When did they do their student teaching? (Sam, certified teacher)

Significant numbers of TFA participants noted that they agreed to take courses two nights per week from the university, as early as the first semes-ter of their rookie year in the classroom, in order to complete the creden-tialing process within that two-year window, just in case they decide to continue teaching with their district, upon completion of their TFA com-mitment. However, Mr. James Finger, director of Manhattanville College's Jump Start program, an alternative certification model for non-TFA career-change educators who wish to enter the teaching profession in high poverty urban schools, disagrees with pushing novice TFAers into teacher-credentialing courses during their first semester in the classroom.

We are aware of the high learning curve that beginning teachers face in New York City schools where our students are placed. That's why we do not ever recommend that they take courses during the fall semester of their first year of teaching. We frontload them with course work, practicum, and observations, four nights per week over the 5 months, from April–August prior to the start of school. Our alternative pathway to the classroom prepares them to teach and allows them to focus on teaching during their first term with their students. Teach For America's model places additional stressors on its candidates. (in-person interview)

Teach For America spells out how corps members are encouraged to take university classes, network, write grants, and promote the organization's national goals for boosting student achievement. While these added responsibilities place stress and burdens on TFA novices (to be discussed in chapter 8), I learned that the prototypical corps member, manages to juggle it all, and are exactly the kind of teacher for which districts are willing to pay.

Districts' perceptions of incoming TFAers are characterized in part, by the organization's long-standing reputation and the excelling track record of only a select group of successful former corps members. Yet, I learned from participants [as well as through my own on-site observations] that the TFA affiliation means upholding TFA's mandate for a finite time frame. Cohorts of incoming corps members know this, and are expected to advertise a public persona that shows that they are worth their finder's fee. But what is so often hidden from all but their closest circle, are TFAers' feelings of inadequacy.

I spent so much of my first 2 years feeling like a failure. I think that just about anyone TFA recruits will have that persevering attitude. We all tend to be over-achievers and perfectionists and, TFA did not have anything to do with that. (Stacey)

The districts' that simply hire noncertified staff and secure emergency certification for them from the state, perceive TFA teachers as a value-added commodity, as their hiring appears to eliminate "stressors" of school districts when TFA teachers are delivered and hired in blocs. Credentialed educators and site administrators allege that districts are hiring and placing TFA teachers in inappropriate classroom assignments and limiting their professional agency when they advocate policies that contradict districts' hiring decisions. Moreover, concerns abound that districts are holding places for TFA teachers, when trained and credentialed non-TFA applicants are available to teach. The e-mail below was sent to me from a credentialed graduate of a teacher education program.

In May of this year, [2009] I graduated from Valparaiso University with a double major in Elementary Education and Spanish. My search for a job, however, began in March when I visited urban, heavily Hispanic schools in the Atlanta area to scope out possible positions. Although I met with several principals, I connected the most with a principal of a school in the Atlanta Public Schools district. She and I shared the same vision for education and were troubled by the same modern issues in our field. The principal urged me to immediately apply to APS via the online system, because she intended to hire me as soon as one of her teachers officially took educational leave. I eagerly awaited her phone call but unfortunately, that phone call never came. I visited the school later in the spring only to have the dismayed principal tell me that she had just found out she could not hire me because she had to accept a Teach For America graduate forced upon her by the district. Only several weeks earlier, the principal had informed the Human Resources department that she intended to hire me, but HR still required her to accept a TFA grad so that the candidates could all be placed.

I was very upset by the situation and also confused. To me, this seemed as though the cycle of inequality in education was only being perpetuated. I was very disturbed by this realization.

Although I graduated with a 4.0 GPA, double-majored in Spanish, took a course in educating diverse populations, completed hundreds of hours of field experience, and student taught in a diverse elementary school, an uncertified individual was hired in my place at that school. I am extremely committed to my profession, while I overheard TFA teachers at the afore-mentioned school make comments such as, "I have no idea what I want to do with my life" and "I'm going to law school as soon as my two years are up here." (Allison, e-mail message received on August 24, 2009)

POINTS TO CONSIDER: DISTRICT POLICIES AND TEACH FOR AMERICA

Districts partner with Teach For America in order to find teachers for subject areas where they have challenges recruiting qualified applicants to teach. The overt expectation that intelligent, TFA teachers, meet certification requirements for the grade level and subject areas they are placed in, is rarely questioned. But insiders know that this is not the case.

Darling-Hammond (1997b) alleges "Districts sometimes hire less qualified candidates over more qualified ones because they are cheaper, viewed as more complaint, or both" (p. 276). Laczko-Kerr and Berliner's (2002) research examines districts that hire emergency certified or "intern" teachers (including Teach For America teachers). Their study concluded that students taught by beginning credentialed teachers achieved higher reading and math test scores than those taught by non-certified teachers, including TFA teachers.

However, districts accountable for providing highly qualified teachers in all classrooms, seem to rely on the "loophole effect" of the No Child Left Behind Law (2002), quite regularly, in the hiring and placement of TFA teachers. Districts assume that they can hire teachers who are taking courses towards certification during a 3-year window. Most TFAers leave the district within that time frame. This appears problematic, when the systemic policy that brings corps members into impoverished regions in a cyclical stream, and holds credentialed teachers to a different standard, is not questioned.

> My school has hired TFA teachers for the last ten years. Not one remains teaching here and no one stayed beyond three years. Last year, I was assigned all of the English Language Learners and the new TFA teacher was assigned all of the proficient English speakers. My students learn beyond what the test scores (which have always been the highest in the district) call for. I am not on the cover of the newspaper. I am not doing this for publicity. But when I am working twice as hard because the principal notes that the new TFA teacher can't handle non-English speakers and I can, I ask, "Why are they hired and why are districts like mine paying for them?" (Mrs. Taylor, veteran educator)

While one district administrator in this study ended his district's three-year relationship with TFA, most succumb to an embedded structure that appears to be motivated by convenience. What appears to privilege TFA corps members over traditionally prepared candidates who are required to document hours in practicum, attend specialized training, and spend out-of-pocket fees for licensure and job applications?

This chapter demonstrates how unexamined district policies impact non-TFA teaching applicants, credentialed mentor teachers (in-district), corps members, and their students. Wirt and Kirst (1989), discuss the concept of "favored values" that perpetuate particular processes and paradigms, privileging some programs over others. They assert that less attention is drawn to policy impact, because it often takes years to unfold, and can systematically and intentionally exclude concerns with issues that relate to the policy. A superintendent's decision influences action plans that favor "accepted" programs while handicapping examination of other programs, and perspectives. This leads to an implied, and structured exclusion that often results in the silencing of policy detractors. Moreover, a "favored values" distinction encourages a "repeat business" policy with Teach For America over time. This appears to cement a reliance on TFA within a district, even when the superintendent who authorized the arrangement retires or moves to another position.

What are the unexamined consequences of these policies? Is it cost effective to hire TFA teachers annually, or is TFA merely an embedded program? Is it a policy that truly brings in highly qualified teachers into impoverished districts, or one that appears convenient? While a range of ancillary benefits appear to be connected to corps member hiring, from the acquisition of classroom computers to mural supplies procured through grants funded by industrious TFAers, the question posed by Dr. Gene Carter, executive director of the Association of Supervision and Curriculum Development, remains, "But, can they teach?" (2003, p. 1). Many stakeholders question why:

- Districts hire escalating numbers of TFA teachers over multiple years through contractual agreement;
- Districts procure TFA teachers, months in advance of the academic year;
- A set number of teaching positions are held for TFA teachers, privileging them over beginning certified teachers;
- Districts routinely place TFA intern teachers in out-of-field positions (e.g., 20% are placed in special education across several regions) conflicting with the intent of federal IDEA [Individuals With Disabilities Act] 1990 legislation and NCLB [2001] legislation);
- Administrators assign proficient English speakers to TFA teachers in higher numbers than their certified teacher counterparts, which negates reliability of student assessment scores of both TFA and non-TFA teachers;
- Districts incur indirect costs related to supporting and mentoring TFA "intern" teachers; and
- Discrepancies surround the substance of "certified" prospective teacher interviews.

As the exemplars in this chapter note, a district's arrangement with TFA raises questions. It appears that hiring policies tend to be hidden from the public, parents, and policymakers. They were hidden from me, too, until TFA corps members questioned why districts would hire them, even before they attended TFA's Corps Training Institute.

CHAPTER 4

BECOMING A TEACH FOR AMERICA TEACHER

A VIEW FROM THE FIELD: CORPS TRAINING INSTITUTE

What is it like at Institute? You're living in a dorm situation with 1,000 other Teach For America people from all over the country. You share a small, dingy, room with one or two people. You're up at 4:30-5:00 A.M. because you have to share the showers, too. Everyone's got to get ready to go to work. You're bussed on school busses and dropped off where you're going to spend the morning teaching, but you've never taught before. In the afternoon, you're being lectured. In between that, you get a premade sandwich, the same sandwich you'll eat every day for 5 weeks. You get home at 4 P.M., if you're lucky, and have to eat cafeteria food that's like dorm food. You have to eat it because it's free. You don't have any money, so there is no other choice. You don't have a car, so you're stuck on campus. After that, you have meetings until 10:00-11:00 P.M., then plan for the next day. You drag yourself to bed, only to be awakened again in five hours and start all over. There are no weekends, no off days. There is no time where you can just lay in bed. If you're sick, that's too bad. Get up. If you're tired, that's too bad. Get up. If you're homesick, that's too bad. We don't care.

Learning on Other People's Kids: Becoming a Teach For America Teacher
pp. 53–66

We were from all over and didn't know each other. But, this is all you had—
really and truly. What I think made so many people stay or stick with it was
the fact that if "they" were getting through it, "you" should be getting
through it too. And, there was really no time to sit and feel sorry for yourself
or question why this was happening like this. What I think gets you through
Corps Training Institute and gets you to wherever you're supposed to go, is
the fact that it is from 4:30 [A.M.] to 11:30 [P.M.] and you don't really have
very much time to really think about what you're getting yourself into. (Nan)

CORPS TRAINING INSTITUTE

I was surprised to learn that Teach For America's corporate culture training and team-building sessions dominated the attendees' days. Study participants referred to the organization's structured approach. Institute was
not intended to be an interactive or participatory-based learning experience. Teach For America's philosophy and mission statement, "One day
every child will attain an excellent education" was reinforced through
anecdotes, testimonials from TFA alums, supporters, and founder, Wendy
Kopp.

TFA's way of doing things, was *the* way of doing things. (Kevin)

Corps members' accounts centered on TFA's training model that
appeared to adopt a corporate-like framework, which included hiring former corps members to train and mentor recruits. A prescribed plan for all
of the organization's incoming TFA teachers [in each of 35 U.S. regions]
streamlined preparation into an efficient 5 weeks of workshops, team-
building, and team-teaching in summer school that was attended by
mostly poor, minority kids. The 20-something recruits assumed that their
TFA training would prepare them to teach well.

First-year corps member recruits were exposed to the organization's
model of content, pedagogy, and classroom management through a compressed time frame. The heightened involvement of former TFA alumnae, along with high-level corporate and media supporters, resulted in
TFA novices' failure to question (especially publicly) the prescribed program. At Institute, a majority of participants noted that they experienced
a "shift" in how they perceived themselves. Trainees were immersed in the
procedures and aspects of "thinking like a TFA corps member," which
seemed to be prioritized over "thinking like a teacher."

You don't have time to sit and reflect and go, "Do I really want to be getting
up at 4:30 in the morning everyday, and teach a bunch of kids who I don't

have any, you know, connection to because in five weeks I am going to leave them and go somewhere else and start teaching again?" (Maria)

The gelling of the organization's philosophy and the concisely packaged content and pedagogical knowledge which TFA leadership deemed tantamount, was supposed to occur quickly and without challenges from new inductees. This mindset to be internalized by trainees was rarely questioned, even when routine procedures didn't make sense to them.

> You're [as a corps member] so afraid that you have signed up to teach, that you believe in your heart that whatever they're doing must be the way that you are going to be trained. And if you just get up when they tell you, do what they tell you, and go to sleep when they tell you, that you will become a teacher. That in five weeks you will know some sort of secret to teaching that will help you. And, so, you do whatever they say, whatever it is. (Bernadette)

The pressure of learning everything in five weeks contributed to an organizational mandate of a zero-tolerance policy with respect to corps members' attendance and corps members' dedication to the task at hand. A heightened state of "get-readiness" seemed to permeate the atmosphere as the corps culture was instilled.

> During Institute a [corps trainee's] family member died and she was told she couldn't go to the funeral otherwise she'd be kicked out. [It was a] family emergency and TFA told them they were going to kick them out.... They didn't end up doing it, but they still threatened her. (Gwen)

CONTENT AND PEDAGOGY: TFA WORKSHOPS AND THE ROLE OF CORPS MEMBER ADVISORS

TFA training at Institute served as a consistent point of origin for any discussion that transpired over the duration of this study. Subsequent groups of first-year teachers, fresh from Institute, confirmed what those in preceding TFA cohorts had shared. The majority of participants entered Teach For America without clinical or educational methods coursework during their college careers and expected to learn *how to teach* at Institute. They reasoned, "Houston, Phoenix, Atlanta, Philly ... or the other training sites will be the place where we'll learn to teach reading and other elementary grade subjects, manage a classroom, plan lessons, and be prepared for what will lie ahead during our first year of teaching."

The first half of each day was spent in the schools; afternoons and evenings were spent attending the workshops. The late evening was spent in planning and preparation for the next day. Participants stated—emphatically—that during the recruitment process, applicants were assured that instructors were experienced teachers of TFA novices. As trainees, they trusted that those who would be teaching them would be aware of their steep learning curve. Yet, participants admitted that they were not aware that those experiences emanated from their instructors' direct participation at Institute, *as former corps members*, less than two years before. Participants alluded to what could only be defined as the fraternal nature of TFA.

> Everybody is TFA. You literally have the school children teaching the classes. It's amazing! Everyone is young TFA, like they just finished their second year and now they are going off to run the school. And, they don't know what they're doing. They're just trying to look good in the end because they are using this for some sort of boost for their own resume and they don't want any problems and they don't want to hear about any problems either. (Sania)

Every participant confirmed that former TFA corps members played key roles in the organization's training of new recruits. Assuming instructional and supervisory roles, they also taught the majority of workshop sessions at Institute.

> Former TFA corps members were our advisors. They were the *only* ones who were with us. The TFA alums presented information, taught workshops, conducted seminars, and observed us in our school assignments, No one came in from any university or school district ... let's just say that no one outside of TFA provided us with instruction during our 5-week stay in Houston. (Lenore)

> Institute was mostly former TFA's. We were partnered with veteran teachers (non-TFA) at our school sites; however, we touched base with them much less than we did with our TFA ties. I don't remember what they (the vets) were called, but our TFA supervisor was a CMA (corps member advisor) and the TFA "principal" was the SD (school director). (Mike)

I wondered, "What classroom experience reserve were Institute trainers drawing from, if, as TFA alums, their teaching was limited to only two or three years (at best) in one grade level?" What type of modeling or range of teaching strategies were presented to novice corps members if TFA alums were the dominant staff conducting workshops and supporting new-to-the-profession teachers?

> We did have workshops in the afternoon but after dinner, more workshops began. You were to choose two or three workshops from a board in the main room that you thought would benefit your future assignment. You signed up

for one. Workshops ranged from things like thematic units to reading programs to how to teach math with manipulatives. (Ashanti)

Few participants admitted to actually observing expert teacher modeling that they felt comfortable applying in their own practice. Over the years, more TFA teachers mentioned how they may have observed an occasional presenter who was "excellent," but were not provided with the grade-level specialists who really were needed to provide them with focused sessions dedicated to their future teaching assignment. Most commented that they were merely viewing their peers (other recruits) presenting lessons, which "turned out to be a highly competitive thing."

All I ever wanted the entire time was for somebody to just show me what it is to write a lesson plan. (Marta)

One of my workshops was a presentation on how to do a thematic unit for lower-age groups. Also, part of the workshop problem was ... The workshops were beneficial, but once again, there were things that we received in Atlanta that were worthy of being read or worthy of taking the time to go through and really understand. But we didn't have that time. And no one wanted to hear it. (Jacqui)

Moreover, with no prior knowledge of the needs or ability levels of the students in their intended grade level teaching assignments, or the communities in which they would be teaching once they arrived back in their region, trainees didn't know which TFA workshop sessions to select. Many, even when immersed in their own classrooms, admitted to not even knowing which questions to ask of veteran teachers.

I think I had about 30 minutes of modeling (from someone who was *not* TFA) and that was it. (Antonia)

CLINICAL EXPERIENCES: TEAM TEACHING DURING SUMMER SCHOOL

Corps Training Institute participants described their experiences as trainees when they were bussed from the dorms at the university to several site locations in the Atlanta, Houston, New York, Philadelphia, and/or greater Phoenix Public School system. Teach For America's intensive summer training was conducted at six Institute campuses in conjunction with local school districts over the years: Temple University (The School District of Philadelphia), California State University–Long Beach (the Los Angeles Unified School District), St. John's University (New York City Department of Education), Georgia Institute of Technology (the Atlanta Public Schools), and Arizona State University (for select school districts in the Greater Phoenix region).

> And it's summer school. So, here we were overdressed, going into these neighborhoods where the kids were barely dressed. How odd did we look? We had no idea what we were doing. We couldn't even connect to parents because we looked like.... They must have thought we were dumb. You know, what are you doing wearing nylons in the middle of the summer in Houston? They [TFA] put us in a bad position to begin with. We looked like little kids trying to play dress up. Really, we looked like we were out of our element. (Nan)

I wondered how these recent college graduates were team teaching with others whom they had just met. I asked, "How did you know what to do with the other new teachers who were teaching the same grade?" "Did anybody model for you or evaluate you?" I inquired, "Who guided or coached you?"

> We had one ... a person that's called a CMA (corps member advisor) and that person, her name is Jane for us. But, she is not just in charge of the three of us. She is in charge of, I think, 20 of us ... 20, 25. And oh, a CMA is just a person who taught as a TFA teacher for 2 years. So, we [now that we finished our second year] are officially CMA material. We can apply for that position now! Can you believe it? (Jason)

> Did I tell you that Wanda was working as a CMA in Philly? They are paying her $5,000 to work at Institute and since she is in grad school, it was a good deal for her. (Denise)

> [The CMA's at Institute] they go through and conference with us about what we [first year recruits] are doing. They observe us. They look at our lesson plans. They comment. We revise, based on what they've written. They observe us in the classroom once a week, I believe. I was observed once a week, I was observed four times in 4 weeks, I believe. (Paolo)

> We had a veteran person [a teacher from the Atlanta public school district] who was kind of our contact. She came in and observed us, I believe once or twice, and offered us very minimal feedback ... basically saying, "Everything looks great." (Ernesto)

> Did you say that you were from Phoenix? Well my Corps Member Advisor was from Phoenix. I mean that's where she taught seventh and eighth grade. But what does teaching there, have to do with me teaching in Philly? I want to learn from a teacher who spent time in my school and knows my kids and this community. Don't waste my time with the TFA CMA! (Claudio)

Participants commented that during their teaching summer school with students in one of the partner public schools, fellow TFA novice team members were always available to take over a class, share the workload and/or assume management strategies.

> I had fifth graders and I team taught with four other people. We were all first-year people, fresh out of college. (Antonia)

> There were three of us in one classroom, so we team taught 20 kids or so. (Gwen)

I was surprised to learn that TFA's "team teaching" approach at Institute served as the *only* experience for the novice corps members who would then assume responsibility for their own classes in public school classrooms, alone. Inductees were learning to teach alongside other novices. This generated other concerns. While many were required to observe roughly 30 hours of teaching upon acceptance into TFA and read articles and educational manuals for background knowledge, corps members who were still completing their senior year in college prior to arriving at TFA training, did not really find that "go-to teacher" to ask questions or debrief with, prior to their shared classroom teaching duties with other TFA novices.

> We each had a whole different idea about why we want to teach and who we are and then we're pushed together in this very stressful situation and we are forced to teach in the same classroom, when all we wanted was to have our own classroom. We all had ideas about how we wanted to decorate, how we wanted to run things, how we wanted to discipline and we wanted to try those out, but you have three people teaching the same children all day long. So, you had to agree on things and it was hard to agree. Because, you know, you just moved across the country and went to Texas to do something you really believe in. You don't want to compromise with the other person. You want to do it your way, the way you think is right and it was hard and we had a lot of arguments. (Monica)

The team teaching approach, which may have been an opportunity to ease new applicants into a teaching scenario, actually presented a false sense of security, which hit the novice teachers head-on upon their arrival in the district.

> We never really had to handle our own class for one entire day, let alone weeks on end, which is what happens when you begin to teach your own class. It was like an unreal situation. (Josh)

> My roommate was assigned a different school, but when she showed up there were no kids. They didn't have enough kids. So, she and a bunch of

other people were not working for a whole week. They didn't have a school to go to. They stayed at the dorm or wherever and went to info sessions and stuff, but they weren't working in a school for a week because they didn't have enough students for them! So, they [district personnel] had to find kids. I don't know where they went to get them, but they did get kids to come in. And then she only had ... I think for the three of them there was only a class of like eight or nine. (Marta)

Participants contrasted Institute's summer school team teaching with their district assignments and noted that, in their "real assignment," they experienced higher class sizes, a fuller load of preparation and management, and a more demanding set of classroom expectations (paperwork, report cards, assessment) than they had faced in their TFA training.

I had 12 kids, all boys, ELL (English Language Learners) at Institute. And then I went to eighth grade and had a class of 37. We now have [in my full-time assignment] around 400 eighth graders and we split them into two teams: 8-1 and 8-2. I have around 200; my coteacher has 200 students. (Ali)

The on-site field experience set up by Teach For America's organization partnering with public schools during the summer was designed to provide TFA trainees with the opportunity to learn and practice how to teach. However, the majority of TFA teachers with whom I worked, stated that their CTI experience presented a skewed version of what teaching one's own students would be like, as noted below.

I had to teach my lesson and then observe three other TFAs teach their lesson. We gave each other feedback, which was OK. But, we were pretty new at teaching and what we thought was a well-developed lesson had some holes to it. (Ernesto)

Many did not feel prepared to translate the Institute experience in form or lived reality to what they encountered when situated in their own classrooms in their assigned region.

So we had this kid crying on the first day. They're pre-K, 4- and 5-year-olds. And, here we are. We are supposed to be professional. We are supposed to be, you know, knowledgeable about what we are doing. And, all you want is for somebody to show you what you are supposed to be doing. (Janelle)

Did corps members benefit from training that was compressed through intense modules? Was 5 weeks at Institute adequate time for information presented to them at "light speed" to be successfully integrated and available for immediate application? Did the team teaching and lesson planning give TFA interns the tools needed to begin their first year of teaching? Would Institute's "class size" (about half that experienced in the field) present a realistic barometer from which to gauge one's beginning practice? For many TFA corps members, the intense format of Institute's training that coupled workshop sessions and a field experience (in a communal environment) provided a less-than-optimal learning condition. In many ways, it cushioned the reality of what corps members would truly encounter when they began teaching in their district assignment and contributed to levels of heightened stress. Was this the best environment for new teachers to absorb, transfer, and apply information for future practice, especially when guided by a high percentage of second-year TFAers and TFA alumnae? Was this the best entrée into a beginning teacher's socialization process? It appeared that TFA's systematic training model, which seemed functional on paper, was not so in practice.

Learning from the corps members themselves about their experiences at Institute, provided me with some answers to my questions. I began to see the relationship between Teach For America's brand of teacher training and TFAers' responses to The Beginning Teachers Top Ten Needs Assessment Survey completed (anonymously) by cohorts of TFA teachers over the years. There appeared to be a connection with one's level of preparation at Corps Training Institute, and the needs of TFA practitioners that differed from non-TFA teachers who were also teaching in high-needs classrooms.

> All of my reading, and even the 6-week summer Institute, did little to prepare me for the reality of the 172 students I would service in my first year teaching. I'd read about students who spoke no English and schools that provided them with little or no support. I'd discussed strategies [with fellow trainees and corps member advisors] for working with middle school students who read on a third- or fourth-grade level. I'd heard that district boards were often governed by politics and failed to serve the students for whom they bore responsibility. What I didn't understand, initially, was that hearing, reading, and discussing, were in no way equivalent to experiencing. I'd learned that many of my "solutions" [fresh from Institute] were not viable. (Betty)

Most, if not all, TFA teachers I worked with noted the correlation between their lack of adequate preparation during Institute and their own perceived effectiveness in the classroom. Furthermore, every study member acknowledged that once they got to their 2-year assignment, self-reliance, hard work, and tenacity figured into the "learning how to teach" equation.

> I really missed having student teaching. Even though we "taught" in Atlanta, it was really not teaching. We were working in groups. A lot of good

that did me when I arrived here and had 36 kids in my class! I had to figure it out on my own. That's what everyone had to do. I would have preferred to just come here for pre-induction in June, stay, and learn here. (Michael)

POINTS TO CONSIDER: TRAINING TO BECOME A TEACH FOR AMERICA TEACHER

What does the research say about teacher training? Who are the best qualified to provide strategies and knowledge for new educators? David Berliner (1986, 1994) delineated what he refers to as the "five stages of teaching expertise." He noted that "novices" (those in the first stage) learn to apply what they learned about teaching during their first year of practicum and observation working in schools. Novices rely on instructional time in academic settings and through their student teaching experiences, to figure out how they will make their teaching work. This phase begins during the preservice period when rookies first encounter the classroom and continues during clinical observations on-site in schools and throughout the student teaching experience. For TFA recruits who arrived at their respective training sites possessing content-based degrees, their five weeks of training at Institute offered an express *novitiate period*, (Berliner's newest term shared in an e-mail correspondence, 2006). Institute exposed TFA corps members to all of the above, which still had to be processed, synthesized and mediated by those who were able to guide novices in practice.

According to Berliner (1986, 1994), novice teachers are usually feeling their way through the experience. Often demonstrating hesitancy and lack of confidence, they try to ingest all that's presented on both a contextual and pedagogical level. Thus, they begin acclimating themselves to the culture of the school and often to the preparatory duties that are involved in planning and lesson follow-through. Novices gradually work to integrate the information and situations that are presented to them when observing experienced teachers.

Viewing TFA teachers through this particular schema, it appears that TFAers are *teaching novices* when they enter their rookie year with less than five weeks to combine all aspects of the preparation experience. Either they must be highly accelerated learners, or there is some serious catching up to do when they enter their first year of teaching.

Berliner's "advanced beginner" (second stage), is still deeply involved in the learning process, usually through the third year of teaching. Prior knowledge references and the scaffolding of one's own teaching experiences, serve to inform decisions and trigger reflection, as to what works and why. Advanced beginners need to learn the content, how to teach it to reach their students, what to do if learning is not happening, effective classroom management, and school routines.

Berliner's third stage of teacher development is the "competency" level, which emerges around year four or five. Berliner (1994) believes that not all teachers attain this level of practice. He asserts that in some instances, teachers become fixed at a level below competency. Berliner's fourth and fifth stages of teacher development are described as "proficient" and "expert." At these levels, the teacher confidently develops in all areas of educational pedagogy. An expert teacher sees the classroom and the experience in a new way. Teachers reaching this level are aware of the intricacies of their work and reflect on their activities as progressively more complex. They possess a schematic system (easily and effortlessly catalogued in their heads and able to be pulled up at a moment's notice) that blends their contextual experience and knowledge gained through years of experience, with reflection. Their knowing is not merely content-based, but multilayered. It integrates both episodic and strategic learning in a seamless manner.

From whom, and under what conditions is knowledge constructed for novice teachers with limited training and experience? Vygotsky's core belief system, as viewed by Moll (2001) centered on the notion that, "Human thinking develops through the mediation of others. Collaboration, direction, assisting through demonstration, leading questions and introducing the initial elements of the task's solution are central components of the 'Zone of proximal development theory'" (pp. 113, 209). For Vygotsky, the context in which the interaction occurs is of crucial importance (Moll, 2001). After a year or two with corps members, I began to understand how the Institute context, which was all that corps members brought with them to their own teaching, lacked both the "go-to" expert teacher and the reflection and learning of traditionally prepared beginning teachers who had already completed a practicum experience in schools. It appeared that TFA corps members' thinking was solely mediated by other TFA trainees and their Corps Member Advisors, instead of those who would be in a position to guide these new teachers to competency or beyond.

> What was needed was a rich description of what happens every day with modeling. (Mrs. Lauria, veteran teacher)

I wondered, "Was rich description with modeling offered at Institute sites?" Over the years, I met with mentors, corps member advisors, and corps trainees whose experiences were representative of several training locations. I was very surprised to learn that veteran educators, who were hired by districts to support TFA novices during Corps Training Institute's summer session, appeared to be in classrooms in name only, as noted below:

> Mrs. Jones: I've worked with TFAers in this district since they came in over 10 years ago. This year there are six TFA teachers on our middle school team. During the summer, I was hired by the district to help train TFAers, who were among the nearly 1,000 [corps inductees] trained in our region for the first time. One of the young men on my team is a "natural," [teacher], but most of the others don't have it, and they are not staying in education beyond their 2-year commitment to really care if they do have it. Another teacher and myself tried to offer feedback to one of the young men who was teaching summer school here. But he wasn't receptive to our suggestions. Then a TFA person, what do you call the one who gives TFA advice?
>
> Barb: A [CMA] Corps Member Advisor?
>
> Mrs. Jones: Yes, that's it. Well, the Corps Member Advisor told the new TFA teacher that I was only in the classroom to cover the district, because there is a requirement to have certified personnel on site for insurance purposes. I wasn't there to give him feedback on his lesson ... that was the job of the TFA people. I was asking myself and other teachers, "How does the TFA person who taught for, 2 or 3 years, really know how to guide a new-to-the-profession teacher who will be faced with challenges in our district? So, it's the same thing over again. We are asked to help TFAers who require a great deal of help to be effective. Most never get there [to the effective stage] and leave after two years.

Limited exposure to lesson demonstrations, observation of expert modeling, and collaboration with more seasoned education professionals than TFA alumnae with two or three years teaching experience, still remains critically lacking in TFA's training system. Many veteran teachers, hired by their districts to mentor the newly arriving TFA novices, posed concerns to me, because they noticed patterns that surfaced in both the questions and behaviors of the corps members that they began to attribute to TFA training.

> You know how experienced teachers ... something presents itself. The child says something or there's a challenge. It's like ... every single morning when you go to school you have a puzzle to figure out or a question. How to handle stuff, like all the time, every day, I'd think, "How am I going to work this?" Cause that's the way teachers think. "What's the best way to do this? What's the best way to go?" And when something presents to you, you've got ... a bunch of stuff in your head. I think it's kind of like a computer where it would go through the options. You go through your options and you pick one. You don't even know that you're doing this. That's how I'm going to respond at this particular time in this particular situation.

Well, that comes from teaching school. And, even people who have gone through fancy colleges of education, they can't do that either, until they have years under their belt. (Mrs. Schendis, veteran teacher)

In surveying the available literature, researchers uphold teacher-training strategies that use interactive discussions to activate prior knowledge (Rinehart, Barksdale-Ladd, & Paterson, 1994). Lev Vygotsky's (1978) theory of learning and development offers a framework for analyzing TFA's training model: "The zone of proximal development: the distance between the actual developmental level, as determined by independent problem solving and the level of potential development as determined through problem solving under adult guidance or in collaboration with more capable peers" (p. 86), provides individuals with greater success in carrying out tasks that they would not be able to carry out alone. "Scholars suggest that the learning process is one in which a more capable peer, interacting with the learner, provides a scaffold to aid learning" (Sperling & Freedman, 2001, p. 374).

As exemplars in this chapter note, TFA's training at Corps Training Institute appears to rely heavily on corps member advisors instead of veteran teacher educators. Yet, by failing to provide expert, experienced teachers who could present alternative strategies and demonstrate how they might be implemented, TFA novices learn teaching skills from advanced beginners (Berliner, 1994). Moreover, Bruner's (1978) research on the learning process can be used to frame discussion of novice TFA corps members. A capable peer, or in this case, a more experienced teacher interacting with a novice TFA corps member, provides a necessary scaffold to (a) model the task, (b) perform part of the task, or in other ways, (c) offer support or guidance, which gradually is withdrawn as the new teacher builds confidence and completes the task at hand, *alone.*

While I worked with TFAers on-site in schools, I was known as "Coach Barb," by corps members and their students alike. One male sixth-grade student asked me what "team" I coached for. As in the game of baseball, I shared with my TFA graduate students, that I would assume the role of "pitching coach," when I visited their classrooms to observe a lesson. While sitting in a corner of the room, I would observe the lesson and take notes as needed, be available to take the "ball" and pitch the lesson to students while corps members watched my delivery, and afterward, hand the "ball" and classroom duties, back to the TFA teachers. My role as "coach" supported novice TFAers who were eager to observe best practice modeling to see how it could be applied to their own teaching. After a while, corps members requested team-teaching sessions for particular lessons– math, literacy, or social studies.

DeWitz, Carr, and Patberg (1987) note that integration of new information results in greater understanding when training takes place with this form of preparation. Teach For America's compressed model of teacher preparation appears to have fallen short on two levels—there was little or no time for interactive discussions that offered reflection on practice, and there were few "experts" to guide the novice practitioner through reflection. Carter and Gonzalez (1993) synthesized the acquisition of knowledge by novice teachers learning to teach into three areas: (a) information processing, (b) practical knowledge, and (c) pedagogical content knowledge. Could each of these aspects of teacher knowledge really be concentrated into a 5-week span? If so, were novices able to retain and then apply all of this information? The commentary below, from a veteran teacher who worked with new TFA teachers, suggests otherwise.

> The TFA corps members are quick learners, but the schema is not there. They don't have anything to hang all of this information on to, and it needs to be really rudimentary, is what I've found. Like "get out the plan book, plug in your specials, fill in all the holes with what you know you're going to do and then figure out what the heck you're really going to do." You ask yourself, "How am I going to put it all together? What are we [as a class] going to study? How am I going to do that? How am I going to do groups?" (Mrs. Lauria, veteran teacher)

CHAPTER 5

LEARNING THE CULTURE OF TEACH FOR AMERICA AND THE REGIONAL ORGANIZATION

A VIEW FROM THE FIELD: ALL-CORPS MEETING

I entered the rear entrance of the Bristol School Auditorium at 6:00 P.M. Once full platters of overstuffed sandwiches, veggie wraps, chicken wings, tortilla chips, salsa, and bean dip covered two oblong tables in the vestibule. The school's personnel were gone for the day, but Teach For America was in the house for the regions' bimonthly All-Corps Meeting.

Voices competed with the blaring music to be heard. First and second-year TFAers took turns making announcements punctuated with verbal endorsements and applause from 100 fellow corps members.

"Sign up with Eric if you are interested in a trip to the Grand Canyon next weekend," advised Missy, an eighth-grade teacher in the Osborn District.

"Let's give a shout out to Dan, the man, who finished the Tempe Triathlon on Sunday!" yelled, Rob, his roommate. High-fives and hugs greeted the lean Colorado native, as he made his way to the stage. Smiling and shaking his head, he graciously accepted a medallion suspended from a satin ribbon crafted by one of his fellow corps members. Raucous

Learning on Other People's Kids: Becoming a Teach For America Teacher
pp. 67–79
Copyright © 2010 by Information Age Publishing
67

laughter signaled peer approval that rippled throughout the spacious room.

I slipped into a seat on the aisle, and was greeted by Emily and Sharon who had requested that I present a workshop session on long-range curriculum planning to their learning team.

But before the sessions commenced, Jared, a former corps member on the West Coast and the regions' executive director, took the microphone. "The TFA organization is proud to recognize second-year corps member, Roberta Jenkins of the Randolph District, whose students' test scores surpassed achievement expectations! Let's hear it for Roberta!"

Rather than leaping from her chair to accept her award and photo opportunity with TFA's regional directors, Roberta, seated in front of me, turned around to accept my congratulations. I was taken by her reaction. Instead of elation, Roberta appeared indignant.

"Last year when I needed help, the people I could count on were you, Lynn, the other 6th grade teacher, and a few fellow corps members. I didn't know how to make it work with my kids, and almost made myself sick, trying. And now TFA is proud of me? Go figure!"

LEARNING THE CULTURE OF TEACH FOR AMERICA IN THE REGION

Corps members were expected to be resourceful, responsible, problem-solving team players that would teach for two years, support Teach For America's achievement goals, and uphold TFA's mission. Teach For America's selection process articulated a formula that considered more than one's GPA:

> Ensuring corps member success actually begins with Teach For America's selection process. We know corps members will face a lot of challenges, and that's why we select leaders with a history of achievement and overcoming obstacles, as well as a commitment to our vision (TFA *Recruitment Manual*, p. 14).

The TFA teachers I came to know, frequently acknowledged the "TFA corps member prototype," and identified how some regional leadership teams prioritized the recruitment of specifically skilled or minority status team members to align with the organization's criteria.

> While we place great emphasis on recruiting students of color to apply to our corps, we don't take race or ethnicity (or any other factors outside our selection criteria) into account at the selection stage. Our experience has taught us that *whom* we select is as important as the training they receive (TFA *Recruitment Manual*, pp. 3, 12).

Seventy-five percent of recruited corps members from one cohort in the regions under study were bilingual and bi-literate, although the corps' racial make-up was overwhelmingly Caucasian. Over time, the corps member profile seemed to change to meet TFA Recruitment guidelines, as the exemplar below notes.

> Proportionately, there are way more women than men in the new corps this year. There are a lot of Caucasians; not many people of color. There are a great number of people who seem to come from very similar backgrounds and really, in terms of their approaches, I think as a group, not as individuals, they don't tend to buck the status quo as much, and are monolingual [English only] speakers. (Renata)

At Institute, Teach For America formally socialized its trainees to *think like a corps member*. Boasting about a 12% acceptance rate for the 2009-2010 corps (Anderson, 2009), TFA affiliation was viewed as a specialized association. The structure and guidelines prescribed by TFA's national headquarters in New York City were in place; *TFA had a model that worked*, so it was followed in every TFA region (Kopp, 2003, 2008; Lipka, 2007; Ness, 2004). Teach For America's national organization noted the importance of staying connected with all TFA teachers on a regular basis. So, when corps members arrived in their assigned region, the local leadership team picked up where Institute's training left off, and facilitated the organization's expectations through All-Corps meetings. These bi-monthly get-togethers promoted TFA team building, monitored corps progress, noted staff development opportunities, offered peer support, and rekindled the TFA team spirit even in the face of mounting challenges, stress, and teaching responsibilities.

All-Corps meetings provided an opportunity for TFA leadership to reiterate that one's affiliation with TFA separated corps members from other non-TFA first and second year teachers in public schools. TFA teachers offered a collective "good" in the community and I was told that this 'special' reputation resulted in celebrities (including politicians, university presidents, sports figures, and media personalities) participating in TFA Week, held during October in all TFA national regions. During this annual event, corps members' students would benefit from guest appearances, scheduled *only* in TFA classrooms, which garnered substantial publicity for the organization and school.

The affiliation with TFA provides "corporate-like perks" for its corps, as TFA teachers are offered opportunities to meet high-profile individuals and participate in organizational outings (similar to corporate events that are closed to the public). Teach For America teachers are presented as a collective entity in their new communities. In this capacity, a corps member's view of "self" seems secondary to their organizational affiliation.

Peer introductions reflect this ingrained TFA corps identification, which appears, at times, to be one's primary signifier.

> He's TFA. He's TFA in the Marley District (pseudonym) and he teaches fifth-grade dual language. She's TFA too, and she teaches in the Randolph district. We're all TFA! Didn't you figure that out? We seem to only hang out with each other. (Colby)

Some participants felt that the overall corporate cohesiveness was beneficial because of the social camaraderie that developed. For most (particularly first-year corps members), the organization served as a familial construct that offered a sense of belonging for those who were not only teaching on their own for the very first time, but were living and working thousands of miles from home. Teach For America's organizational affiliation continues to offer offer social, collegial, and, in some respects, communal integration. Teach For America's organizational design is reminiscent of a college lifestyle, which fosters a peer network of young, single roommates often sharing multilayered experiences. For some participants, this arrangement proved to be ideal, but for others, this system suggested dependency.

> Yeah, we all lived together in one house. All of us were TFA's. We were all first-year TFA's. TFA sort of conditions you for that. You're all in a new place. You are just out of college. This is your first job and you tend to hang around with others who are like you. (Robbie)

> There were parties and social gatherings on weekends and it was good in the beginning, but after a while it got old. (Rene)

> Barb, Aria is going through a tough time. She was dating Greg and now he's seeing Janel, so she's not okay now. It's corps stuff. Just giving you heads up. (Lila)

> TFA wants you to be a good corps member and that means hanging out with other TFAers. But, I had other things to do and people outside of TFA who I could learn from. (Justine)

> I brought some of my research with me. They took issue with the fact that I wasn't getting involved in many of the social networking opportunities. (Tony)

For those who did not get the opportunity to interact with other corps members except those they lived or worked with, All-Corps meetings offered a welcoming venue. All-Corps meetings were always conducted at a set time and place. Attendance for both first- and second-year TFA teachers was and remains mandatory. These routine gatherings provided peer socialization with TFAers from all district schools, along with refreshments and often dinner. More importantly, however, All-Corps meetings presented a face-to-face forum where the regional leadership emphasized TFA's national goals and outlined localized action plans. Teach For America's sponsored activities, announcements, staff development, and fundraising opportunities were often highlighted.

Yet, I learned from participants (as well as through my own on-site observations), that with the perks and privileged status of corps membership, TFA affiliation carried additional responsibilities. Promoting organizational goals seemed to weigh heavily on the minds of TFA newcomers, as Teach For America's strategic plans spell out how corps members could network, write grants, and promote the organization's national goals for boosting student achievement. These added performance expectations placed stress and demands on TFA beginning teachers.

> For me, sometimes Teach For America is imposing on what I am doing. Like last night it was "learning teams." But last weekend we had university classes [on] Thursday, Friday and Saturday. We had "learning teams" yesterday and we have class again tonight. "Learning teams" need to be at a time when there's nothing going on. When was I supposed to get grading done? You want me to achieve significant gains? When I am going to do so, if these little insignificant things come up? (Curtis)

Participants noted how All-Corps meetings served as a stage from which outstanding Teach For America teachers, who met or surpassed student achievement goals, were celebrated. These public displays of recognition, in front of the entire corps, propagated the organizational message on the regional level that even first-year novice teachers are responsible for bolstering student achievement. The organization capitalized on competition and corps' character traits.

> They make us believe, "We are doing it better [than other teachers trained in education schools] and here's evidence. Look at what this one did!" I started to feel, like what's wrong with me, if I don't measure up. (Lenore)

> At one time, we had a more relaxed way of boosting morale, in the form of "shout-outs," that were ways that we could say something good about everyone in the corps group every month without the appearance of competitiveness. But then the leadership changed and even the TFA newsletters took on a more "polished" look. Now there's a spotlight on a single corps member for each issue and what they did in their classroom. (Brandon)

Novice corps members, aware of TFA's "mission statement" from Corps Training Institute, admitted that organizational goals were continuously echoed in their regional placement cities. All-Corps meetings enabled

TFA leadership to reinforce the organization's "mission"—in-person, to the entire corps, perpetuating an Institute-like atmosphere. Teach For America's cohesiveness and teambuilding was accomplished in part, through Teach For America's "learning teams" who assumed the organization's brand of in-house mentoring. Second-year TFA teachers were teamed with novices from the same grade level or subject area placement and shared strategies, their own successful teaching approaches, disseminated thematic plans, and created activities for the benefit of their peer-learning group. While the second-year TFAers (still learning teaching themselves) were viewed by the organization as experienced enough to provide in-house support (similar to a business' corporate mentoring of new employees), first-year corps members were not as convinced. Participants' feedback on this programmatic element of TFA's method of support, was mixed.

> That's the nice thing about our meeting with the learning teams. They [second-year corps members] bring their units and they do talk about that and for me those are always the most beneficial meetings. As far as TFA, we have the community groups where we talk about issues in school and they are o.k. But I've always benefited more from the Learning Teams. I mean, I've been given some worksheets and some ideas to use that were great. (Ali)

> Are they [second-year TFA's] really experts in teaching? (Jamal)

In addition to the "learning teams," support consisted of periodic classroom visits by TFA Program Directors, who, as alumni of the organization, completed two years of teaching through Teach For America, themselves. Program Directors were hired and compensated by the TFA national organization and were considered experienced in guiding novice practitioners. While some corps members accept the site visitations as routine, it appeared that the overwhelming majority of first- and second-year TFAers regard these observations with skepticism.

> If you're not in my classroom every day, how much can you help me? I just felt that the notes the woman [TFA Program Director] gave me the other day, it wasn't like anything really. So, I said, "What's the issue? How can I control 33 people?" No one can control 33 people unless you want to start from the beginning and treat them like an army. These are eighth graders! I don't care what they [TFA program directors] come in to find! They can find all they want. (Ronnie)

> Now, during my second year, I've been observed once (by TFA). I told my P.D. that because TFA was not involved at all last year, it felt intrusive this year for me to be making time for them because they didn't provide support last year, when I needed it, so I found my own. (Lorena)

As the demands of teaching escalated, one's own time was viewed as a precious commodity. Participants expressed concern that Teach For America's "command performance" gatherings covered nonessential matters, infringing on time that could be better directed to classroom preparation. Others had a unique way of prioritizing TFA's demands and attendance at mandatory organizational functions, over more teacher-related responsibilities.

> I don't mean to miss class tonight and next week. I know how important it is to attend, but I have to recruit for TFA and then the next week is a TFA fundraiser. Can I make up some of this, reading the text? (Aisha)

When corps members voiced concern as to the frequency of these mandated meetings, one's dedication to the organization, Teach For America's mission, and commitment to students, was questioned.

> All-Corps meetings were not useful. They could have just sent out another e-mail. Do you know that I got a nasty e-mail because I said that I couldn't attend one meeting? They questioned my commitment to the organization. I was really ticked off about that. Here we are going in there and teaching the kids and doing the extra after-school stuff, running clubs, and taking college courses so we know a little something, and then ... they [TFA regional directors] berate us like we're kids? Please! (Miranda)

A concern shared by many corps members related to the AmeriCorps vouchers, on which the organization signs off. I learned that the voucher can be withheld if corps members short-changed their TFA responsibilities. Attendance at All-Corps meetings was, and still remains, one of the requirements.

> If we didn't go to the All-Corps meetings we would get into trouble. They held that AmeriCorps check over our heads, saying that we wouldn't get it, if we didn't show up to those meetings. I'm working with kids, taking classes and tutoring, yet they tell me that I have to go to these events too, and be a "good corps member." I didn't have time for it. (David)

A few corps members shared that they felt that TFA's All-Corps meetings and some events were "meant to indoctrinate" (as some term it), or rally for successful corps members' accomplishments. Some TFA teachers admitted to assuming a level of "agency," within the context of the larger affiliation, and noted how they felt compelled to prioritize the needs of self and students over the organization's expectations. Many emphatically stated that the TFA organization wasn't really advocating for corps members or their students. Some took matters into their own hands and adopted a version of self-efficacy, as offered by the exemplar below.

I was up front that I had a life outside of TFA, and that I had other things I had to do. I had to complete a project, it was my master's thesis, and the government funded it. But, the TFA program directors said, "You're not going to get this done. You're going to be too busy. We're going to run you ragged. You're not going to have any time." They were telling me I couldn't do it because TFA was now going to be my life. It's true. (Trudy)

Some members admitting to a more pronounced social change agenda, related that Teach For America was concerned with maintaining the status quo, rather than truly advocating for students in the high-poverty communities with which they contract. As the passage below asserts, this "branching off" may have been viewed (by the regional TFA leadership) as subverting the mainstream organizational mission of Teach For America.

If I were on a list of troublemakers, it would have been from my association with a group started by corps members inside Teach For America called "Always Adelante." We created it to address issues of power, perspective, privilege, and oppression in the classroom. And, part of what that involved was talking to TFA about things that we saw as problematic within TFA ... about their narrow definition of diversity. So, I think that a lot of people in that group have a stigma of being slightly outside of the TFA circle. (William)

Implied within the organization's explicit and covert messages initiated during Corps Training Institute, and reinforced by the regional directors as a component of TFA's ongoing enculturation, is the furthering of Teach For America's "corporate-like" organizational agenda. While "hidden" from outsiders, participants overwhelmingly acknowledged that "following the TFA way of doing things" was overtly linked to not only *becoming a TFA teacher*, but being recognized as a *good* TFA corps member.

Initially, most rookie TFAers assumed a posture that is *compliant* (at least outwardly) with the organization's goals. Some even *embraced* TFA's organizational platform and continue to do so as Teach For America alumni. Yet, I came to learn how corps members *negotiated, counter-crusaded, detached from*, and even *subverted* their association with Teach For America.

I just don't agree with some of the TFA ways. Personally, I'm not in it for Teach For America! I'm in it for myself and for my students. So that's what frustrates me. I'm not here for you. So, you helped me get [to] this place. I'm going to do what I have to do, to make sure that you're not down my back about stupid things. I'm not here to do this for you [TFA]! And, to be quite honest, I feel that's a lot of people's opinions. Like summer time [training] you can do the TFA way, then, during the school year, bump that; doesn't work, movin' on. (Curtis)

Teach For America's leadership listens to some people and not to others. Sometimes it's bad. I don't mean it to sound this way, but it's *almost like TFA is a cult.* If you're not all for it, all for one, then you're a bad person. Some of us that are outside that main core group get the attitude that we're not good people; that we're not trying as hard as we possibly can for the kids. But it's not true, because most of us spend 15 hours just doing curriculum and planning for our kids. (Natashia)

Barb, Carmen quit TFA. She is a second-year corps member, like me. She will finish out her course work and teaching at her school here, but strongly disagrees with most of TFA's diversity ideas. Carmen and her entire family picked fruit all over the West Coast. She told me how her fingers would be stained from the strawberry juice. Carmen is someone who takes action and does what she believes in, even though it might not be convenient for her. She wants to be able to teach her students without as she put it, "TFA breathing down my neck." By quitting, she forfeits the AmeriCorps stipend, which she could really use. (Breanne)

POINTS TO CONSIDER:
LEARNING THE CULTURE OF TEACH FOR AMERICA

I can't believe that some of these kids are going out there to recruit others and they don't even have the basics of how to teach a reading lesson! Some of them have such sporadic attendance in [graduate methods] class and it's not their fault. They are asked to go and do the TFA thing. How is that helping their students? (Mrs. Keneer, literacy instructor)

The Teach For America rookies enter teaching from a different point of origin than those trained in traditional or even alternative teacher education programs. Teach For America teachers are members of an organization whose corporate culture presents a construct of the prototypical TFA teacher. The regional organization ensures that this brand of teacher exercises its presence in the community.

Teach For America's model, as noted in earlier chapters, perpetuates an identity, that is viewed as a value-added commodity by school districts. It is interesting to note not only *how* TFA prepares its teachers, but also, *who* is assigned this important duty. When new corps members enter Corps Training Institute, and attend All-Corps Meetings, they recognize immediately, that former TFAers assume primary responsibilities for enculturation of applicants, candidates, and eventually, first and second-year corps members. They notice the TFA network and chain of command that includes TFA's recruiters, corps member advisors, and regional directors. Some corps members aspire to follow this career path during their post-TFA teaching years either locally or through TFA's network of affiliates, such as the 60-plus KIPP academy charter schools founded by TFA alumnae (Mathews, 2009). The culture of TFA is perpetuated through interactions with former TFAers, who not only assume leadership and decision-making roles on the local level, but also often work to support initiatives of the national organization. Teach For America's corps members are aware of, and witness how one is able to reap benefits in post-TFA careers, if one is a member in good standing.

> Greta is working with TFA in Chicago as a recruiter and Ben is working in New York City as a Program Director. There's a huge group that's teaching with Kipp too. (Ryan)

Goddard, Hoy, and Hoy (2004) offer a fitting analysis:

> Although the expectations of peer groups do not always win the day, organizational life is nevertheless filled with social exchanges that communicate expectations, sanctions, and rewards to members. Part of the organizational learning process deals with the acquisition of requisite orientations for satisfactorily functioning in a role. Hence, expectations for action set by collective efficacy beliefs do not go unnoticed; rather, these expectations are an important part of organizational socialization and fundamental aspects of an organizations' culture and influence on group member performance. (p. 6)

It seems to me that a mutual dependency is built into the TFA model. The organization is dependent upon corps members to fulfill TFA's expansion goals, and corps members are dependent upon TFA to place them in their classrooms, train them to be teachers, garner legislative support on the federal and local level, and run interference for them in each region. This leads novice TFAers to expect that their needs, (from placement to support), will be handled by TFA's regional directors. Conversely, Teach For America's administrators expect its novices to *think* and *act like "a corps member"* (Kaplowitz, 2003; Kopp, 2003). This equates to loyal corps members being responsible, proactive, willing to keep issues private, and agreeable to uphold the organization's goals and ideals.

The regional directors attempt to support the growing numbers of young corps members, but at times, this is a daunting task. I noticed that the ratio of corps members to TFA regional administrators is rather high, considering that one program director is often responsible for supporting 50-75 corps members in their new-to-teaching site placements. Besides teaching concerns and school-based issues, other personal matters are mediated by TFA regional directors. When issues escalate and/or dissent enters into the mix, TFA's regional administration handles all matters, including public relations, in the same manner that any corporation or institution manages "damage control," by addressing concerns, containing the matter, suppressing complaints, and keeping a lid on any malcontents.

> TFA had these organizational expectations. All TFA people must sign their name when they give input. The pressure is there to not tell all that they are feeling. If they make comments, they are called in "to discuss it." It's usually not pleasant. (Cassidy)

There is evidence from the exemplars noted in this chapter, that the organization's ideology filters into TFA teacher beliefs. Richardson (1996) suggests that beliefs play a significant role in not only organizing knowledge but, defining behavior. Goddard et al. (2004) writes: "As defined in social cognitive theory, all efficacy belief constructs are future-oriented judgments about capabilities to organize and execute the courses of action required to produce given attainments in specific situations or contexts" (p. 3). *Social Identity Theory* refers to how an affiliation with one's group creates both an identity (telling us who we are) and self-esteem (making us feel a certain way about ourselves) (Ashforth & Mael, 1989; Tajfel & Turner, 1986). This theory might be used to describe the manner in which corps members identify with the national organization in such a way as to maximize a positive and distinct presence within the community, and nation. (Teach For America looks to develop educational leaders, and as of TFA's Annual Report for fiscal year 2008, 15 former corps members hold political office across the country.)

According to Bandura (1997), collective efficacy involves a judgment or belief about group capability, as participation actively engages groups to achieve a goal. Hoy, Tarter, and Hoy (2004) broadened this theoretical construct to include teachers in schools working toward a common level of attainment, such as promoting gains in student achievement. Goddard et al. (2004) found that, "Perceptions of group-capability varied more than 40 percent among groups and suggest that individual perceptions of group capability are what really matters" (p. 7).

It is my observation, that TFA's corporate model typifies collective efficacy theory from two fronts. The first builds upon the research of Goddard et al. (2004) which discusses "an organizational culture and its influence on participants and group outcomes" (p. 4). Teach For America presents its "culture" at the onset of a prospective corps member's application, through its advertisements to candidates, and in the public domain (more on this in the closing chapters). If thousands of young corps members follow the TFA model and are disbursed among TFA's national and international regions advocating the organization's mission and goals, then the advertised benefits (to the community, sponsors, and corps members) appear to outweigh any perceived liabilities. The regional culture is in place to systemically ensure that procedures are followed as planned, through outward appearances in the community, which involve creating alliances with local business, board members, school districts, and university partners.

But, when things get tough, and they do, (as noted in chapters 6, 7, and 8 when corps members learn the cultures of the community, school, and teaching), the burdens of TFA's goal attainment are placed squarely on the shoulders of young corps members. Teach For America teachers are obligated to embrace the organization's mission, even from within the scope of one's condensed TFA preparation. Regardless of the personal costs involved, TFA teachers are expected to be effective teachers and meet student achievement goals.

Bandura (1997) asserts, "A capability is only as good as its execution. Insidious self-doubts can easily overrule the best of skills" (p. 35). Goddard et al. (2004) note, "Efficacy judgments are beliefs about individual or group capability, but not necessarily accurate assessments of those capabilities" (p. 3). Teach For America's novices initially hold onto and replicate the beliefs of the organization's founder and supporters, but, as first-year teachers gain familiarity with their routines and classroom duties, their collective experiences as novice TFA teachers initiate alliances within the ranks of their fellow corps members.

It appears that the second aspect of collective efficacy theory becomes evident with the passage of time. Participants affirm that collective efficacy takes on other forms, too, as self-reliant and tenacious individuals, accustomed to viewing situations with a discriminating eye, align with each other and proactively advocate for issues that are at the core of their critical philosophies. At times, their concerns challenge regional corps leadership and prior ways of thinking. Initiation of this level of efficacy does not always manifest fully during the first semester of teaching for first-year corps members. The noted exception involves issues of support and stress (discussed in chapter 8).

Collective efficacy is sometimes viewed, as a reaction to what researchers term, a "hidden curriculum" or "agenda" that exists in most institutions. The outward message, plan, agenda, programmatic model, or appearance, often differs from what is explicitly professed inwardly, experienced by insiders, or viewed from behind closed doors. Michael Apple (2004) discusses the construct of a "hidden curriculum," a term he attributes to Philip Jackson and others (p. 47).

Teach For America appears to systematically perpetuate their message, which filters into the ongoing models presented to TFA novices through All-Corps Meetings and through TFA communication. Teach For America's "hidden curriculum" is not explicitly advertised to corps members, but includes a high priority placed upon being a "good corps member." Participants seem to translate this directive into a pressure to conform, follow the prescribed TFA model, and perform above the "average" teacher, even when faced with challenging situations. Each newly initiated cohort of corps members' noted that they were still in grade school when TFA made its debut on the educational landscape. Why would *they* [novices] challenge the organization's line of practice? How do they know (upon applying) that TFA's teacher training does not replicate the model that prepared their own teachers, or themselves, for that matter?

It appears that over the ten years of my discussions with corps members, that TFA still relies on its own programmatic version of reproduction theory. Teach For America's organization controls information disseminated to both the press and the public. As documented in *Teach For America's 2006 U.S. Treasury Form 990, Schedule A, p. 2, Part III, Statements About Activities*, which reads, "During the year, has the organization attempted to influence national, state, or local legislation, or include any attempt to influence public opinion on a legislative matter or referendum? If 'Yes,' enter the total expenses paid or incurred in connection with the lobbying activities," Teach For America reported $120,177.00 on the aforementioned U.S. Treasury Form 990 (see Appendix B).

Teach For America's public image is explicitly reinforced by TFA's regional directors and is one to which corps members are aware of once they begin their teaching.

> You know the TFA leaders in our region tried this [getting veteran teachers into our classrooms to support us] since so many of us had asked for it. There were veteran teachers who came into our classrooms and they had so many negative things to say about what we were doing or not doing. We knew things that we were expected to do wasn't happening, and TFA pulled the plug on it. They didn't want "bad publicity." So, there we were again, not getting any feedback, from anyone other than the TFA learning teams. (Rosa)

Implied within the organization's explicit and covert messages (initiated during Corps Training Institute and reinforced by the regional organization as a component of the TFA's ongoing enculturation) is TFA's own 'curriculum.' Although the organizational agenda may appear to be "hidden" from outsiders, participants acknowledge that it is overtly linked to their expectation of success, and recognition as a good TFA corps member.

PART II

THE SOCIALIZATION OF
TEACH FOR AMERICA TEACHERS

CHAPTER 6

LEARNING THE CULTURE OF COMMUNITIES AND SCHOOLS

A VIEW FROM THE FIELD: UNWARRANTED VISITATION

The classroom was still. Markers left askew dotted computer printouts of student writings on "Tolerance." Tablecloth-sized sheets of rainbow-colored poster paper obscured the linoleum and offered evidence of a lull in student activity as works-in-progress were temporarily placed on hold. Gina eased into a canary-colored chair with a satisfying but reflective sigh.

"You did well," I offered. "Your eighth-grade students were engaged in group projects. This served as an assessment of content you taught earlier in the week."

Gina outlined plans for next period when the door flung open and a middle-aged policewoman, clad in navy uniform and shiny black boots, invaded our private space. Catching us off-guard, we stared in silence as she proceeded to grab random student backpacks from their hooks at the room's exterior.

"Officer, can I help you?" Gina offered. "Those bags belong to my students and they're at gym." Stunned, yet inquisitive, I inquired as to what was going on. The blonde, pony-tailed officer directed her ice-blue eyes at me.

"There's been gang activity in the area and I'm just doing my job."

Learning on Other People's Kids: Becoming a Teach For America Teacher
pp. 83–98
Copyright © 2010 by Information Age Publishing

Visibly shaken, yet protective of her students, Gina challenged, "Do you have a warrant?"

The officer ignored queries from both of us as she stormed out of the room with students' backpacks in tow.

LEARNING THE CULTURE OF THE COMMUNITY

The world of students taught by TFA teachers provided its own unique knowledge "independent of school" (Friere, 1998). If students of corps members had limited exposure to life outside of their community, they didn't lack for experiences that others only read about in Jonathan Kozol's (1991) work.

> One morning in the second month of school a fifth-grade girl is outside my classroom crying with family members. Her big brother was shot by the police a few hours before. I was just out of "Institute" and I had no bag of tricks. How did *I* know what to do? Unfortunately when it rains it pours. It turns out that her 6-year-old cousin was also killed a couple of months ago from a hit and run. Crazy, the things [that] some of these kids are forced to go through. (Jay)

Systemic realities (large class size, inadequate supplies and funding, frequent administrative and teacher turnover, inconsistent support, external mandates that dictated a scripted curriculum, and a myriad of community issues) comprised the teacher professional landscape of Teach For America first-year teachers.

> I don't have enough textbooks for everyone and they can't take textbooks home. (CJ)

> I never knew all the policies, the politics. How things ... it's just a mess and my students are labeled under-performing or failing. So the pressure is there. I guess I didn't really have an idea. So, I was imagining it to be terrible, absolutely terrible and for me to be miserable. And, so, I was ... sometimes. But I've just learned a lot about how to relate to people and how the school system is just so incredibly messed up. (Ali)

Many students of TFAers were children of immigrants or recent arrivals into the community. Other students were children who regularly witnessed the effects of families and communities in crisis. TFA novices were presented with recurring opportunities to learn how teaching involved more than arriving with prepared content-based lesson plans. Teaching students whose lives were impacted by grim social realities on a daily basis lent a deeper meaning to novice TFAers learning about the culture of the school, and the community in which they had committed to teach for two years. For most corps members, the region's site-based environment was not familiar to what they had experienced back home or in school.

> I don't think of my students as kids. I have to remind myself everyday that they are only 12 and 13. They seem to me to be 15, 16, or maybe even 17. They keep telling me they are from the "ghetto," the "South Side." I am realizing more and more that they have seen more in their short lives than I have seen in twice as long and in a million more places. (Melanie)

At times and in light of certain challenges faced by their students, TFA rookie teachers inquired as to what course of action to take. They were inexperienced with outer manifestations that signaled a child's internal response to challenging social and personal circumstances. In other words, TFAers were not good at reading situations that faced them on a daily basis. While at Corps Training Institute, TFA's trainees were learning to assess students' academics, but, figuring out their students' body language or facial expressions was another level of competency that was learned while on the job. Teach For America novices noted how these unrehearsed events affected them at depth, and influenced their teaching.

> Yesterday, Adriana was not in school. So, today she came up to my desk and whispered, "I was at court." Then she started crying. I knew that this was one of those moments where I had to be a shoulder. It was in the beginning of the morning, so the rest of the students were doing their daily seatwork. I took Adriana outside and we sat on our step. I asked her if she would like to tell me what happened. She told me that her dad got caught drinking and driving and that he had to go to jail and stay there in the detoxification tank for the rest of the night.
>
> She started crying again and I hugged her. It was a shock to me to see her shaking so badly and see tears, but hear no sound. I wondered if she had to do that a lot. I asked where she was when this happened and she told me that she and her baby sister were in the car. When she said that, I was not prepared for it. I heard about some of the shocking things that your students would go through (from TFA stories) and I knew that some of my students probably went through some of that, but I did not really want to face it. Here I was facing it. What did I do? What could I do, but hug her and tell her that I love her? I have a stuffed elephant that my students get on special days, so I let her have it for the day. I also made her a super star at some point during the day. It seemed to make her feel better, but at the end of the day when all of my students left ... I sat at my desk and cried for her, but my tears were not silent. (Hailey)

The majority of Teach For America teachers were less familiar with certain constructs and expectancies of schools impacted by poverty, based on their own upbringings, but sought to build relationships with their students.

> I taught seventh- and eighth-grade SPED [special education] classes at the Van Buren School in the Randolph District that borders the West Mountain area. It was so weird, Barb. As you know, my population of 13- to 15-year-olds were 90% Hispanic, with a few African American students and two White students. They admitted to me that they never had personal contact with an Asian person before.
>
> I mean, it was like I had two heads, the first time the kids saw me! And do you know what really freaked them out? I let a few weeks go by, then I couldn't hold it in anymore. I returned a comment in fluent Spanish. You should have seen their faces! "You speak Spanish?" they questioned incredulously. "Why didn't you tell us?" It was amazing! I never realized how I would still feel like an outsider in a school with kids who were all outside the mainstream. (Sara)

> I have 13 monolingual Spanish-speaking students. I have many others who are English language learners [ELL]. Rich and beautiful as their native language may be, these students are living in a society where their education is dependent on their ability to speak English. At least once a week, I overhear them complaining about teachers who have yelled at them for speaking Spanish in class. I've witnessed adults get in my monolingual students' faces and accuse them of failing to pay attention or being disrespectful. (Marguerite)

Corps members who reflected a cultural connection with their students recognized the importance of building community in spite of site-based realities that posed challenges.

When I first arrived in the region, the corps members that I met were familiar with Central American cultures and the majority (70%) were fluent Spanish-language speakers. This greatly impacted their enculturation into the community. Because of their language fluency, many of the cohort members advocated for their students over and beyond what their districts or TFA viewed as appropriate. Many corps members funded weekend field trips to cultural events from their own personal resources and embraced families through home visits.

After a few years, I noticed that the regional leadership team accepted greater numbers of applicants who were predominately *mono-lingual English speakers*, which was a significant departure from the make-up of the earlier cohorts. Although actively engaged in empowering their students and the community by writing grants and attending school board meetings, their experience and familiarity with students' cultural backgrounds was limited. Some accounts reflected an initial naiveté with respect to the realities of teaching in a high-needs school setting, and, while TFA teachers were pressured to focus on achievement and organizational expectations, while becoming acclimated to teaching in high-poverty school settings, some TFAers appeared to blame students, cultural mores, site-based factors, other teachers, or all of the above, for their students' academic problems. When particular issues presented, such as poor parental attendance at a parent/teacher conference, some corps members exhibited a heightened sense of personal commitment for student agency. But others' perceptions reflected not only an academic superiority, but also, perpetuated stereotype and judgment.

> My students are 13 and 14 years old. When they first walked into my class, they read at anywhere from a second to fifth-grade level. They have every problem that urban kids are rumored to have—drugs, poverty-ridden households, teenage pregnancy—as well as the problems you never hear about—neglect by both teachers and parents, ongoing self-esteem issues related to being labeled as "poor inner-city Blacks or Latinos," and the responsibilities for caring for many of their younger siblings, as well as their parents and other family. My students walk into the classroom every day, take off the red or blue jackets and bandanas that keep them safe on the street by association, and start reading the books that they should have read in the fourth grade if their teacher hadn't given up on them back then. (Klima, 2003, p. 1)

> These students seem so lazy. I don't think the laziness is inherent; I think it comes as a result of the educational experience they've had. Last year they had two official teachers and a series of substitutes. No teachers were effectively able to handle them, and they've just been shuffled around for a really long time. I don't think they've ever been expected to push themselves in the classroom. And that shows in their unwillingness (I really don't think it's inability) to memorize spelling words and multiplication tables. (Jeannie)

> I keep sending work home with her brothers and sisters who are all thin and dirty too—but, wow they have the best smiles! (Lucy)

A great many TFA teachers admitted that their initial perceptions of students' school experiences were predicated in part by TFA literature and messages received before arriving in their assigned region. Applicants were provided with scenarios of what one might expect as a TFA teacher during the interview process, initiated during TFA recruitment (as discussed in chapter 2). Many admitted that a preconceived picture of what their students' challenges might entail and their image of what teaching in high poverty rural and urban public schools would involve was gleaned from reading TFA's websites and hearing accounts from

TFA's Corps Member Advisors. In the absence of prolonged contact hours spent on-site in urban and or rural classrooms (other than TFA's compressed five-week student teaching) initial perceptions tended to be measured against TFA's own literature and publications. Generally, corps members' own language, race, ethnicity, social class, teaching assignment, and levels of support bore greater weight in the long run, and impacted how one viewed their work and their students.

> I survey my students. Does Nina come to class every day burning with questions relating to math? Does Jose engender that sense of wonder and awe in the face of a vista of knowledge just waiting to be discovered? Unfortunately, I must respond in the negative. Out of my 82 students, maybe a handful are truly enraptured in the positive sense of learning to continually ask questions. (Miguel)

Roughly 80% of the corps members in this study reflected different social class profiles than their students and viewed site-based realities through their own personal lens.

> But looking around my classroom, I realize that classes that would directly pertain to my job now just don't exist in an education major. Deciphering gang fights from Regular Fights 220 isn't in the curriculum plan. Coaching 13-Year-Olds Against Planned Pregnancies (and Trying to Convince Them Not to Get Pregnant on Purpose) 301 wasn't offered. And Appreciating Latino Culture while Teaching Kids English 441's professor must have been on sabbatical abroad when I was at UM. The reality of my job is that lesson planning isn't the part I'm least qualified to do here; it is the life lesson planning that I struggle with, and even 4 years in an Ed school wouldn't have helped me with that. (Klima, 2003, p. 1)

Yet, corps members who were (a) children of immigrants themselves, (b) conditioned by societal inequities, or (c) familiar with urban and rural communities impacted by poverty, sought to embrace the needs of their students.

> The very first day, my students entered my class; I talked to them about the meaning of a community. They learned that our class is a family ... a community. Ever since then, every Friday we have "community circle," in which we give compliments to each other, make apologies and have class meetings. I conducted them for about 15 weeks, but for the past three weeks, the students conduct the meeting. Today, I noticed how mature my students are. They take responsibility for their wrongdoings and, most importantly, appreciate each other. I noticed that they have all become more expressive and respectful during community circle. I can still remember how dependent on me they were at the beginning of the year. Now, they can conduct their own meetings ... independently. (Cortina)

Teach For America teacher's site-based realities were often sobering. The day-to-day lived experiences of the school and community culture served as eye-openers for so many, as noted below:

> On the first day of school, I invited my students to write down a question they would like me to answer on an index card. A child in my homeroom wrote, "Are you going to be here all year?" I wondered why he would ask this question. This simple question was drawn from the hat and aroused as much, if not more, curiosity than the others. I answered it with a simple, "Yes, of course." Hushed whispers of "Yes!" rippled through my classroom. Instead of moving on to the next question, Juan asked "Next year, too?" My "yes" was again returned by another round of "Yesses" from my students. Daisy chimed in. "All the way until we graduate?" "Yes."
>
> Today I learned that my students have been left with permanent subs for half a school year in the past. Most of their favorite teachers spent only a year or two at Jackson before moving on. In fact, most of my students have been at the school for longer than the majority of teachers. I have mixed feelings about my own commitment here. On one hand, I am just like the others. I will likely put in my time and leave, if not within two, then within three years. On the other hand, it seems as though even my few years of commitment is providing some type of consistency for my students.
>
> What a difficult situation! I believe it affects student morale when teachers come and go so quickly. Our students are very in tune to our thoughts and attitudes. If Jackson were an excellent place, why wouldn't teachers stick around? Why would they [teachers] suddenly leave? (Heather)

Teach For America novices were trained to think like corps members and this exacerbated challenges. Novice TFAers were determined to handle, even serious situations, on their own. For many, thinking of their students was prioritized and often contributed to a heightened sense of social commitment. But others noted how their levels of preparedness, and in some cases, lack of sustained support at their school, influenced how they reacted to the range of site-based realities they were immersed in as Teach For America teachers. Most were tenacious, determined, and hardworking, but was that enough?

A VIEW FROM THE FIELD: HALLOWEEN MORNING

Muted lights set the stage for groups of pantomiming fourth graders who reacted to scary sounds emanating from a Hollywood, sound-effects CD. It was Dave's way of reinforcing a lesson on descriptive language for his mostly Spanish-speaking students on this Halloween morning. Tiptoeing to a corner desk at the opposite end of the classroom, I found a seat to observe the high-interest lesson.

The excited mood of the students was charged by an unrehearsed event that tested Dave's reaction time. Suddenly, amid screams, which I sensed were *not* part of the teacher's script, blood drenched the white, cotton uniform shirt of a male student and the immediate vicinity … desk, books, and floor. Instinctively, with tissues in hand from my purse, I attended to the student, applying pressure to the artery above his two front teeth, stemming the blood flowing from Marco's nose. Dave telephoned the office to "follow the procedure." Twenty-seven kids were either crying, trying to calm them, quiet, or laughing nervously. The 5 minutes that Dave was on hold seemed like 50. He talked his students through the situation while holding the phone to his left ear. "Thank you, boys and girls, for being dependable in an emergency," he complimented in both English and Spanish, trying to keep his cool. "What am I supposed to do?" he whispered to me, as his blue eyes rolled upward.

The slow-moving, middle-aged nurse arrived about 15 minutes later with tissue box and emergency kit in hand. Her plump face registered more annoyance than concern as she rebuked both of us with her curt remark.

"I hope you were wearing your gloves, Mr. O'Brien. You never know what kind of diseases and stuff these kids have."

Site-Based Realities: Learning the School Culture

> Thirty-three of the nation's top college graduates have come to the West to nurture young minds in various school districts. Their common goal: to ensure all children in this nation have the chance to receive an excellent education. The group is part of Teach For America and these outstanding recent college graduates commit to teach for two years in disadvantaged urban and rural public schools. Teach For America is serious about educational excellence. (Estes, 1999, pp. 1-2)

The learning curve was steep. There was no gradual easement into site-based responsibilities. Participants admitted that they had a lot to process.

> I taught fourth grade at Institute and here. But it didn't really matter. It wasn't easier for me when I got here. It's not like, you know, you somehow got some information that you really could use at Institute. It wasn't like that, because when you got here you got a whole new set of standards and you had … to figure it out. (Marili)

Site-based realities included navigating each school's culture, or way of operating. Variances in protocol occurred at each district, school, department, and grade level. TFAers, new to the school culture, were learning how to deal with personnel (other than their students and parents). These included: superintendent, principal, school secretary, mentor teachers, grade team leader, colleagues, and custodial staff.

> Every district is different. Every school is run differently, so when we got here I had to really go by what I was being told by my district and my principal. (Jaqui)

> When I arrived, there was not one veteran teacher on the fifth-grade level at my school. I didn't know who to go to. Luckily for me, the principal helped me out. (Jared)

> What I learned from other TFA's is that I was lucky to be placed at my school. My principal hired a lot of TFA's over the years and hired someone to help us with the basics, like filling out trip forms, [and] reviewing class lists and students' individual needs. He tried to pair us up with someone in our classes to co-teach with. None of the other corps members were so lucky. When I heard them talking about what they were going through at their sites, I kept my mouth shut. I knew that, relatively speaking, I had it good. (Antonia)

Teach For America novices were among the newly initiated; trying to read the social cues inherent with any organizational culture, of which schools were one. They stated that they had plenty of questions, as noted below, but were not sure whom to ask or if asking was the appropriate strategy.

> We would like to know some things that are very basic, but no one sits us down and tells us this stuff. You know, like you're supposed to have someone approve any notes home to parents. And no one tells us what you are supposed to do when one shows up and wants to talk to you and you have to do afternoon bus duty. (Jesse)

Participants had plenty of questions with respect to procuring supplies, utilizing the copy machine, negotiating requests for student services, and, getting a handle on the school's daily routines, such as bus evacuation drills, sudden student emergencies, and procedural things that require a teacher's immediate action.

> I had no idea as to who was going to cover for me when I had to use the restroom. We had "specials" canceled [art, music] all the time, so when that happened, you couldn't just leave your kids. You had to wait for lunchtime. (Nan)

Teach For America novices arrived in the region with their heads overloaded, with informational how-to's germinating from Institute. The district employee handbook and school site procedures (to be referenced as needed) added to it. Unlike other non-TFA first year teachers, novice corps members didn't experience student teaching from which to develop a familiarity with daily school-based routines. Many of the participants relied on TFA's organization to provide them with that foundational teacher-learning.

> I didn't outright face any challenges to my self-confidence when I first entered teaching, primarily because I really had no conception of what I was getting myself into! It wasn't until the end of the first week that I began to face the possibility that I wasn't cut out to be a teacher. (Mike)

> Last year, I was just flying by the seat of my pants. (Cassidy, second-year TFA)

> So, what I learned at Institute was OK, but not necessarily OK here. So, really it just ... it was like two completely different teaching experiences, regardless of the age of the children. What it did do was frustrate me, because I was teaching kids that were at the same level as I was supposedly going to teach when I got back, but I wasn't learning anything because I was, you know, so lost there. It just frustrated me even more because I thought that I would get some good experience that I was going to be able to use and I didn't. I didn't have a clue. (Martina)

Expectations that their district would provide mentors to provide guidance didn't seem to materialize either. When that didn't pan out, novices admitted that they were on their own and relied on each other.

> Thank God, I had Marta [another first-year corps member] help me out. She came into my room and the two of us put up the bulletin board paper. I had never done that before. I had less than a day to get my room ready. You want to talk about panic? (Nan)

> Some of the second years [TFAers] helped me out in getting my classroom ready. They were as helpful as they could be. But, they had their own class to prepare. (Dave)

First-year TFA teachers were unsure about relaying concerns to the administration of both TFA and their district, even when they involved serious matters. They were accustomed to the TFA prototypical teacher who proactively solved problems.

> Barb, I'm shaking, but I had to talk to you. I don't know who else to go to. One of the seventh graders at my school threatened to kill me. He said, "I'm gonna get you, bitch." I sent him to the office. I wanted to see the principal. He was busy. The principal had him in the school in an in-house suspen-

sion. I see him every day. He just leers at me. I don't know what to do. No one is helping me. I am not a kid. I need to know. I went to TFA and they said that the administration is handling it. How do I know that? Only the other corps members are there for me. (Trudy)

I had my car vandalized at Southport School. They poured paint on it. I can't get to school now. I went to my principal three times! Where is the accountability? I am carpooling with someone. Students in my class are smirking. Three of them are involved. They are "getting away with murder" and no one does anything. (Nancy)

We need a course on school law. We need to really know the chain of command to go to if things get out of hand. (Jeremy)

Others seconded Jeremy's concern. Study participants admitted to me that they were dealing with a predetermined set of district operating procedures that made little sense to them and appeared generic when application was called for in their daily practice. Likewise, most didn't feel comfortable contacting TFA's leadership team.

We were told that we (TFAers) were responsible legally. If issues involved legality, corps members had to make a decision to either comply with the school's policies or leave. (Trish)

What are we liable for? How do we handle this? How do we know what to do? (Jennifer)

What are the roles of the people in the school? The guidance counselor, the police officer, etc? (Marcy)

Some corps members were admittedly outspoken in their undergraduate careers and were inclined to voice concerns to those in a position of authority. A few bypassed their school administrator when they felt that things were not proceeding to their expectations. As noted below, corps members alerted me to their contact with the district superintendent to complain about site-based issues, just weeks into their first year of teaching.

Barb, I know that this is going to sound inappropriate to you, but I called the superintendent and told him that the administrator at my school is utterly incompetent. He leaves at 2:30 and is never available when you need him for anything. (Eric)

How do we approach the superintendent with our concerns that have gone unrecognized like legal issues, class sizes, case loads [special education students] too large to handle? (Vickie)

> Three [out] of four of our corps members are experiencing lack of class-room and administrative support. What is TFA willing to do to assist? If need be, would TFA remove corps members from sites and reassign us? Can TFA administration sit in with corps members and principals if issues are not being resolved independent of TFA? (Erica, Tina, Justine, and Molly)

Teach For America corps members were self-reliant and socialized to solve problems that surfaced. This course of action (or in some cases, inaction) wasn't always a prudent navigational technique. Some internalized TFA's mission philosophy and set out to offer what they perceived to be support of their own students. Yet, graduating from college and beginning to teach, with only a 5-week intensive program that combined coursework, field experience, and social advocacy, exacerbated the site-based realities of TFAers. Many TFAers admitted that their picture of schooling was based on experiences as a student in their own community of origin. This served as the major point of reference by which TFAers determined what schooling should look like. Lortie (1975) referred to this experience base as "an apprenticeship of observation" (p. 61). It is the means by which one constructs an image of teaching and learning. While some corps members did travel or volunteer in national and/or international school settings, researcher Lisa Delpit (1995) noted how upper- and middle-class teachers view school differently than their students who attended schools in high poverty communities.

POINTS TO CONSIDER: LEARNING THE CULTURE OF COMMUNITIES AND SCHOOLS

For a majority of study participants, site-based teaching realities sharply contrasted with their own K-8 schooling experiences. The cultural climate of one's students was, in most cases, significantly different from that of most TFA teacher's own social class and life story (Dewey, 1938). Connelly and Clandinin (1995) discuss the influence of a teacher's personal experiences on their teaching:

> Personal practical knowledge is in the teacher's past experience, in the teacher's present mind and body, and in the future plans and actions. Personal practical knowledge is found in the person's practice. It is, for any one teacher, a particular way of reconstructing the past and the intentions of the future to deal with the exigencies of a present situation. (p. 25)

Not only were TFAers learning the background and multiple subjectivities (gender, race, religious affiliation, culture, and family background) of their students, but often they were trying to negotiate district policy—

which differed from building to building—and often from changes in administration. At times, these policies (less likely to be influenced or scrutinized in more affluent districts) took on elements of a "hidden curriculum" (Anyon, 1980; Apple, 2004).

Teach For America's first-year teachers were not aware of some of the legalities or what I term, *"pot-holder"* (too-hot-to-handle) topics that are part of any teaching situation, but are more intense in high-poverty urban and rural schools. Prior to corps members' arrival in their district, might first-year TFA rookies have been well served with a full course in school law? Would one more compressed session integrated into their studies during Institute have even been deemed effective? Districts provided a new employees' handbook that outlined policies, but did corps members have time to process the contents with a rather compressed entrée into the school setting, as foremost on their minds were responsibilities of setting up a classroom?

The literature discusses the inadequate training that teachers for low-income children receive (Berliner, 2009; Children's Defense Fund, 2003; Darling-Hammond, Hammerness, Grossman, Rust, & Shulman, 2005; Delpit, 1995; Haycock, 2002/2003; Hilliard, 1991; Kaplowitz, 2003; Knapp, 2001; Knaupp, 1995; Laczko-Kerr & Berliner, 2002; Ladson-Billings, 2001; Lankford, Loeb, & Wycoff, 2002; Zeichner, 2003).

With a compressed training model and team teaching at Corps Training Institute, how were TFA teachers equipped to deal with some of the issues that surfaced in their classrooms? How were they able to protect themselves and their students and know how to advise and counsel them? Where was the line drawn between teaching their students and safeguarding their own well-being? Was a line to be drawn, at all? If so, who would go to bat for corps novices if an issue did arise? Was Teach For America's organization going to run interference for its teachers?

Haberman (1995), Ladson-Billings (2001), and Viadero (2009) identified experienced teachers as those who know how to teach well in challenging circumstances. How experienced were corps members who went through TFA's training? Dilworth and Brown (2001) observe, "We frequently find that the sole responsibility of teaching disenfranchised students is placed on the classroom teachers" (p. 653). Was there a better way of providing TFA novices with a background into what would lie ahead?

> Right now our main focus is on new teachers because we have so many in our schools. Next year, we're trying to plan where maybe our non-certified TFA teachers could come to us in the summer, and work with our kids during a district summer school. They would work alongside a mentor in the classroom and in the grade level that they are going to be working in for that year. I also want to try to work with the mentors during the summer so that the new teachers have a strong buddy that they can work with on a daily

basis when school starts. One of our administrators, in the district, Dr. Pineela (pseudonym) wants to start a jump start program in the summer and have these teachers come in and work in our district. If that could be worked out, TFA teachers would get to know their schools; their administrators, and the support staff that would be there to help them. But I don't think that the TFA people want to go that route. They like things the way they are. (Mrs. Ortega, veteran teacher)

Dilworth and Brown (2001) recommend, "A need exists for teachers who are consciously responsive to their students cultural backgrounds and learning styles; it is considered crucial by many scholars in their efforts to improve academic achievement" (p. 659). Mercado (2001) advises:

> Current scholarship suggests that teachers need to be knowledgeable about the social lives of the children and the conditions of their lives outside of school. What teachers know about the lives of children outside of school affects their pedagogical practices (p. 690).

Eisner (1983) discussed how teachers [need to] know how to "read" students, respond quickly, and reshape the flow of events. "Teachers who function with aesthetic vision, perceive the dynamic nature of what is unfolding in front of them at any given moment" (p. 4). Paolo Freire (1998) asserts,

> Educators need to know what happens in the world of the children with whom they work. They need to know the universe of their dreams, the language with which they skillfully defend themselves from the aggressiveness of their world, what they know independently of school, and how they know it. (p. 72)

Darling-Hammond and Sykes (1999) argue that, "New teachers need 'case knowledge' to accumulate much more detailed qualitative information about what transpires in classrooms in order to build a more reliable knowledge base" (p. 103). The question of "what teachers do" assumes a more serious tone especially when a teacher's landscape heightens the stakes. Grimmett and MacKinnon (1992) noted the difference in teacher's knowing "rules," as opposed to knowing what drives practice:

> Craft knowledge is the accumulated wisdom derived from teachers' and practice-oriented researchers' understandings of the meanings ascribed to the many dilemmas inherent in teaching. Craft knowledge has a different sort of rigor, one that places more confidence in the judgment of teachers and distinguishes between "knowing that" and "knowing how." (pp. 428, 437)

How, then, did TFA's model integrate research on teaching students impacted by poverty in America's urban and rural schools? Garcia-Gonza-lez' (1998) work examines teachers biographies as an influence on their beliefs and practices. The questions posed are insightful and informative:

> (1) How do we as teachers educate so that we do not replicate existing social inequalities and (2) How do we avoid the twin pitfalls of (a) stressing the obstacles of economic success, thereby encouraging defeatism and (b) stress-ing the possibilities for economic success and thereby encouraging the view that those who have not "made it" have only themselves to blame? (p. 40).

Researchers, experienced with issues surrounding teacher preparation and retention for high needs communities, realize that there is a com-plexity to effective teaching that involves layers of knowing that are inte-grated with timing, circumstance, context, place, culture, and condition.

This integration of learning the culture of the community and how to meet the needs of the students one teaches, involves more than what a "social mission" will remedy; especially when limited opportunity for exposure to the community is presented prior to one's beginning to teach there (Dilworth & Brown, 2001; Zeichner, 2003).

Good teaching is not only shaped by a teacher's knowledge, but by a teacher's beliefs. Pajares (1992) suggested that beliefs are not easily defined and not readily measurable. It comes down to what a believer holds true or false. Graber (2001) wrote, "Beliefs represent what is true and what is false to the believer, and are developed through personal experience over time and often form the substance for an opinion or point of view" (p. 493).

> Knowing about the community, knowing about the students you are teach-ing, their background, where they come from, what prior knowledge they have, if any, about the subject that they're going to be teaching [is neces-sary]. But, I think [above all] you have to understand the culture of the chil-dren that you are teaching. (Mrs. Egan, veteran teacher)

Berliner (1990) notes that teacher thinking and actions are insepara-ble. "Thought and action are so inextricably linked that it is really a fic-tion to maintain their separateness" (p. 341). Teach For America teachers act primarily from their beliefs during their first year, because they have such limited practical experiences in classrooms to draw from. The proto-typical corps member, who advocates for his/her students, demonstrates the internalization of TFA's mission in high poverty schools. But are corps members acting from a solid foundation that is grounded in best practice research in teaching children impacted by poverty, or are corps members acting out the organization's belief, that by simply placing TFA teachers in high-poverty classrooms, students are provided a quality education?

CHAPTER 7

LEARNING THE CULTURE OF TEACHING

A VIEW FROM THE FIELD: CARA'S QUESTIONS

Cara teaches sixth grade in the Middletown School District. In February, Cara's principal placed her on an improvement plan. She was written up for classroom management and lesson presentation skills. "Well, this is the first year that TFA placed any teachers in our district. I need help. Right now I have 26 students in a class with tremendous fluctuation. New kids come in probably once every 2 weeks. That's been a problem, especially with the English language learners since I don't speak Spanish. I only have two kids who are fluent Spanish- and English-speakers and neither one is really willing to take their time to be translators for the new kids. They can speak Spanish, but they have a very hard time explaining things, so they say, "I can't do it." So, that's a struggle.

On top of that, both of my Robert's are new to the school. They are off the wall and constantly up out of their seats. I have questions. Like, when do you do the team meetings? What kinds of things do students talk about? Do they talk about things they want to talk about or things related to teaching stuff? Also, are there ways to approach these meetings? Is it something that if a student is having an issue with another student, issues are brought out? While we're on the subject, how do you do group work? What number [of students] works best for groups? My high kids are tired

Learning on Other People's Kids: Becoming a Teach For America Teacher
pp. 99–125
Copyright © 2010 by Information Age Publishing

99

of working with groups when the other kids are goofing around. Oh, and I feel like there's this rush to get through everything. I have to get through geometry. I have to get through fractions. I have to get through this, this, and this. Can you give me strategies? I need something to use with my students that works for them and me. Something lasting that I can figure out."

CONTENT AND PEDAGOGY: THINKING LIKE A TEACHER

Teach For America partnered with districts challenged in recruiting qualified applicants. TFA recruiters often prioritized outreach to undergraduates majoring in math, science, and technology over those possessing pedagogical backgrounds. While these candidates seemed to fit the Teach For America profile, corps members reported being assigned to teaching positions in elementary or middle grades. Participants noted that their content area background, which might have proven beneficial for those teaching secondary school, did not totally prepare them to teach students in their assigned grade levels, as noted below.

Instructional skills: I lack greatly. (Charles)

My instructional skills are lacking and I think I know why: This is my first year teaching and I have no formal education in educational instruction. (Jessica)

I never had any education courses before I went to Institute, not ever. I thought that teaching was just naturally maybe knowing a little bit of how to give a good lecture, how to have an activity. I have read some books, but reading how to do something and then being put in that situation, you know is completely different. I think that having classes, seeing people model lessons for you, I mean these are all things that no matter how good you are, you can always benefit from really seeing how it's done even when you try it yourself. And, I would almost say that with teaching, I think that less content and more pedagogy is needed. To me that means, you understand like how is the best way to convey your information. (Ali)

Study participants alluded to expectations which assumed that TFA novices knew not only what to teach, but, *how* to teach it. Curriculum and instructional practices, which involved learning the content for each subject, its connection to the state standards, and application for a range of student abilities, surfaced as one of the top three needs that novice TFAers listed over five consecutive years.

It all depends on the grade you're teaching. You realize that you need to know certain things. Like, how do I organize the classroom? How do I set up things? Even knowing things like, how do I access materials? How do I sift through? Because it's all those little things with knowing how to teach that if you don't know how to do them ... you have problems. (Ali)

I'm trying to figure out how to teach math to three different ability levels. I've been trying to find endless handouts of varying levels, and I just plan to pass them out to the appropriate group of students. I will try to get around to each group and give one-on-one instruction. (Lydia)

I'm finding that a main concern of mine right now is differentiating instruction. I have such varied needs in my classroom and I have quite a few bored kids. I certainly do not have enough time to work with students who really need my help. (Stacey)

I just wish there was a "Centers for Dummy Teachers" book that I could get to help! There is such an overwhelming amount of information to process. (Jeannie)

I need organizational tips! How do I set up an effective classroom? (Gabby)

I was surprised to learn from several participants (who stated in recorded interviews) that they didn't know how to plan lessons for their kids. Teach For America's regional administrators seemed to suggest otherwise. "Barb, they all know how to plan lessons. That's something we stress at Institute" (N. Baker, former TFA program director, personal e-mail correspondence).

Teach For America's novices appeared to be: a) spending most of their time planning lessons; and b) planning for segmented portions of their day. Study participants noted that, as teaching novices, they seemed to be continuously focused on *having that plan*, as something on which they could hang their hat, and were disappointed when their efforts did not measure up to their expectations.

I really don't feel any more prepared this week than last week. I need to get into a routine for preparation and planning. The most difficult part of that is I don't even know where to start! (Stefania)

Even if I planned one lesson really well, what was I going to do for the other lessons? I just didn't have that time! (Cordelia)

I planned this lesson and it didn't last as long as I thought. So, now the kids are acting up and I am waiting for lunchtime to save me. (Jana)

Participants admitted that they relied on pragmatic approaches as the foundational tools that guided their practice. These included context-free decisions about instruction, textbooks, teachers' guides, borrowed plans from other teachers and routines that previously worked for them.

> To begin the class, I always have the day's objectives on the board, like the agenda for the day, so they [students] always know what we are doing. You always have the one or two kids that need to know exactly what we are doing. I will have a quick-write type thing to try and activate prior knowledge. [For example] I'll have a picture of stars and have the students make lists of the many different things you can see in this picture or have them tell me what the stars look like. (Ali)

TFA novices also stated that they employed a trial-and-error approach to pedagogy with an emphasis on self-correction as referenced from their TFA training.

> You would like "guess" to do something and then okay you'd ask yourself, "Did this work?" If not, what am I going to do differently? I mean, as TFA [administration] would say, "use constant reflection." So I asked myself, "OK, what is working, what is not, what do I need to change?" And, that's one good thing about teaching when you're hired. You do it once and you realize, okay or this is terrible. Then when the next group of kids would come in, you'd try something different. (Janelle)

While corps members counted on me to provide feedback and ideas, some first-year TFA's relied on me to not only model or team-teach, but take over completely, which I did in a few cases. When on-site coaching was requested, I taught the lesson, and then metaphorically handed back the ball (class instruction duties) to the rookie teacher.

> Well, I planned for one lesson or maybe two. But I have a 90-minute language arts block and now I don't know what to do. Barb, I was hoping that maybe you'd have something you could do with them to fill up the next hour. (Tess)

Since TFA training offered only 5 weeks for its corps members to learn content, pedagogy, classroom management, and learner strategies before their real teaching duties commenced, participants admitted that lingering questions persisted with respect to teacher know-how.

> When I came in [to teaching] I didn't exactly know [what kids at this age were able to do] so I gave them something of what I thought maybe an eighth grader would know, realizing it was going to be difficult. I mean that's how I finally figured out teaching through trial and error. But, trying to find that level, that's challenging. (Ali)

Novice TFAers shared that they were not prepared for all that they were required to know. "Teacher knowledge" involved learning the curriculum prior to each day's teaching, and making the lesson content interesting. Many admitted to reading the textbook the night before to familiarize themselves with the next day's lesson.

> As a fifth-grade teacher, I have more than sufficient knowledge of all six subjects that I teach. My lack of scientific knowledge and educational methods requires that I read the night before I give a science lesson, so I don't delve too far into the subject knowledge. This would never work in some other school district. (Charles)

How one transitioned from one lesson to the other during the course of the day was a noted pedagogical concern. Most corps members shared that they were not adept at figuring out the pacing of lessons, the integration of several subject areas into a block of time, or long-term projects. They relied on the ready-made lessons presented in textbooks. With the multiplex demands on a novice TFAers time, all admitted that as beginning teachers, they were reading the prompts in the teacher's guides verbatim, just to keep up.

> I don't have time to plan for everything, so I am using the textbooks to teach from. I know I'm boring the kids, but what else am I supposed to do? I am a first-year TFA teacher! (Tia)

> I was handed a set of textbooks, but I'm having trouble breaking those down into individually engaging lessons. (Katherine)

> The textbooks with teachers' guides are boring and my kids know it. (Melissa)

> I feel like, I at least have the book [teacher's guide]. (Carmen)

> Is there something besides teaching straight from the text and worksheets? (Stephen)

> I know that all students learn differently. I know that giving a lesson solely using my voice helps only a small percentage of my students. I know that I have made great efforts to incorporate individual work and group work, as well as visuals while instructing. I have the full attention of my students, hardly any management issues or discipline problems. But I have run out of ideas. I have (in a sense) hit a wall. I feel that if I don't find more interesting ways to engage them, I might lose them. In other words, if you were to spend a week in my class now, you would be impressed at the variety of activities I present in my teaching. But, if you were to come back to my class two months from now, I fear you would wonder if you had gone back into

time, two months prior. The activities wouldn't have changed one bit because I don't know any other activities. (Charles)

Many TFAers realized soon into their teaching assignment, that pedagogical know-how required more than what a textbook could provide. A novice's planning often necessitated becoming familiar with their students' learning curve as well as content areas (math, reading, language arts, science and social studies). Those who were not content to just follow a script and attempt to figure out an alternative game plan *while in the process of teaching their lesson* felt that going with the flow would, actually, be a useful tool in motivating students. Creativity was the intent of this approach. But participants admitted that as teaching, novices their intentions of teaching through improvisation fell short. Modifying an existing series of plans to meet the needs of their students without an idea of where that route would take them posed other challenges (as noted in the next section on classroom management). When their efforts (or lack of tiered lesson plans) didn't work out, participants frankly confessed to using "fillers" or less academic or grade-level activities to just get through the day.

> Eighth grade is definitely another world. At least I have five or six students who consistently volunteer in class. Story time is also another highlight that saves me in the afternoon! (Jessica)

> I was chewed out today by my assistant principal. He came in this morning and wanted to see my plan book. I have to be honest with you, Barb, I didn't have time to plan. I was busy this weekend. I was intending to get to it on Monday night, but he came in today. I was sort of winging it. Some of the stuff turned out pretty well. He [the principal] was not amused. (Derrick)

> To say that the start of my school year was hectic is an understatement. I literally moved to ____ one day and began teaching the next. Needless to say, my planning for the first few weeks of school left much to be desired. (Marguerite)

The newly hired corps members were required to prepare activities that introduced the lesson, hit the academic standards, and, include an assessment that indicated that the day's objectives were met within an allotted time frame. Participants noted that timing was a factor in learning to teach. Many inquired as to how to pace a lesson for student engagement.

> I understand my standards [state/national academic benchmarks]. But I don't know how to get there. What order? How long? (Jenn)

> I tend to go over my lesson plan time. How do you fix that? (Cortina)

Not enough time in the school day to teach and give adequate time for project or worksheet assessments. Not to mention I have no time to do all I need to get done. I feel like I need someone to sit me down and help me organize so I can stay on track. (Lila)

For many novice TFAers the answers to, "How is it done?" and "Why does this work today, when it didn't work yesterday?" were stored in memory in the form of *flashbacks from their own teachers* teaching during their elementary and junior high school experiences. I was surprised to learn that many lessons and/or teaching strategies that they wanted me to observe, were recalled from the methods modeled by *their* former teachers from over a decade ago. Some even contacted family members, who were teachers, to coach them long-distance by phone or e-mail. It was truly amazing to see the lengths that TFA teachers assumed to try to meet their students' needs.

I mean, in a lot of ways, how I am teaching right now is what I remember doing in high school. It's what makes sense to me. It's a kind of...prior knowledge. I guess it is just that. (Ali)

I remember Mr. Salazar from fourth grade in Connecticut. He was the reason I tried TFA and I admit that some things that I did with my students (also fourth grade) I remembered from being in his class. I never forgot the things that made learning fun from his class. (Nan)

Teach For America's training workshops seemed to provide a generic model for its trainees. It seemed as if participants stated that what they needed most was more specific demonstration of how to teach subject matter to specific grade levels of students.

My friend who is still in the region [he was TFA five years ago] meets with current corps members every week. The district pays him for this extra role. He told me, "I'm spoon-feeding these people weekly lessons, and, Sania, they give me a blank stare. They don't know what I'm talking about. I forgot that they just go through the TFA program and are expected to figure out teaching when they get here. Nothing's changed." (Sania)

I told TFA people here that I want to observe. I want to see how it's carried out just like my students need things to model from, I need things modeled for me. You could read a book, you can write a lesson plan, but until you see it. (Ali)

Teach For America's novices who entered their classrooms with only minimal resources in the form of their own teacher-made materials noted that they had little in the way of field-tested lessons from prior classroom teaching experiences to pull out and confidently use with their students.

> I have all of these great ideas and things that I want to do with my kids, but when will I have the time to create this stuff? Definitely over winter break. (James)

> I am going to take the time to give my classroom a make-over. I will get to it during the winter break. I can just about keep up right now. (Lauren)

For the majority of study participants from consecutive cohorts, the teaching of reading proved to be a major concern. Although they themselves were avid and proficient readers or *content knowledgeable*, this crucial skill was not automatically transferred. It required subject, grade level, and learner-specific strategies. Most reiterated that when they left CTI they were not experienced in the intricacies involved with literacy development.

> My recommendation is that when we arrive in a region, we are given a course in reading and language arts, then phonics and teaching decoding strategies for those teaching the lower elementary grades. (Lenore)

> Some days I do reading. But, I do reading differently. Like some days I actually read almost like an elementary school teacher because they really like it. They like when I read and show pictures to them. Some days they read in a group, some days they read independently. It's just to get background for the subject. Is that okay to do with eighth-graders? (Ali)

My housemate Mark, and I sat down and planned. We shared some of our similar challenges and successes in teaching junior high reading. We decided to tackle the reading curriculum routine and established it for 2-week sessions where students would study and practice vocabulary, elements of a story, literary terms, reading comprehension, and summarization. Every class period would be divided into three 15-minute sections that we broke down like this:

> - 15 min. silent reading
> - 15 min. book report study sheet/vocabulary development
> - 15 min. shared reading

> We discussed how we thought a routine every day would improve student achievement and management. (Rob)

Even those with a content-based degree in the sciences, for example, were not prepared to teach content that they had never seen before *and* translate it to the learning levels of their students. Most participants acknowledged the distinction between content (i.e., knowing science) and pedagogy.

> I mean, you could be the smartest person in the world, know everything about science. My co-teacher had a good science background. He would lecture the whole time about these concepts none of the kids understood. He was way beyond them. I mean he was great at science and brilliant. But, the kids, honestly did not understand a thing he taught because he just stood up there and lectured about things that they couldn't relate to or had no prior knowledge about. So, really, they [the students] got nothing out of it. The other teacher [who I teach with] doesn't have a science background, but she can read the chapters and get enough of an understanding about science to be able to teach it, because she has the tools to teach. She knows how to present information to the kids and so the subject matter isn't that important. You still need an understanding of science, but I feel in my grade level [eighth] that's less important. In the junior high situation, I would probably put it at maybe 35% for content and the rest for pedagogy. (Ali)

> You can know everything in the world about science, but if you can't... if you don't know how to set up a lab or how to give directions clearly (because you're just lecturing) and if students are just being given a worksheet, then that's not knowing how to carry out those labs and not knowing how to manage them efficiently. So, I think there definitely needs to be a balance. (Trudy)

Often, unexpected events occurred. Participants realized that a teacher's plan could be interrupted or postponed for one reason or another. Teach For America's novices learned that the effortless shifting of gears along with a workable backup plan (kept in one's pocket at all times) called for a set of teaching strategies that required countless hours of practice for ready application. In becoming a Teach For America teacher, novice practitioners noted that pedagogical know-how required adaptability to the teaching situation at hand and administrators offered little tolerance for lapses in learning-time.

> Today my class was supposed to go on a field trip. Unfortunately, we did not go because it was raining. We were supposed to take the city bus, but I felt that taking 23 third-graders out on a rainy day would turn into chaos. Since I was not expecting the rain, I did not plan for today. Therefore, I was completely unprepared. As a result, after giving my students the sad news that the trip was canceled, I gave them free time to relieve the energy they had for the trip. Then suddenly, the principal shows up and my students are playing checkers during the reading and language arts block. She was pretty upset and not moved by the fact that my students needed some free time since their field trip was canceled. I told her that the class was going to be

ready in 5 minutes for writing workshop. She left. Approximately five minutes later, she returned. I was pretty upset that the principal expected the
class to drastically move their mentality from being ready for a field trip to
plunging into reading and writing. (Cortina)

Some participants' teacher thinking appeared to rationalize their
experiences that were the result of, or related to the complexities of learning both content and pedagogical expectations within their placement, as
the commentaries below illustrate.

If I were given more than a day to prepare for the first week of school I'm
sure it would've run smoothly. (Teresa)

I cannot speak with previous science teachers about what curriculum has
been covered. They are long gone, leaving me with both the 7th and 8th
graders and the mystery of what to teach them. The same holds true in
other subjects. In a district where curriculum is debatable and standards
seem to be met or not met depending on the whims of the teacher, (especially in science), this type of communication is very important (not that I
would condone such attitudes, but they exist none the less). (Marguerite)

I was a computer science major in college so it was not that difficult to
assume the duties of a computer teacher for middle-schoolers here. I mean,
when the principal asked me which assignment I would prefer … teaching
third graders or being the computer teacher for fifth-eighth graders, I knew
that it was an easy choice.
    I love teaching this subject area. I know the content. I knew what I
wanted to teach them. Most are very interested in learning about computers. But, while I am still teaching the same grade level in the region that I
arrived in, I moved to another school district that wanted me and other TFA
alums. This is my sixth year as a teacher here. (Nancy)

Incoming corps members were required by the state to pass tests
related to not only content knowledge, but, pedagogy and professional
practice. Teach For America's teachers possessed high cognitive abilities
and tended to do well on Praxis Exams, designed in part to assess content
knowledge. But did the tests suggest that TFA novices were ready to perform the multilayered tasks they faced while teaching?

Barb, some of them will pass because they are smart and test taking comes
easy for them. But based on my own experiences, teaching for 2 years, how
does a passing grade translate to teacher effectiveness, or as you say, teacher
"know-how" without ever having spent time in a classroom? Without any
education courses how would you know what you should be doing and how?
There is no test that I could have passed that would ever indicate that I was
prepared to teach. And they are being given these tests before they go to

Institute for any TFA training. I *definitely* didn't know what I was doing. I had to learn on the job and by taking university courses. That first year I was just trying to figure it out. (personal conversation with Olivia and Darnell)

How then, did content knowledge alone provide novice practitioners with pedagogical direction? And why, according to those in charge of educational licensing standards across the country, is it so heavily favored as criteria enough for entrée into teaching? The rationale behind this stance that content knowledge is *the* criteria that matters appears to be challenged by study participants. Teach For America teachers, whose pedagogical and experiential development consisted of a 5-week compressed model, were relying on their own content knowledge backgrounds, and their own grade and high school experiences, to anchor their teaching. They were operating under an organizational paradigm that inferred that development of critical pedagogical skills, with application, would occur during their first "100 days" of teaching.

However, as the data seems to suggest, the learning curve was steep. Was it assumed that plunging young, intelligent candidates with limited teaching internship experience into a classroom of poor children would acclimate them to teaching? Was content knowledge really all that mattered? John Dewey (1938) offers a different view:

> It is a mistake to suppose that the mere acquisition of a certain amount of arithmetic, geography, history, etc., which is taught and studied because it may be useful at some time in the future, has this effect. And it is a mistake to suppose that acquisition of skills in reading and figuring will automatically constitute preparation for their right and effective use under conditions very unlike those in which they were acquired. One trouble is that the subject matter in question was learned in isolation. It was segregated when it was acquired and hence is so disconnected from the rest of experience. It is contrary to the laws of experience that learning of this kind, no matter how thoroughly ingrained at the time, should give genuine preparation. (pp. 47-48)

Teach For America teachers' 5 weeks preparation comprised both pedagogical training and field experiences. Then they were hired by high needs community schools to the dismay of more experienced teachers who wondered about their qualifications.

> I was told that they were qualified. I asked, "Are you serious? *By what criteria?* What happens with special education and elementary education? They don't have any of that kind of thing. I don't know what to say about that. They're smart; they're dedicated; but they haven't got a clue. It goes back to what I was saying before ... they don't think of themselves professionally as a

teacher. It's like they're playing like they're a teacher. (Mrs. Schepis, veteran educator)

A VIEW FROM THE FIELD: BEN'S BLOWOUT LESSON

Ben caught himself repeating idle warnings, "Settle down, listen up, okay now," as he tried to teach a reading lesson to his students. A prolonged exhale preceded his systematic glance at the plan book resting on the podium. From behind it, situated front and center of the room, his body language betrayed his efforts at control. He cleared his throat and readied his next pitch.

But, intermittent student outbursts penetrated efforts by the young teacher to manage the class. His TFA program director suggested that he create consequences for students who called out answers or comments. So, even though his heart really wasn't in agreement with the suggested form of behavior modification, male and female adolescents who shouted out responses to questions in class were met with the consequence of standing behind their chairs, for this infraction.

When I entered his classroom, middle-schoolers, some with changing voices, laughed loudly as scrunched paper balls, crafted from white loose-leaf sheets, flew across the room, and made contact with standing human targets.

"Ooowww! That hurt!" whined a girl with a flair for the dramatic who was hit in the back. The more serious-minded students rolled their eyes and shook their heads.

Sweating and eyeing the clock, Ben privately wished for the quick passage of time, or perhaps, lunch, art, music, or physical education, to rescue him and close the chaotic scene. The seventh graders were not impressed that Mr. Barro, 7 years their senior, had, only 5 months earlier, earned a double major from Brown.

CLASSROOM MANAGEMENT

I was supposed to pick up teaching skills over the summer from Teach For America (TFA) which places mostly recent college graduates with no ed-school background in disadvantaged school districts. In its training program, I learned lesson planning and I internalized the TFA philosophy of high expectations for all students. But the program skimped on classroom management. As a complete teaching novice, I was ill equipped when I finally stepped into my own fifth-grade classroom. (Kaplowitz, 2003, p. W13)

Webster's 3rd New International Dictionary of the English Language (1993) defines *management* as: "a. a skilled handling, conducting or supervising of something and; b. the function of planning, organizing, coordinating, directing a project or activity with responsibility for results" (p. 1372). As participants noted, becoming TFA teachers involved integrating all of the aforementioned skills and duties. Classroom management expectations, as one participant summarized, were intricately entwined with "getting the content across while keeping a handle on what was going on with every student in one's charge for the entire day." This included moving groups of students across campus, maintaining order during an emergency, providing for the flow of experiences from full class lessons to group activities, and a list of other tasks, all of which necessitated that a visual inventory of the happenings within the classroom be continuously maintained.

Classroom management proved to be one of the top three needs of first year TFAers over seven consecutive cohorts whose classrooms I visited in both the middle Atlantic and Southwest regions. Furthermore, nearly all participants admitted that they needed to prioritize pedagogical knowledge over content knowledge. Many viewed the connection between responsibilities related to management, and engagement of students, as key to their teaching effectiveness as noted in the Top Ten Needs Survey of Beginning Teachers. At the onset of one's teaching, however, many TFA novices viewed management as a separate category of responsibilities that were unrelated to teaching and planning. Teach For America's "bits" curriculum met its counterpart in classroom management strategies.

> As a member of the Teach For America corps, I was instructed in the intrinsic value of a strict linear educational platform, which meant follow the plan, state objectives ahead of time, use the textbook and maintain control! The short teacher tutelage of TFA which involved 6 weeks in the barrio sections of Houston ingrained in me the need for a static taxonomy, unrelenting discipline and consistent management within the classroom. Ideally, this control was congruous to earned respect of the students, applause of the administration and fulfillment of teaching duties. (Delah)

Participants shared how the TFA system with its limited experiences in classrooms resulted in corps members' adapting the TFA model in the hope of maintaining the ideal classroom environment. When I walked into TFAers classrooms, I noticed identical wall charts that sent very specific messages. Amid the banners from a number of universities, handmade poster board placards, "Work it, work it, work it," and "We achieve 85% on all achievements," signaled the goals to be met by both students and TFA teacher. Students who were attentive, cooperative, and on-task during direct teaching were favorably viewed. But an overly vocal class, whose students were constantly mobile, demonstrated a perceived loss of class control.

> The main problem I've experienced so far is keeping my students quiet when they should be. I've definitely got some kids who like to talk! Rearranging them [seating locations] helped to some degree, but for some of them, I don't think it matters who they sit next to. They are very social. (Sally)

Novice TFAers admitted how they were "tested" by students across all grade levels. Some in the middle grades even challenged corps members in my presence, inquiring, "Ms. Lee, are you a *real* teacher or just a TFA teacher?"

The students' quips often alerted corps members to the inferred reputation that Teach For America teachers presented in the schools—on the one hand they were *the* teacher for the year and probably the next—but many students, experienced with successive TFA rookies sensed a relatively short turn around on the part of the mostly young TFA teachers, when compared to veteran educators.

Corps members shared their continuous efforts to balance relationship building (with students) and an achievement-oriented classroom.

> Now that the end of the year is winding down I do feel more comfortable. I have established certain relationships with my kids so that I can do more now. But I had to go through so much to get to this point. You burn out. (Nan)

Those who felt inadequately prepared or lacking in confidence as a teacher, admitted to holding onto what worked from a management perspective, such as established routines, even into their second year of teaching. These characteristics reflected in practice, influenced their teacher thinking. Those TFAers who were not adept at assuming a management style that worked for them admitted to experiencing heightened stress factors.

> I get frustrated when they don't listen to me, or when they don't understand what I'm trying to teach them. In the first case, I have to remind myself that they might very well listen if they were engaged in the lesson (i.e. that means I need to make it more interesting) and in the latter case, well, that's my fault too. I have to somehow figure out another way of explaining myself, of meeting all the students where they're at—not where the textbook says they should be. (Lydia)

What kind of teacher do I want to be? At Institute I went to a workshop and the guy said that you don't have to be yourself as a teacher. You can be any kind of teacher you want. I want to be myself in the classroom, but I also want to give my students what they need. I suppose we all want to be the fun teacher, the teacher everyone likes, but I am learning that if I am concerned with just that, then I am not doing my job. I am here to teach, not to be liked. (Cameron)

Most admitted that there wasn't a teaching "formula" to remedy what was ailing in their management plan. What worked for one teacher, even a TFA peer, or program director, wouldn't necessarily work for another. Stress factors exacerbated management issues and perpetuated a recurring cycle. Once that a management deficit model became habitual, the cycle was hard to break.

Today I realized that I need to scream less. I scream at my students for no reason. Maybe it's because I don't have any children of my own. I don't have any experience with kids. (Lorie)

It takes so such energy to try to keep those kids under control. How long is it supposed to take to teach your students to follow the classroom procedures and system? How long does it take to teach them how to be responsible and work independently? (Ryan)

Thinking like a TFA teacher meant that any approaches offered by program directors, even short-term strategies, were welcomed. Some hoped that a mentor would bail them out, but when this type of support was not forthcoming, those challenged with management concerns relied on their own intuitive strategies with varying outcomes. Many participants implemented a reward system modeled during Institute.

Friday was a good day, but by no means perfect. I started a new reward system Thursday. We started a weekly drawing for those students who were able to earn reward passes. It's amazing how a new mechanical pencil or a soccer ball shaped pencil holder can motivate a child. I hope this isn't too much of a bribery system, but my discipline system was starting too much on the negative. (Meryl)

I have found that candy is a great bribe. Who knew eighth graders would be quiet and hard working for Starbursts and Kisses? (Miranda)

For some, the external reward system ran counter to their personal philosophies. Others sought to promote intrinsic motivators that built relationships with students and their families.

I have been using positive praise/attention in my classroom and have seen encouraging results. If a student is off task/ talking and another is on task/ quiet. I will give attention to the positive behavior. (Rob)

I find parents every day on campus to tell them how loved their children are in my classroom. I called home nearly every day for over a week to see how my student was doing after his father had died just a few days before school started. (Matt)

My experiences proved that balance, and not control, was imperative to maintaining a successful classroom. This is a core tenet of my educational philosophy. Balance is allowing for ebb and flow between teacher and student, capitalizing on unforeseen educational experiences, and negating stringent control methods. Balance creates a boon for agency and power to prosper within an individual's educational attainment. (Delah)

Eventually corps members surmised that they were responsible for their own management style. Maximizing student safety and engagement required preparation and facilitation, as opposed to simply wielding control and discipline.

For the TFA interview we read many articles, and what I remember the most from all was that students wanted someone who cares. They defined a good teacher "as someone who listens and cares." But I thought to myself, "How do I define a good teacher?" (Andrea)

Participants noted that opportunities to observe effective classroom management in-action, was limited to team teaching summer school classes during Corps Training Institute, or stolen moments sitting in on a veteran teacher at their school, during their prep period. In reflecting on management styles that TFAers sought to embrace, several reverted back to what I term, "the flashback model." These were memories of the teaching strategies and activities presented by TFAers' own former teachers, when they attended grade school or high school.

What qualities did my favorite teachers have? My second grade teacher was kind and soft-spoken. She never raised her voice. She was kind and everything in her class was important. She respected us. I remember my fifth and sixth grade, my teachers reading aloud to us. I remember warm-up assignments like reading between the lines. I remember a lot of brain-teasers, puzzles. We had jobs and earned fake money. (Terry)

Furthermore, the majority of TFA novices reported that strategies that they adopted, and knowing what to do in situations, appeared to be rooted in a foundation initiated during their own grade school years.

Mrs. Schendis: Many times in meetings, the TFA first-year teachers will say, "I've got this great idea to do with my class. My fourth-grade teacher did it and it was so much fun."

Barb: Their fourth grade teacher? They're going back to modeling when they were ... (10 years ago?)

Mrs. Schendis: Yes, because that's *all* they know. That's what they're drawing on. The things they did in school because, in 5 weeks ... What are you going to know? And, they haven't been out of school for that long. Plus, they've come through schools since schools have ... there's been a revolution in schools, no matter what anybody says. I think they had a lot of good teaching. So that's okay, to remember their great school experience. But that's their training in my mind. *Their own schooling experience was their training!* No matter what TFA [organization] thinks they are doing. (conversation between Barbara and Mrs. Schendis, veteran educator)

POINTS TO CONSIDER: LEARNING THE CULTURE OF TEACHING

Detractors from traditional teacher education minimize pedagogical training, expecting content area knowledge to suffice. Yet, research (Bereiter, 1995; Berliner, 1990; Berry, 2002; Carter, 1990; Clark & Peterson, 1986a, 1986b; Eisner, 1979, 1983) suggests otherwise. "For new teachers, learning to teach well is difficult work. Managing a classroom, deciding what skills and knowledge to cover, designing lessons and implementing them effectively, accurately assessing student understanding and adjusting to student needs are complex tasks" (Kauffman, Johnson, Kardos, Liu, & Peske, 2002, p. 274).

You have to have content knowledge in all areas. Literacy and the teaching of reading is complicated. You really learn to be a better reading teacher by taking classes in literacy training and reading. (Mrs. Schendis, veteran educator)

One might question as to how and when TFA teachers' personal practical knowledge (Connelly & Clandinin, 1985), practical knowledge (Duffee & Aikenhead, 1992; Elbaz, 1983), and "ways of knowing" (Shulman, 1986a, 1986b), were developed for novice TFA teachers. Participants admitted that few had opportunities to acquire prior knowledge of classroom procedures other than their own schooling and an abridged team-teaching experience at TFA's Institute (as noted in chapter 4).

Teach For America's beginning teachers admitted to building a prerequisite base (of teacher knowledge) from which teacher thinking evolved during their first year of teaching. Only through practice, which took the form of teaching their own students, did participants admit to having a base to anchor old (from Institute) and new information. Furthermore, as noted in this chapter, the majority of Teach For America novices admitted having limited pedagogy and teacher knowledge.

Shulman's research (1987) discusses seven categories of teacher knowledge of which content knowledge is but one. The other six include: general pedagogical knowledge, curriculum knowledge, pedagogical content knowledge, knowledge of learners and their characteristics, knowledge of educational contexts, and knowledge of educational ends, purposes and values. All of the above seemed by participants' accounts, difficult to acquire during their TFA compressed learning program.

Content knowledge assumes proficiency that's measurable, tested, and associated with high cognitive ability. Eisner (2003, personal conversation) notes the dialectic between "knowledge" as a noun as in knowledge of scientific principles and the identification of subject matter content, from "knowing," which suggests a process. Viewed as a verb, teacher knowing comprises a merger of performance, timing and procedures.

The process of knowing how a class works or what a student is doing, is viewed as one of the hallmarks of excellent teaching. But it is not developed overnight. A teacher's reference for making decisions on practice and teaching is based on prior experience that is catalogued in a teacher's mind for instantaneous retrieval as needed at a later time. As with every professional practice, some type of filing system chronicles one's operating procedures. Eisner (1998) suggests that, "the schema-theoretic perspective" tends to activate prior knowledge and is a tool for practitioner decisions. A schematic is that set of translucent instructions stored away and retrieved automatically by those who think like a teacher. Eisner (1998) describes "the development of "connoisseurship" in a domain (i.e., teaching) as a stock of schemata whose use often looks like a search but is more like the seamless, almost effortless moves of a skilled practitioner. Those with refined sensibilities and an appropriate schema see quickly. They understand the significance of what they see" (p. 231).

> TFA [novice] teachers don't think they can adapt these lessons to work in their own classroom. They don't see that and some don't even believe that it can be done until I go in there and model for them. Part of their training courses should include, "This is what I'm doing now. I would like people in different grade levels, during the course of this evening, to adapt this." They need more make and takes in their course work so they can experience how it works themselves and feel confident in teaching from that base. (Mrs. Lauria, veteran educator)

Yet, Teach For America's novice practitioners didn't possess the "cognitive schemata" (Shulman, 1987) or automated brain coding for the range of teaching conditions that they would be presented with. As an untrained teaching novice hired to teach their own class, they were banking their first-year teaching experience deposits into an account from which to draw from at a later date. To put it bluntly, they were learning to teach on their students. But did that paradigm support their teaching or their students, if they were in fact, operating at a level lower on the scale than most pre-service teachers who had logged observation hours in classes for extended periods, and who developed as a beginning teacher, during student teaching? Those who had a more focused clinical teaching opportunity had some resources (teacher-made activities, lessons that were field-tested, unit plans) to draw from, as well as the benefits of modeling from an expert, whose directed feedback offered an initial framework of teacher knowledge on many levels.

For Shulman (1996) pedagogical knowledge is specialized, inferring the combination of both knowledge of subject matter, mathematics for example, with its teaching for specific audiences. Cochran and Jones' (1998) research found that "the process of teaching itself increases teachers' subject matter knowledge. Experienced teachers have more complete pedagogical content knowledge than inexperienced teachers and the connection between content knowledge and pedagogical knowledge becomes more clear, sophisticated and complex with teaching experience" (p. 881). For Barr (2001), teaching is "a constructive process in which learners [beginning teachers] modify their knowledge through transactions in social and cultural contexts, including programs of instruction" (p. 398). Shulman and Quinlan (1996) assert, "Excellent teachers transform their own content knowledge into pedagogical representation that connects with the prior knowledge and disposition of the learner" (p. 409). Grimmet and MacKinnon (1992) define "pedagogical learner knowledge" (p. 888) as a knowing on the part of the teacher of how particular students learn best. It may be less finite than content knowledge, but is nonetheless identified by those who lack it.

> By year's end, the lack of teacher training was evident and one of the TFA teachers was asked to leave. She had no control of the kids and did not know anything about classroom management or how to reach our students. As time went on, the situation wore on her. She was the one who didn't have any educational coursework or field experience under her belt. It is a shame. How can you just think that this works for anyone with a college degree? (Mrs. Damon, Rock Ledge Indian Community School)

So, does TFA's training model provide enough of a richly contextualized experience for corps members to make the connections that embody the complexities of teaching? Study participants suggest that as TFA rookies, they are lacking in pedagogy (by their own admission). Hurrying its acquisition or minimizing its importance (as determined by Teach For

America's organizational programmatic corporate model) appears detrimental to first-year teachers. Corps Training Institute's intention is to prepare the framework for constructing TFA's "Cognitive Anticipatory Schemata" (Eisner, 1998), which exposes novices to TFA's methodology as it meshes content instruction, pedagogy, diversity training, and classroom management. Yet, participants' application of both content and pedagogical strategies from that model, which is supposed to serve teachers entering a range of grade levels from kindergarten through junior high school, falls short on practitioner oriented approaches. The TFA organization opts instead for a more systematized model, or a 'one size fits all corps members' approach to training.

Popkewitz (1998) found that Teach For America classrooms favored a "bits' curriculum, which entails teaching through segmented approaches that compartmentalize instruction into prescribed modules. Popkewitz recalls, "the textbook was made into a real thing that sets the pace, provides the criteria of learning and defines the formulas" (p. 104). Popkewitz, who observed TFAs training and teachers on-site in the Los Angeles region, describes the formalized curriculum model:

> Knowledge is broken down in to its smallest constitutive elements with an organization of the different bits into a hierarchy whose progression leads to understanding. The learning theory that emerges from this practice is that the sum of the elements "makes" the whole. While the bits curriculum dominates the ordering of things in the classroom, there are times when this curriculum seems less than central in [the] construction [of] teaching. We could think of the bits curriculum and the recipe knowledge as different from the scaffolding of ideas.... The organization of school knowledge seemed to consist of sets of pragmatic responses. (pp. 103, 113-115)

Critics of this approach cite the "lack of attention to the 'interactive character' of teaching with its unpredictable aspects and how different teachers work out the generic script" (Barr, 2001, p. 400). Veteran teachers who observed corps member practice noted how teaching involved more than merely following that generic script.

> I think that if a person ... [say they have a degree in anthropology and they want to be a teacher, all of a sudden] should have instruction structured around what is most needed when they walk into that classroom. They need a lot more instruction.... Right off the top! Like, really writing a lesson plan. They can start by telling me the materials they're going to need to teach the lesson. I ask them questions: How will you engage your kids? What are your objectives of this lesson? How are you going to evaluate them? How are you going to assess these students to know whether they've learned your lesson?

They just look at me, like it's the first time anyone asked this of them. I think these are the essential elements that they have to have.

A big part of it is when they're planning, they don't make a connection...of okay, here's this lesson, but what can I shoot out of this lesson that's going to teach all of these different areas to my students. They look at a lesson and they think, " Okay, this is a reading lesson and that's it." But it's not. That reading lesson can turn into a writing lesson, it can turn into a social studies lesson, it can turn into all kinds of lessons in the classroom, but a new teacher doesn't have that mentality of broadening that lesson. They look at it as a reading lesson or a language lesson or a writing lesson and they don't see how they can branch it out and make it something different.

They don't see that need to plan the specifics, like, "I'll do this, do this, do this." They need to say to themselves [and their students]: Step one: Take out the paper, Step Two ... that's exactly what they need. (Mrs. Lauria, veteran teacher)

I believe [in our district] we should have our teachers' manual for all of the curriculum right there. At the beginning of the year we should have an in-service for a week, where those TFA and veteran teachers sit together in grade levels and they say, "OK, this is lesson one. This is what you have to teach. Read through this and tell me, How are you going to do it? What are you going to need? How are you going to get the kids to learn these objectives?" (Mrs. Schendis, veteran teacher).

Teachers need to know, in the beginning of their career, how to plan lessons. They need to organize those lessons and they need to know how to deliver those lessons so that students are engaged in the activities that they want them to be engaged in. So I believe that instruction, curriculum guidance, knowing what to teach, and how to present a lesson, are extremely important for the beginning teacher. (Mrs. Lauria, veteran teacher)

Those thinking like corps members viewed their successes in terms of living up to the organization's prototypical model as it translated into teaching and classroom management routines. Participants' perceived deficits in their readiness for teaching not only impacted virtually every other area of their classroom practice, but also their beliefs about their effectiveness as TFA teachers. After learning how to reflect on their practice, it seemed to me, that TFAers viewed their day with transactions that were marked upon their mind's register. Many seemed to tabulate their successes or shortcomings in the classroom.

Popkewitz (1998) noted how corps members discussed "*their* thinking in terms of *their* successes and failures" (p. 142). Yet, in spite of the bits curriculum training that Popkewitz characterizes as "moving from containment to containment, adapting an almost pragmatic, just follow the model, because it works, response to school practice," rookie TFA teachers were not as successful as they assumed they would be.

Building upon Popkewitz's research, the data suggest that Teach For America's novices opted for a routinized model that favored a classic linear platform. It was particularized, predetermined (either by Institute or textbooks) systematic and controlled (teacher directed).

> I've found that some had what they would think of as the "A" lesson plan from their prior background. They were spending hours on one segment of the day and not having something for the rest. (Mrs. Lauria, veteran educator)

Participants affirmed that in the early stages of their teaching they defined being effective if student performance in the classroom manifested outward signs of prescribed socially acceptable behavior coupled with growth as measured on standard instruments of assessment.

> I'll walk into their classrooms and it's supposed to be silent reading time and I'll see 16 children that aren't doing anything, they're just sitting there. They're supposed to be reading. And I'll approach the teacher and she'll say, "Oh, but they are reading." And I'll say, "No they're not, because I walked around the room, and they're on the same page that they were on 20 minutes ago. (Mrs. Lauria, veteran teacher)

Elbaz (1983) viewed a teacher's practical knowledge as knowledge *of* practice mediated *by* practice, suggesting that rules of practice are clear statements of what to do in specific commonly occurring situations. For Elbaz, (1983) *rules* guide practice for teachers in a methodical way, *principles* guide action in a reflective way, and *images* guide action in an intuitive way. Goodlad (1990) writes, "*How it's done* towered over research and theory in addressing the particular problems teachers face in their practice" (p. 224). Carter, Cushing, Saber, Stein, and Berliner (1988) offer a summation.

> The education of a teacher takes place not only in teacher education classes but, through experience. When novices and experts look at classrooms, experts tend to generate more hypotheses about what they see, qualify their observations and interpretations, weigh the relative importance of certain kinds of information, and take into account the complexity of problems that exist in classrooms. (p. 29)

These qualities inherent in experienced professionals, namely that of "reading" what's going on in one's class and then predicting what will occur in order to adjust to each situation, were not integrated into beginning TFA corps members thinking about practice as the data suggests.

As noted in the previous chapter, beginning teachers (Berliner, 1992) revert to strategies employed during *their* student teaching and field observations, not the strategies of *their former teachers'* when they were in grade school. Moreover, trained beginning teachers were taught to reflect and question their practice. They ask themselves, "What occurred here and why?"

Britzman (1991) asserts that novice practitioners lack transfer ability and notes that a distinction between the acquisition of knowledge and how it "plays out" or transfers into the practitioner dimension of teaching exists. This concept (illustrated below) suggests that the methods employed in preparation of TFA teachers seemed to run counter to the overall intention of equipping corps members with the practical teacher know-how on which new teachers would come to rely.

> If I tell them something that might be specific to one age group, all of a sudden they'll say, "Well that's great for second grade, but I teach sixth grade." They don't know how to take a lesson and adapt it to their grade level. With the type of children that we teach, in one classroom, whether it is first grade, second grade, sixth grade, or eighth grade ... you're going to have a span of ability levels. You're going to have a first-grade ability and you're going to have a grade-level child. But they don't see that, they are not transferring one grade level activity and applying it to another. (Mrs. Schendis, veteran educator)

> I've given my new teachers a whole stack of poems every month. I tell them, "Put these on charts, use them for reading, use them for writing, use them for phonetic reasons, you can use it as a creative writing after they read this poem." I tell them to make it into their own. I go into the classrooms and I don't see them. I don't see the poems, I don't see the kids using them. I don't think they can take a tool and use it, without being shown how it can be used very basically for their age level of students. They can't see the many layers that *seeing* and *knowing* entails. (Mrs. Egan, veteran teacher)

But, I wondered, "Don't *all* beginning teachers have problems trying to figure it out?"

> Yes, but your certified teacher has had student teaching, usually in the grade that he/she is going to teach, whereas the TFA's come in after their five week program that they have in the summer. They're put in a situation where maybe they have adults or upper grades and maybe little children during that time. Then they come into a public school and they are teaching in a kindergarten, first or second grade beginning reading, when they've had no experience in that. TFA teachers' *biggest challenge* is lack of experience. (Mrs. Lauria, veteran teacher)

According to the data, 100% of study participants appeared to agree with the aforementioned statement. Teach For America novices were not experienced and were challenged in presenting a quality plan to get them through each day. They were building their foundation [of teacher knowledge] one day at a time, with not much in the way of banked reserves to fall back upon.

> I think teaching is something you have to learn how to do on the job, but first you need education. And you need to be a certain kind of 'teacher person,' But I don't think a lot of them are teacher people. Some of them turn into it. But they didn't think of themselves as being a teacher. So, it's hard for them to get a mindset or an attitude or a worldview of themselves as teachers. So that's my theory. I'm thinking, maybe they hold back a little bit because they know it's not their life's work. Maybe you would try a little harder and be a little calmer if you had decided that teaching was your career. But for most of them … it's not their career. I definitely think they were really surprised at how hard it is. (Mrs. Lauria, veteran teacher)

Kane, Parsons, & Associates conducted an independent survey of principals and over 90% of them rated corps members as above average to excellent on a scale measuring a range of criteria from choosing effective instructional strategies to creating a classroom environment conducive to learning. This same study reported that principals felt that TFA teachers were as or better prepared than other first year teachers as reflected in student achievement categories (Kopp, 2003; Lewin, 2005).

Lewin (2005) reports, "While most parents do not know that their children are being taught by Teach For America members, some New York City principals say, they love having Teach for America members assigned to their schools," (p. 2).

This contradicts research from Teach For America teachers who rated their preparation more poorly than did those from traditional programs (Darling-Hammond, 2001; Laczko-Kerr & Berliner, 2002). How is this reconciled, one might ask? What constitutes better preparation? Were principals basing their judgments upon the intelligence levels of corps members, or their overall value to their school, to gauge their levels of classroom preparedness? Participants in this study tended to color their abilities and readiness for teaching based on several factors, one of which was comparing themselves to their own teachers who, in contrast, were highly prepared to teach.

Researchers note how beginning teachers have difficulty controlling students, shifting instruction to meet student needs and motivating pupils (Broadbent & Cruickshank, 1965; Codell, 1999; Lortie, 1975). New teachers require support and opportunities to learn the varied elements that contribute to expert practice on a continual basis. Corps members were especially aware of these criteria for success in the classroom as two of their mentors noted.

> So, I tell them that yes, discipline is important. But of course, classroom management, all phases of that ... organization, materials, procedures, routines all those kinds of things you have to have in place and be prepared. One needs to learn how to discipline with love, how to discipline with caring, to have a nurturing environment for the students. You have to be firm, yes, you can't be a friend, you have to be ... the teacher. You have to let them know their parameters and you have to let them know what's expected of them. (Mrs. Schendis, veteran teacher)

> There are a few things that I think are of essence. I know that a lot of beginning teachers believe that classroom management is the most important thing. However, classroom management would not be an issue if instruction and organization were in place. (Mrs. Cordova, veteran teacher)

Popkewitz' (1998) research noted, "A TFA corps member's commitment to students needed to be accompanied by strong classroom management techniques if one was to overcome students' perceived skepticism toward school and weaknesses and deficiencies of children's upbringing" (p. 67). Management strategies presented at CTI (Institute) were designed to assume an organized and systematic routine that was generic across grade levels and student populations. Popkewitz (1998) noted how novice teachers integrated aspects of the bits model into their classroom management and how control of students was connected to a corps member's perception of effectiveness as perpetuated through the training and TFA mission in urban and rural schools.

> An argument that appeared frequently in interviews with corps members is that they are attempting to teach students who do not want to be there; students who are not there. Students who should learn now, so that they will be able to get a better job or acquire some social mobility later. Discipline and the management of behavior are embodied in a grid of practices from which the urban/rural child and teacher are constructed. Teaching-as-management, which focuses on the organization of lessons and classroom behavior, and teaching as managing the personality, attitudes, and beliefs of individuals were connected. (Popkewitz, 1998, p. 103)

Berliner (1992) notes that novices' thinking is mediated through interactions with experts. These individuals know how to translate the language, symbols, activities, and the real life world of students. Hammerness, Darling-Hammond, and Shulman (2002) agreed and carry the premise further:

Building on Berliner's work, we identified five elements that appear to be characteristic of expert thinking. Experts shared nuances and details about learners and their learning, generated multiple hypotheses, offered connection to theory and other's experiences, provided elaboration that expanded on those connections, qualified generalizations, observations or hypotheses, and included concrete evidence of student learning. As novices get beyond their concerns with self, they begin to focus on their students and to appreciate the difference between engagement and learning. (p. 227)

Teaching a few weeks within one grade level or subject area, alongside peers who were also novice teachers, provides limited opportunity for corps members to learn how to teach. There were no quick fix diagnostic or prescriptive formats or "Centers Teaching for Dummies Book" that novice TFAers could consult, (as suggested by Jeannie in the previous section). When consecutive cohorts in more than one region express concerns based on their own experiences in learning how to teach with a content-based degree in hand, and TFA's training behind them, a warrant exists to examine the agenda that fuels the content versus pedagogy debate. Participants' statements seem to illuminate what constitutes less-effective preparation for the critical work of teaching in high needs schools. As Linda Darling-Hammond (2001) asserts,

The professional conception emphasizes the appropriateness of teaching decisions to the goals and contexts of instruction and the needs of students. It assumes that practitioners inquire continually into the usefulness of their actions and revise their plan in light of these inquiries. In this view teachers construct knowledge about their students, classrooms, and subject matters in the course of practice, just as they use knowledge that has been developed by researchers and other teachers. (p. 760)

TFAers' "teacher know-how" account was short on backup plans and strategies, despite high cognitive abilities and problem solving skills. Study participants realized that there was no manual that could walk you through procedures; and, even if there was ... when would rookie corps members have the time to reference and make meaning of it? Some corps members entered professional development courses, sought experts in their schools, observed teachers at off-site locations, and interacted with university instructors and those outside of Teach For America's organization. They were intrinsically motivated to merge both content and pedagogy into their practice. Only after countless hours spent adapting their newly acquired teacher knowledge to practice, mediated by colleagues, veteran teachers, and university instructors, who supported TFA novices' discovery, did corps members begin to "see" differently. They began to think like teachers. This subtle, yet telltale sign was evidenced when they began thinking of their students *all the time.* And, what it would take from a preparatory standpoint, to make their lessons effective.

There is no question that Teach For America recruited highly intelligent, quick learners for its corps. But these data suggest that time and quality of training, on-site coaching, and levels of stress factored into their opportunity to teach, process, and apply information to their own practice. I often wondered, "If TFAers admitted to intense challenges, does content knowledge deserve to remain the primary criteria for being considered highly qualified?" As one participant confessed,

> I went through 4 years at Harvard, and nothing was as hard as this. (Michelle).

CHAPTER 8

LEARNING THE COMPLEXITIES OF TEACHING IN POVERTY SCHOOLS

A VIEW FROM THE FIELD: THURSDAY AFTERNOON

Twenty Teach For America corps members, who seated themselves around brown, laminate-topped tables—which were pushed together to form a stretched oval—greeted me with an array of expressions. Some barely had energy to wave as they dropped into padded armchairs with body language that transmitted a sense of, "Don't ask me to *do* anything!" The resilient ones were more playful, grabbing snack items and hurling them across the room to those arriving late. It was a Thursday afternoon in November, and it had been one of those weeks. Even the conference room was hot.

Sasha caught us off guard with her fiery tone of voice: "These kids have been terrible since we got back from break! I don't know what to do. They all talk when I am trying to teach; don't complete homework or class assignments; tattle on each other (even though they are in the sixth grade), and never get anything done. I finally told them that if they want to keep this up and do what they've been doing, then it's fine with me. They can grow up to be *losers* and it's their choice!"

An awkward silence permeated the room. Monique's ebony eyes widened as hers met mine. Then Rob, somewhat thinking out loud for the rest of us, commented, "Wow, I can't believe you said that!" Mendoza asked incredulously, "You actually called them *losers?*" Another inquired, "*To their faces?*"

"Yes!" she yelled, almost indignantly. "I couldn't believe I said it, either. I was so ... frustrated! I didn't know what to do!"

Stress Factors

> My principal met me immediately. "I want you to cover the TFA teacher's class. Will you take her and tell me what you think?" I can hear through the wall. I can hear! I know she is having a hard time. I can tell by the look on her face. She is a brand-new TFAer teaching first grade! (Mrs. Egan, veteran first-grade teacher)

The complexities of teaching came as a shock to many of the TFA rookie teachers who were armed with good intentions, binders from Corps Training Institute (CTI), tenacity, enthusiasm, and intelligence. Yet, the responsibilities involved in assuming their multi-faceted teacher work, on a daily basis, caught many by surprise. Teach For America teachers acknowledged how stress factored into their teaching. For many, it was a carryover initiated from pre-induction in the region, escalated during their compressed training session at CTI that continued through their teacher socialization process. Feelings of uneasiness, anxiety, self-doubt, and pressure hampered personal well-being, and ones' perceived effectiveness as a Teach For America teacher. For some, this contributed to persistent angst, while others identified stress factors as situational. For the majority of the TFAers in this study, contributing factors to their levels of perceived stress, which infringed upon their coping skills in the classroom included: the complexities of teaching, internal and external expectations, and support levels.

> I admit it. Sometimes I wish for a job that I could actually leave at work, a job that wouldn't consume my mind relentlessly, invading even my dreams. (Jeannie)

> ... And, part of the problem is, I just never know exactly if I am doing what I am supposed to be doing and that creates a lot of stress. (Kyle)

> I didn't give my teachers enough credit. I realize that now. This whole teaching thing is *damn hard.* (Lydia, Stanford alumna)

TFA rookies' daily routine involved kids to manage, curriculum to figure out, and lessons for all subjects to be planned, presented, assessed, and geared to students' ability levels. Additionally, there were parent communications to relay, grade-level meetings to attend, school assignments, and mandatory districtwide responsibilities. These external factors, coupled with the organization's expectations, mandated furthering gains in student achievement and advancing TFA's social efficacy mission for under-served students. All of the these examples contributed to different types of stress factors than those experienced by non-TFA first year teachers, who were not subjected to the outside responsibilities of TFA affiliation and weren't teaching far from home.

As with any beginning teacher, however, Teach For America novices were finding their way with respect to classroom management, planning, curriculum, differentiating instruction, and learning the culture of the school and community of their students. Districts and universities, conducting professional development courses that were necessary for state-mandated professional development hours, per contractual agreements, added one more ball to juggle for first-year TFA's. (TFAers emergency-certified status required the completion of 15 credit hours during their rookie year). Some TFAers felt overloaded with the demands placed on them and opted to withdraw from university classes or "extras" that infringed on their time.

> What does TFA want me to do? Attend UPenn classes four nights in a row, grade my students' papers, and prepare for teaching, or listen to them? I'm done with it! (Curtis)

> Some of the university classes were a waste of time and money. (Kaylie)

Most of the participants viewed university and district courses as lifelines for their teaching. These initial courses followed TFA novices right through their second-year teaching commitment and culminated with a master's degree with teacher certification.

For a significant number of study participants, the juggler metaphor was not only apropos, but a signifier with which they identified. If they were to be successful, they had to learn to juggle. But for most novices, the challenges of balancing the range of complexities of teaching with the external factors of university classes, All-Corps Meetings, and personal issues (such as living with roommates who were also TFA teachers), escalated stress levels and contributed to the internalization of self-defeating emotions.

> At the beginning of the year, I felt that I could do anything and everything for these kids. Then September came around and I felt that most days, I

couldn't do anything at all. Often, I would question why I began teaching. (Hilda)

When will the vacation come? It seems that even when the students are being good they are still driving me nuts. I just keep thinking only two more days, but let me tell you those two days can't go fast enough. (Lee-Ann)

I know you say I am pretty together. And I do feel that way. I have things pretty organized, I really like my class and I have a handle on what I am teaching. But I'm one of the lucky ones. I have a great principal and parents that support me and I really mind my own business and take care of my students. That's enough. I can't get too involved in the TFA thing. I have to pace myself. (Charlie)

Participants admitted that external demands placed on TFA novices teaching in high needs classrooms came from both their districts and the Teach For America organization, both of which were pushing student achievement and teacher accountability. These added pressures proved to be greater than TFA novices anticipated. High-achieving young trainees, fresh from Corp Training Institute assumed that they, too, would fit the TFA prototype of "a good corps member," by boosting student test scores. But they felt pressure to succeed and be recognized. This led to reflective moments as the exemplars note:

I find myself questioning myself as a teacher. I keep thinking that I should have been dismissed from Institute instead of you. The West region's corps has lost three [corps] members already, one voluntarily, the others were asked to resign ... considering the massive teacher shortage, I never thought that would happen. (Tammy)

My friend, Trudy, is the best TFA teacher I know. She does whatever it takes for her kids. She literally spends all weekend planning and then is up for hours. I mean she works until 1:00 or 2:00 A.M. so that she can read and comment on her students' journals and stuff. I tried to keep up with that, but I can't. (Rachel)

When feelings of inadequacy manifested, participants' doubts were actualized as negative self-talk. Many of the participants noted that they resorted to fault-finding when stressed, which was initially turned inward. In reflecting upon these experiences however, several participants noted that it was at this stage, which often arrived in the midst of challenging circumstances, that they were opened to the self-reflective process that ushered the onset of *thinking like a teacher*.

I should be able to handle all of this, but I am falling short. (Paul)

I find myself in a constant state of quandary, streaked deeply with self-doubt. What am I doing here? Am I making any positive contribution to the lives of my students? How can I call myself a teacher? I consciously try to push aside deprecation, and end up wallowing in it. (Javier)

For others, stress was related to their perceived inability to meet their students' individual needs.

God! My students all have special needs and it's crazy figuring out how to reach them all! (Meggie)

Seven students (out of 28) speak limited English. Two students speak no English, two are resource (special education) students.... Kids range in skill from K-6. Help! (Cristina)

All of my students are at such different levels! It's hard to involve everyone and try to keep my students interested—either half of them are bored or half of them have no idea what's going on. (Dana)

Meeting student needs did not stem the emotional overload. Evidence that stress was triggered by a flow of events and expectations that, dependent upon one's assignment, carried to the end of not only the first year, but manifested into their second year.

How do I survive next year? How do I receive support from the administration? I called my mentor to discuss the bad day/nervous breakdown yesterday. I have anti-TFA sentiments at _____ School. (Ernestine)

Many first-year TFA teachers exhibited higher stress levels during their first semester when they realized that their TFA teaching experience was nothing like what they were dealing with on an everyday basis. When I visited the TFA regional headquarters in April of 2004, I was surprised to note that Teach For America's regional administrators posted those stages for all corps members to view on the wall of its local offices. Teach For America's teachers not only lived these stages, but became familiar with them, especially, "disillusionment":

Many of you are aware of my struggles with stress. I still love "my children" and I think that is why it's *sooo* hard sometimes. This week was an incredible roller coaster ride of tremendous lows and minor highs. Disillusionment has set in. Despite a few bad spells, my kids moving in and out of the district, illnesses, irate parents, stress headaches, thoughts of, dare I say, quitting. Fortunately, I spoke to my principal and coworkers. My "cycle is over" and now I can see myself managing and staying in teaching. (Meryl)

Often, instead of receiving encouragement when stress issues surfaced, TFAers were referred to the "wall chart" to learn that they weren't experiencing any emotions that were out of the ordinary. Moir (1999) chronicled the emotional roller coaster experienced by all new teachers and described the stages of anticipation, survival, disillusionment, rejuvenation, and reflection—these stages played out with great intensity for TFA's first-year novices.

By the TFA administration's acknowledgment of these stages for first-year teachers, the stressors were minimized into expectations. In other words, stress seemed like a common cold, something that all beginning teachers would get eventually. But, as noted throughout my involvement with the cohorts, TFA novices were pressured in ways that their peers weren't. This contributed some additional stressors. Some corps members felt that they were expected to deal with the stress by themselves, as the districts and TFA's organization dismissed these stages as "normal" for novice teachers, rather than as concerns.

> Being proactive is an ingrained TFA thing, Barb. When you ask for help, you soon hear TFA's patented response that sends you back with your tail between your legs. It goes something like this, "Did you try to solve this problem with your school before coming to us?" After awhile you don't even bring it up to them. You just resolve it somehow, or it goes unresolved, or it gets to you on the inside. They [TFA regional directors] don't want to hear it. (Olivia)

Corps members assumed that they were supposed to meet broader goals in becoming TFA teachers. When these perceived benchmarks that covered many areas were not met, participants found fault with themselves, especially when routines weren't running smoothly. In spite of outside factors (i.e., limited supplies, large class sizes, and lack of sustained support) which were not within an individual corps members' control, TFA rookies tended to feel *personally responsible* when things weren't working and had to assume support for themselves. Participants noted that stress factors were not limited to teaching scenarios. Internal stress played out in their mindset as "reality," and affected the perception of their successes in their role as TFA novice teachers.

> As the weeks mounted, I lost more and more self-confidence. Even though I can't say, its back to the pre-teaching level, it has begun to rejuvenate somewhat. I interacted mainly with my roommates to sort through common issues plaguing our classrooms. (Mitch)

I learned that all TFAers were affected by stress factors in one way or another. For many second year corps members, at the tail end of their two-year commitment, other concerns surfaced. Participants shared how stress symptoms cropped up sporadically until they concluded their two-year TFA commitment.

> It's the end of my second year and my psychological state is not doing them [students] any good. I mean I'm getting the stuff out there to them... But, I'm sick of the nonsense with my school. For example, our science fair has been canceled four times already. Now we're supposed to have it next Wednesday.
>
> Well, next Wednesday they're doing this construction thing, so we're not having it at all this quarter. Well, their projects can't last three weeks without being taken care of, like plants or animals. So they [students] want to have it right after break, so it's not going to happen.
>
> So, I told my kids that we have to have our own little, private science fair and they were so bummed. I don't know what I can do anymore. I told my kids, "I am trying for you guys." I said, "I'm trying to put things together but it's just always falling apart." So I said, "We're just going to try to get through the rest of the year without having everything you know, collapse around us. We'll get through ecosystems; we'll do our projects; and, you know, that will be it." (Trudy)

TFAers experiences viewed either positively or negatively, seemed to be colored by their lived realities. For some, these judgments served as a barometer from which attitudes about self, students, and teaching, were generalized. Teach For America teachers exhibited stress over their perceived duty to develop solutions to *change broader situations* (as noted in Table 8.1).

Efforts that fell short by corps members' own standards (and that of some administrators, both within the district and TFA's region) led to heightened feelings of disillusionment. For several participants, these internal factors mushroomed and impacted their physical and emotional well-being. On numerous occasions, I heard comments in recorded interviews such as the following:

> This is making me sick, literally. I call home and tell my mom that everything is OK. What else am I going to say? Here I am in a new area, living with TFA roommates, and I just can't get away from it. It's teach, eat, plan, correct papers, make it to TFA All-Corps meetings, talk to TFA corps members, take classes, do more work, and try to sleep. What social life? There is none. (Sunny)

Stress levels from the complexities of teaching and external factors (i.e., living with four other corps members, adjusting to the new environment, districts' and TFA's expectancies, and/or personal relationships)

Table 8.1.   Teaching Cons, Pros, and Ideas for Change
(Casey, Special Education Teacher)

Bad Things About Teaching

• Out-of-control kid	• Feeling out-of-control	• Working all the time
• Some other teachers	• Self-criticism	• Feeling incompetent
• Yelling from next door	• Discipline	• Fighting
• Swearing	• Not feeling human	• Tired all the time
• Haggard	• No friends	• Alone
• Mean kids	• Unhappy kids	• Can't sleep
• Can't get away from school	• Feeling like I'm getting nowhere	• Can't rest
• Worrying about people who could give two shits about you		

Good Things About Teaching

• Teaching math	• Helping students after school	• When "they get it"

What Can I Do to Change This?

• Don't put the world on your shoulders	• Be well planned	• Be assertive
• Don't yell	• Move their clips down	• Ask for help
• Focus on—at least—one good thing each day	• Get a life	• Go out and have fun, too
• Follow your rules, kids will follow	• Work hard one day on the weekend and enjoy the rest of the time	

metastasized internal stress levels. For several corps members, the stress presented as serious illness:

> I'm not sure where Mariah will be, but she's sticking around here and I'm sure she would appreciate the visit or anything you may send. She has been really happy with the help she's gotten from TFAers and the supportive relationships, but not so much with the lack of sympathy from the actual organization. I'm not one to comment either way, but at least the friends are making her feel better about it, which is good because she's very far away from home. (Sharon)

> Everything went okay. They actually ended up having to do open abdominal surgery. They had to remove 18 inches of the colon—the tumor had grown since the colonoscopy, but the surgeon believes we got it just in time. They took out my appendix just for fun while they were in there! Recovery has been slow. I tried going back to school after 4 weeks off, but it was too much. All in all, I am very lucky and I appreciate you sharing your story about your misdiagnosis with me. Thanks again, and have a wonderful summer. (Mariah, personal correspondence)

External expectations from the organization whose corps track record and hype preceded one's arrival in their own teaching assignment, was often internalized into self-imposed lists of criteria to be completed. In the absence of sustained support, deemed minimal and sporadic at best, negative self-talk spiraled into pressures to perform, as evidenced in these passages:

> Okay, I've been a teacher for 3 whole months now, and well, I am exhausted! It's Sunday night and here's what I still have to do before I get to drop into bed:
>
> 1. Write lesson plans for the week, including a whole "lotta" handouts and tests;
> 2. Read my students' journals and write supportive comments in them;
> 3. Correct papers from last week, including zillions of times-table tests and those fun-filled spelling tests;
> 4. Fill out the progress reports, which really should have gone out on Friday, but I didn't have enough time to finish them so they're going home on Monday and that will have to do. (Lydia)

> If I am honest with myself, when I look over the past quarter, I have allowed my teaching to consume me. Completely. The situation I am in seems far too urgent to allow for anything but complete devotion to my students and their learning. It is because of this that I spent last quarter feeling that the very best that I could, the very best that I knew how, simply was not enough. I didn't get enough sleep or eat well.

> How could I [sleep or eat well], when by the end of the semester I was spending 12 or 13 hours a day at school and still bringing work home with me? Before I began teaching, I ran at least 5 days a week. These days I consider once a week a major accomplishment, and I can see the difference in myself. In college, I never allowed even the heaviest of class loads to interfere with my social life, my valued time spent with friends and with family.

> Over the past months, I've felt guilty for spending time making phone calls to these people. My weekends all follow a similar pattern: Friday–*Sleep*, Saturday–Grade papers and notebooks and sleep some more, Sunday–Plan for the coming week. I am learning that there is a fine line between doing the best that I can for my students and going to extremes.

> If I had the past semester to do over, undoubtedly there is little that I would change. I refuse to function without a certain level of professionalism and I had to work as I did to reach that level. Next quarter, however, now that things are somewhat under my control, I need to step back and begin living a normal life (at least somewhat). (Marguerite)

Points to Consider: Learning the Complexities of Teaching

Veenman (1984) summarized the large body of literature on novice teachers into over 20 categories, which he described as the "reality shock" of the first year. Crosby (2002) notes, "For the vast majority of novice teachers, that first year is baptism by fire" (p. 171).

Roehrig, Pressley, and Talotta (2002) assert that beginning teachers are "immersed in layers of potential challenges," which they attribute to five sources: self, students, professional, other adults in the school, and outside of the school (pp. 18-19). Within the "self" category is lack of knowledge about teaching and curriculum, conflicts with school culture, personal life issues, unconstructive attitudes and perceptions, and induction and mentoring issues.

Reynolds (2004) cites research by psychologist Robert Sapolsky, who concluded that prolonged psychological stressors are not aided in the long run by negative self-talk. The rebound effect is often worse than the initial stressor. "Often people just give up, creating a state of learned helplessness due to a perceived lack of control. They quit trying to make things better" (p. 51).

Certainly the concept of "overload" surfaced as a common element among all cohorts. It was—more often than not—related to not having "the whole teaching thing under control." Stress levels of Teach For America novices' were the result of compressed training, team-like student teaching, challenging site-based realities and external expectations that were linked to becoming a Teach For America teacher. Corps members admitted internalizing TFA's *thinking like a corps member,* which suggested that TFA teacher trainees could assume any position or school-based assignment that they were given, even with limited or unrelated levels of training. Many, who experienced heightened stress levels were often teaching in out-of-field assignments to the surprise of more veteran staffers.

A VIEW FROM THE FIELD: JACKIE'S KINDERGARTEN

Jackie turned 21 in July. She taught seventh graders at Teach For America's 5-week training site and admitted that she was not remotely prepared for the challenges and responsibilities of teaching *Kindergarten* in an urban setting. Pre-school was not part of the landscape for her 27 students, who were mostly children of immigrant parents.

"By Thursdays, Barb, I don't even care what they ask me! They are all shouting, 'Teacher, Teacher!' all week, that I don't really listen to them. They could ask me something like, 'Can I leave the room or punch a kid?' and I am so oblivious that I say, 'Yes.' Not really knowing what I am saying yes to."

Her chest heaved and her lips quivered. She casually brushed stray, dirty-blond hair away from her face. Attempts at muffling her sobs were not successful. She received a hug from a fellow corps member seated next to her, as she admitted that the revelation was better off of her petite frame and onto the groups, who could bear it collectively. Twelve other first-year, uncertified Teach For America teachers listened in awkward silence, some nodding their heads in agreement, others staring silently with that glazed "I'm wiped out, too and I know what she means" look on their faces. Others, like Kay, who fixed her warm, brown eyes on Jackie, waited to offer a response, a positive comment, or this worked for me and you should try it too… the mark of TFA solidarity.

SUPPORT

I get by with a little help from my friends.

—John Lennon and Paul McCartney (1967)

A desk calendar that I kept with me offered two support sayings that I shared with my TFA teachers. "Support is the fuel that keeps you going when you want to stop," and "Supporting another means giving with no agenda."

To say that support was varied from corps member to corps member, even within the same district and/or school, is an understatement. For the majority of corps members, support was either in place nominally, not highly prioritized, or nonexistent. Many of the corps members felt strongly that all parties involved, from TFA's organization to the districts and their administrators, paid lip service with respect to support. There seemed to be confusion regarding whose responsibility it was to support corps members in the region each year and what support should look like. Ellen Moir (1999) the director of the Santa Cruz New Teacher Project concludes, "Teachers who are hired outside their teaching area often have a more difficult introduction into the profession and require different types of support."

Even though TFA's organization generated interest and an endowment for expansion, noted glitches in the model surfaced. One was the issue of sustained support by knowledgeable veteran educators familiar with urban education who were willing to provide it and work with TFA's leadership team.

> TFA has the potential to be a really positive force. I don't think it is right now. And this is what I've been saying to TFA administration. This is what I've been saying to the staff. We can make a portion of the master's program an observation part when you are getting non-TFA people to come in and do long term plans and they [TFA directors] tell me, "No, we have the pro-

gram directors. They do long-term plans if you want them to." They don't understand no matter how many times I say it, that it needs to be someone who's got more than two years in a TFA classroom. And so, that's what I've been talking about. So what has that meant for me? It means that all these things are sucking my time. (Roberta)

School administrators, tended to "hand off" TFA novices to the tutelage of identified site mentors, who were often teaching full-time, or were mentors "in name only."

I mean, my mentor, honestly, is the person who I spend a lot time with. The CPT [collaborative peer teacher] for ELL [English language learners]. So, I've talked with her. I've watched her teach a lot and I started working with her after school, teaching ELL, but that's language, and not science. I need a little bit more support and I think the best way is to ask me like, "What would you want?"

I would want observations on what I've just done, or some type of introduction to what I should be doing. I mean it's nice to know what I need to do. Everyone likes to be told or be given some guidance and to know ultimately what they are supposed to be doing. There are a lot of times where I feel like, I am teaching them, they are learning things. Whether or not this is what they really need to know, I honestly don't know all the time. (Ali)

I could use on-site observations by people who know this grade level. (Lynette)

Some corps members were fortunate and received continued support from excellent veterans who were hired by the school administrator or district superintendent to support TFA and/or other new teachers specifically.

My district was good. We had an assigned coach who did come around and stayed with us for our first year. She observed us for four months. (Kim)

Rookies were told by TFA's local and national leadership team, "Be proactive. Find a mentor on-site, observe someone whose classroom and leadership style is exemplary and ask them for support."

We were told we have to be self-starters. But they [TFA directors] seem to have this understanding that we all have mentor teachers because I remember them asking us on several forms who are mentors were. Those weren't set up. I don't understand if TFA was supposed to set them up or if our school was supposed to set them up, but my school didn't set me up. I just got lucky. I found support in a veteran teacher on my grade level, at my school. She had been teaching in the Raleigh District for 12 years. She has been employed as a teacher ... pushing 20 years. And she was great. She would sit down with me, talk about anything. I mean, it's stupid the stuff that you have to ask when you're a first-year teacher. Like okay, this kid just decided to spit in the face of another kid—like, what's an appropriate punishment? And you have no idea what an appropriate consequence would be—just stupid things. (Stephen)

I really believe that there are TFA's who make a significant impact. But I think they are the exception to the rule. I think we are not given support. I think the ones that do make it are the ones that find support in other places.

I've also come to the conclusion that there are three categories of corps members; effective TFA, lucky TFA, and hard working TFA. But you can work until you are blue in the face, but if you don't know what to work on, you're lost. I think that it's the veterans [experienced teachers] who help you realize what you need to work on, where to focus your energies, where not to. (Roberta)

Support was viewed as varied and situational, even by those who offered their experience to helping novice TFAers figure it out.

It seems that the TFA organization itself does not do much following of their folks. Is that the case? I don't think they [corps members] feel supported by the TFA organization that brings them here. I don't think so. I know they have meetings, but I don't know what they do there. Do you know? Do they do in-service stuff? (Mrs. Lauria, veteran teacher)

Barbara, TFA doesn't know what they [corps members] need! (Dr. Willis, Randolph District Superintendent of Schools)

Over the course of this study, participants became more accustomed to inconsistent support. Many managed on their own, but it was noted by several mentors that TFA teachers' self-worth appeared diminished when support was lacking. The greater the level of stress, the more intense those perceptions appeared.

We need modeling, "make-and-takes" and specifics. Expose us to binders full of activities. (Jenna)

I need instructors who will guide me through it. (Josh)

I learn best by taking in a ton of random information from every possible source and filtering out what I think makes sense. That means reading, that means talking to people, that means trying something and watching it flop or watching it succeed and going from there. For discipline it kind of helps to have a model. When the veteran teacher pulled over the student to talk to him, you kind of want to be close enough so you can hear what they're saying to the kid. So you can go, oh yeah. I'm going to use that! But sometimes there are things that are too in depth to really understand if you're just hearing it, like a specific reading technique or something. You know, you really need to see it, to understand how it's going to work. And what works for me is pulling out the concept—what I like about one technique and pasting that with something else I like and going with it. (Roberta)

I couldn't rely on mentors at my school, because some of them were worse than me. I mean, they had no training either. (Darnell)

Without promised support from districts and the TFA organization, corps members' stress manifested in quiet reflection, absences, more concentrated efforts, or feeling jaded.

I advised my principal of my personal thoughts–the potential of my leaving, not as a threat, but how this environment is affecting my personal life and that I cannot continue to receive the existing levels of support. I am keeping Rebecca from the TFA organization aware of my actions. (Erin)

You're trying to get the good stuff out of them—ideas about what they want to do with their students. But when I can get her to talk–she explodes. (Mrs. Egan, veteran teacher)

For most of the corps members that I came to know, finding personalized and consistent support was an issue of concern. It seemed as if both the districts and TFA's organization shirked responsibility when it came to providing the support that corps members requested in their process of becoming Teach For America teachers. Even those mentor teachers who were trying to support TFAers discussed this:

I asked one of the TFA teachers, "What kind of help did you get from TFA?" and she said, "You know what the deal is with TFA when you sign on. They tell you straight out. You're on your own when you get your job. You know we'll help you get your job. We'll take you to the summer thing [Institute training], but then you do it." (Mrs. Schendis, veteran teacher)

TFA teachers were left on their own to figure out teaching, management, and "the whole teaching thing." Rookies resorted to seeking and finding support any way they could get it. Some even resorted to locating friends and family who were teachers from "back home."

During the break I went back to Connecticut. I had a chance to visit my fifth-grade teacher. She was so helpful. She gave me all of this stuff I can use. She sat down and listened to me and offered suggestions. I wrote all of this down. Now I can't wait to try some of this. (Lee Ann)

Do you really want to know who supports me? My mom. She is a kindergarten teacher back home. I am on the phone with her and she sends me some of the things she is doing with her kids. I have used most of her ideas. She even has her friends sending me goodie packages of teacher things. (Kendra)

Teach For America's All Corps Meetings and TFA's Learning Teams offered support. Second year TFA corps members presented lessons and approaches that were beneficial. They offered ideas and "stuff" that worked for them to their first year corps buddies.

It doesn't work, though. I have no faith that [second-year corps members] really knew what they were doing. Like my buddy that first year was supposed to be this woman named [Vickie]. [She doesn't teach anymore.] The Program Director, assigned her to me because I mentioned to TFA that I wanted to be in contact with people who really knew what they were doing. But, after we talked, she said that she didn't really know what she was doing. She was just finishing out the year. (Sania)

Some second-year corps members were helpful, but they too, had their own classes to teach and viewed themselves as advanced beginners. All participants noted that levels of bonding and support occurred frequently during the socialization of first year cohort members who shared a commonality of intelligence, academic background, age, social proclivities, and similar challenges. But did rookies supporting one another professionally, contribute to their teacher effectiveness?

I received most help from other new teachers, who were TFA's. (Maura)

Oh yeah! Me, too. It was easier to ask one of us how to handle something or work with a student or take suggestions on an administrative or parent problem. (Dave)

And, if you trusted your TFA buddies, like I did my housemates, they would keep your stuff private until you were able to work it out. (Javier)

As far as support goes, I went to my housemates. We talked for hours about planning. (Ryan)

POINTS TO CONSIDER: SUPPORT

Another expectation that wasn't met, although promised was that each TFA teacher would be "heavily supported" (TFA *Recruitment Manual*, p. 12). But, just what *did* that entail? And who was going to do the supporting and fund it? Each TFA rookie teacher tended to have a preconceived expectation about support, namely that they would be working with a trained veteran teacher who would be available on-site to target their specific concerns, as opposed to someone who was in place to offer generic advice in a group setting.

Participants noted that they were expecting someone who was effective with adult learners *and* experienced in supporting beginning teachers in high needs' districts. Wouldn't "rookies" in other fields, be it baseball or cosmetology receive "coaching" at the onset of their career? Who, then, did TFA novices go to for modeling of strategies? Whose practice, during the critical stage (at Institute) and during their socialization process in the region, when they were learning to become TFA teachers, did they observe? Who provided the demonstration lessons with time for reflection on one's practice?

Breaux and Wong (2003) defined that process of preparing, supporting and retaining new teachers as Induction. Induction is a systematic initiation into the workplace culture of how one does what they do in a particular setting.

For teachers, induction includes responsibilities, missions and philosophy of not only their district and schools, but of the grade level and community. The literature suggests that quality induction programs include structured training that commences before the school year begins and continues beyond the first year (Darling-Hammond & Sykes, 1999; Feiman-Nemser & Remillard, 1996; Johnson & Kardos, 2002). Some districts (whose TFA teachers participated in this study) did take steps to provide their own support programs as noted below.

> I don't go in there as an evaluator. I go in there as a support person. The TFA teachers are very open to suggestions for my visiting them, for my meeting with them and my discussing what's happening in their classrooms. I think they thrive on the support that I give them. After I go in to the classroom I make an observation, sometimes I just drop in for two or three minutes and I'll leave a little note on their desk ... always a positive statement. Sometimes I comment ... you might want to think about this, or think about that.
>
> When I go in for a long observation, by that I mean 30-45 minute observation, I script what the teacher says. Then I usually spend about 20 minutes that same day letting that teacher know what I observed, and then I make recommendations as to what I think would help her/him in their situation. They seem to be open to my suggestions and when I go back into the classroom, I see them doing some of the things I told them to do. I do have a cell phone and they all have that number and they can call me at any time. I told them that my phone is on. (Mrs. Schendis, mentor teacher)

My district (Philly) hires me to work with beginning teachers at our school. Some are TFA. We provide incentives (materials for their students, gift certificates to a bookstore) to any new teacher who attends the weekly professional development sessions held after school or during lunch. I go into their classes. I see what they are doing. I provide specific feedback on their practice. Curtis is one of my teachers. He is doing a great job. He has a street-smart instinct that wasn't gleaned from TFA's manuals. His classroom management style and rapport with the kids is real. They know that he grew up in an urban area and went to public schools. But, he's coachable, and wants to learn from someone who knows the kids, the community and the curriculum. The support provided by my district administration, that sees the importance of having someone like me with thirty years of experience working with new teachers in an almost one-to-one situation, is the support the TFAers need the most. (Mr. Porter, mentor teacher)

Those who did have district support personnel available referred their fellow novices to these knowledgeable veterans who helped them reflect on practice, refine management strategies and develop curriculum plans.

Some TFAers who benefited from my knowledge and experience recommended others who asked for help. I'd say a TFA-word-of-mouth-network was happening, especially with the second-year TFA's. I know that in conversation with them, they've said that they told so and so to ask me about this, you know, to get help from me regarding a certain situation in their classroom. I do feel that they spread me around by word of mouth. (Mrs. Schendis, mentor teacher)

However, most novice TFAers did not have a Mrs. Schendis or Mr. Porter to mentor them. Nearly 75% of participants admitted to not having a supportive "coach" or mentor to contact when needed. Most had minimal interaction with an assigned mentor. Many noted (see chapter 3) that during their hiring process they had met with mentors who said, "Don't worry, we'll help you."

In the absence of this promised support, many corps members, acting pragmatically, decided to seek out other corps members to serve as their primary source of support. The majority of participants (from all cohorts) affirmed that TFA rookies were supporting other TFA rookies. This practice, initiated during Teach For America's Corps Training Institute, not only continued, but became solidified for 98% of this study's participants during their TFA teaching. Novice TFAers were encouraged to turn to other corps members for ideas, suggestions, clarification, problem solving, and how to's in the absence of coaching support provided by the experienced mentors they felt would be there for them.

Olson (2001a), found that, "Those who did not go through an induction program were roughly twice as likely to give up as those who had support" (p. 11). At a 3-day seminar for qualitative researchers in Palo Alto, California, I happened to be seated next to Lee Jacks Professor of Education and Professor of Art at Stanford University, Elliot Eisner. He imparted words of wisdom to me that relates to teacher support:

> If Pavarotti, with a voice touched by the gods, could have a voice coach, don't you think the rest of us can benefit from feedback on our teaching? (personal conversation).

Would on-site coaching from trained teachers dedicated by their district to assist corps members in learning and applying best practices, work? And, what kinds of "help," help? What support frame offers the best contextualized opportunity for movement from tacit knowledge to a more explicit consciousness? One veteran teacher noted how her administration assumed a proactive role in supporting novice TFAers.

> My job was invented by the principal at our school. It's localized to the school and it was partly, I'm sure, in response to the numbers of TFA's he had. Yes, because he needed somebody to help them. He invented this job and it was called Teaching and Learning Facilitator was what he called it and it's one of those jobs that was a mentoring job, basically. It's one of those jobs that was a great idea. I got into almost all the classrooms, and I also do a lot of curriculum design and model teaching. I just try to do anything I can to help them, relieve the load that they have and help with their teaching. I have grade level meetings where they meet as a group and hear what people are doing, see what resources I can get for them. (Mrs. Lauria, veteran teacher)

TFA teachers expected support from districts, Teach For America's organization, site administration and veteran teachers. When this promised support fell short of their expectations many expressed feelings of abandonment. The lack of sustained, reliable, teacher centered support was cited as a major contributor to stress by nearly all study participants.

Darling-Hammond (1997a), Haycock (2002/2003), and Feistritzer and Chester (1998) cite insufficient support for novice teachers. Ballou and Podgursky (1996), Roza (2009), and Stover (2007) provide evidence that districts are not hiring the most qualified candidates. Dr. Ronald Lewis, former deputy superintendent for Atlanta Public Schools and former state education commissioner in Pennsylvania and New Jersey offered,

> You can't hire a new teacher and expect them to know what to do. You have to show them the way. And with a teacher, who has never stood on their own during student teaching, like the Teach For America folks, how can they see how things happen? And then TFA sends them into schools in communities that expect them to hit the ground running? (personal conversation)

Can levels of "learning" [on the part of novice practitioners and their students] become reduced, confused or even muddled when rookies learn from rookies? Did Teach For America and districts' support programs for novice TFAers promote reflection, professional development, and practitioner growth that is deemed so necessary for effectiveness of beginning teachers?

Part of my job is mentoring everybody. But, as a new teacher support staff person, I'm drawing back from them [TFA]. I'm thinking if I only have so much time in a classroom to work with people, should I invest my time and energy in somebody who's not going to be here in another year? But then, by the same token they're the most needy. A couple of them still cry, I mean, they break down at least once a week. They miss school, because they can't face it in the morning and they're really, really floundering. Part of it is that they're people who have always been high achievers. So they come to school and they can't do it and it's horrible for them. I think teaching is something you have to learn how to do on the job, but first you need education. (Mrs. Lauria, veteran teacher)

Gina, a TFAer who I supported from Georgia, had no experience with our population: inner city, poor kids who were mostly African American and Hispanic. She was here early and stayed late, did her best to be kind and teach math. But, you know, Barb, the middle school kids just walked all over her. And she couldn't really get help from the other TFAers, because they were overwhelmed themselves. Even with my coaching, it didn't work. She just about made it through the year. She didn't come back. I felt really badly for her. She had all of the TFA posters up in her room, but it wasn't enough. And, in some instances, it wasn't safe for her to be here. (Mr. Porter, veteran teacher)

A VIEW FROM THE FIELD:
TEST SCORES LIKE NUMBERS ON A FOOTBALL JERSEY

A glistening whiteboard provided a backdrop for Carla, a 21-year-old Teach For America teacher who hailed from New York City. Her dark hair framed her face and accentuated her Latin features. She held a dry-erase marker in her right hand and several sheets of paper in her left hand.

"Okay, let's review. The grades on this math test are terrible! I want you to make the corrections on your paper, as we go through the steps, so next time you'll get the right answers."

Moans emanated from the students who suggested a host of alternatives to pass the time until dismissal. Two actually crafted a paper airplane from their test paper, which landed near the teacher's desk. She wasn't amused, but that set off some members of the class. It was last period on Friday and it was not easy to command the students' attention.

Students read their scores aloud while the teacher recorded the data in her grade book. The scores of 90% of the end-of-quarter algebra tests ranged from 12 to 77.

Dustin, an athletic-looking adolescent with dirty blond hair, was unfazed by the red markings on his test paper and was sketching in pencil.

"I didn't get it," he shared spontaneously. I nodded and surmised correctly that his age surpassed his test grade.

"Well," I offered, "Twelve is a good number for football jerseys, but maybe not for a math test grade." He smiled at that.

Carla coached her students from the front of the room, "Order the integers from least to greatest. The choices are: −15, 0, -5."

Dustin looked my way and asked, "Hey, what's an integer, anyway?"

Student Achievement

Each TFA region offered inspiring accounts of corps members who surpassed expected achievement goals. They posted such profiles on the organization's web site:

> The corps members in our region are determined and committed individuals who work relentlessly to achieve dramatic gains in student achievement for students. A recent Kane, Parsons & Associates, Inc. independent study cites that 97% of Teach For America principals surveyed said that corps members have made a positive impact on student achievement and that having corps members was advantageous for their students and their schools. (www.teachforamerica.org)

All Teach For America's Corps members, even beginning first-year teachers, were expected to push student achievement, measured by at least two years' growth on standardized tests. Achievement goals were stressed by the Teach For America organization and were touted in public messages.

> I've learned that much truth lies in the advice I received in training this summer. Begin with the end in mind! As I've advanced in my planning, I've come to see that it is important for me to develop my assessments before I begin a unit, so that I can be certain I teach *exactly* what I expect my students to do. (Rene)

Most corps members started the year with students' reading, writing, and math skills below grade level. At the end of the year, a few noted to me that their students averaged 1.7 grade levels worth of growth in reading. In math, the majority of one TFAers sixth graders scored an 80% or higher on the district math test to assess mastery of grade-level standards. Many of the corps members interviewed shared how they pushed themselves to push assessment goals.

When I taught my kids in the summer [Institute], I fell short on assessment(s). Now I dedicate nearly one full day a week to assessment. Friday has become test day. We work very hard Monday through Wednesday learning new material; we participate in a full day of stations nearly every Thursday reviewing new material and working on challenging group work activities, and Friday we take exams. My students have been doing so well on my exams that I have begun to assess my assessments. Am I assessing the right skills? Do my exams require single word responses? Am I not challenging my students enough? I will guarantee that I am challenging these students and making them work as hard and harder this year than they have before (by my own speculation as well as student complaints—which I take as compliments).

My personal assessment of my assessments has led me to believe that although my assessments truly do test knowledge gained, they do not stretch the students enough. Instead of simply asking "who" the protagonist is in the story, I now ask, the students to "describe" the protagonist. (Charles)

Some participants noted that they wrote down their goals early on, even during Institute or their first All-Corps meeting in the region. Successful corps members possessed high expectations for their students, took steps to get them there, and achieved results, which were important components of the organization's mission in poor urban and rural schools.

For those becoming a Teach For America teacher, embracing the organization's achievement ideals contributed additional stress factors. Performing up to TFA's prototypical corps member standards, especially when TFA highlighted corps member's successes in public forums (like All-Corps Meetings) presented an overwhelming message that rookie corps members internalized. Namely, "If one corps member could do it, (achieve two years' growth on standardized tests) then I, too, should manage to accomplish similar results."

I want all of my students to have the opportunity to show me what they know and experience success in doing so. To express their knowledge, I may ask my students to draw, act out, or verbalize the things that they know. I must admit, though, I sometimes struggle with this concept. At what point should I draw the line and recognize that, right or wrong, standardized tests are vital to my students' futures? It is imperative that they are able to perform on these types of tests. Am I only hurting them in the long run, if I don't emphasize those assessments?

This aside, I do feel I have come a long way in my ability to accurately assess my students. I must also admit that I have much more to learn if I am to reach the lofty goals I set in July at the end of Corps Training Institute. (Geneva)

The predetermined goals related to student achievement were prioritized for all corps members, even those fresh from Institute. Some confided in me that even though they created engaging lessons and built relationships with their students, they felt like "failures" when they didn't emphasize preparation for tests. This tended to become all that corps members focused upon, and when internalized, it added another layer of professional "pressure."

Teach For America's [program and executive] directors always make you look at the things you need to improve. You become so programmed with that, that you think you're not good at anything. You can really be feeling like, if a student drops out of school in two years, it's your fault. (Andrea)

The Guilt! I'm always feeling it. Like, what if I didn't do enough? (Marty)

I never knew that teaching was such a competitive thing. I thought they [TFA] were all altruistic and everything ... but it's all about competition. (Teresa)

Corps members noted that just because they focused on assessment, concepts, grade-level content, and teaching test procedures, their efforts didn't automatically guarantee high student achievement. There were other considerations that contributed to gains, some of which were not related to the efforts of individual corps members during their transition to TFA teachers.

Am I making science real and exciting for them? Absolutely! Have I helped them to believe in themselves and set goals for their future? Yes, I think so. Can I dry their tears and provide a listening ear? Of course. Be a positive role model and help them make good choices? Naturally. I have found that I am more adept in these areas than I had ever imagined I might be. What I do question, is whether or not I am really preparing them academically for the future, raising the bar, setting high standards. (Marguerite)

There is little consistency in the makeup of the staff at my school, and this inconsistency directly affects student learning, student achievement, and me. (Roberta)

Many TFA novices resorted to reflecting on models from how testing was conducted when they were in school. They soon realized however, that simply giving a test at the end of the book chapter, and holding high expectations, did not equate to student comprehension and high test scores. Teach For America's novice teachers who, themselves, possessed a natural proclivity for high academic performance, admitted to feeling challenged when their lessons' assessments fell short of their intended expectations.

> I feel like crying. *No* wait, *I am* crying. Today I administered a math exam on long division after teaching it for almost four weeks and I only had four students *pass* the damn exam. I think what I'm going to do is have them retake the exam using multiplication tables. That way, I can figure out whether the problem is that the students don't know their multiplication tables, or if it is that they don't know the division process. (Jeannie)

> Trust me, it is *not* a simple matter of high expectations. I expected these kids to be able to work on their own better. I expected them to know how to be responsible. I expected them to understand concepts like "expectations." I thought to myself, am I being "played" by my kids? Am I being too nice? And, I feel so confined by this push to increase standardized test scores. I can't believe they want me to give my students major assessments in reading, language, and math every four weeks. I understand the importance of standardized tests and I know and accept that it is my responsibility to teach my students to perform well on them. But … I feel like there's no time left to teach anything else! (Stefania)

Some participants noted that the test atmosphere and methods of measuring student academic growth was prioritized in discussions with fellow TFAers and the Regional TFA administration. Even TFA's continuous agenda promoted systematized planning during All-Corps meetings that reinforced the importance of test strategizing by novice corps members:

> For our TFA grade level meeting [at All-Corps meetings] we discussed standardized testing. We conversed about our concerns and fears. I learned that preparing my students with practice tests and teaching them test taking skills was something I could do to properly prepare my students.
> So, the following day, I spoke to my students about a "big test." The subject intrigued them, but they were mostly concerned about the outcome after the test was taken. We discussed how difficult it would be and how important it was to prepare for it. They now understand that the test is very important and that it will also be mentally exhausting. But I told them, it's like practicing their favorite sport. If we go over this stuff it will help them achieve excellence. (Cortina)

We were taught early on, I mean really early on, to focus on testing strategies, So, 2 weeks into the quarter, I decided it was time I gave a test. I looked over the material we covered, developed questions I believed were fair to my students, and created my test. In the middle of the night, I remembered my Spanish speakers and jumped up to create a Spanish version.

The next morning, I remembered my non-readers and rushed to find the special needs teacher to come up with a solution. As I administered the test, I realized that in a room of 36, where students were practically sitting on top of each other, it was near impossible to prevent cheating. (Valerie)

First-year TFAers were ingrained with the image of the high-achieving corps members noted in national media. The student achievement issue remained a front-and-center concern. Many participants noted how district administration also reiterated that message and enticed even first-year corps members with monetary incentives that targeted certain subject areas.

Because AIMS is tested and third grade is the grade that they use SAT-9 scores that reflect the whole school, third grade is a huge year ... huge ... huge! All you hear at every meeting is testing, testing, *testing*. What are you doing to prepare your kids for testing? You must prepare your kids for SAT-9. You must prepare your children for AIMS. Third-grade scores count the most. That's all I heard over and over and over. (Martina)

But, as noted earlier, TFAers admitted learning [teaching] on the job. Most felt that the mandate to boost student achievement was taking its toll. Some TFAers who really did work hard fell short either personally or because of their school's cumulative scores.

My boyfriend, who taught at Garfield worked his ass off all year to get those kids' scores up. His kids improved significantly in math but the 301 money is only based on an increase in reading, so he didn't get paid his 301 money, even though over half of his kids jumped over that 50th percentile. (Olivia)

My school has been on "maintaining" status for the past 3 years. I found out that the teachers are still eligible for the 301 money if the whole—regardless of individual classroom performance—increases the percentile of kids who go over the 50th percentile by 5%. So some TFAers will be in schools where they will not be so great but are carried by good teachers. Yet in other places, the TFAers really work hard but the school falls short. (Jennifer)

You know, TFA pushes this testing thing and I wonder if they really care about the kids. I mean, I'm teaching middle-school reading and language arts in Philly. [He led me to the hallway outside of his classroom where poems written and illustrated by students were posted on a bulletin board.] Here's one poem written by a 13-year old girl who is talking about how she has no place to go after school because her parents kicked her out. So you tell me, what's more important, getting the test scores up, or trying to do things to keep my kids together? (Curtis, personal conversation)

First-year TFA teachers looked for immediately applicable strategies from staff development within and outside the district. Some corps members shared how they strategized to achieve assessment goals for their students, and devised plans for intense review methods to help students succeed. They sought advice from veteran teachers who were experienced with district tests and state assessments.

I want to know how to find out what AIMS and Stanford 9's [state achievement tests] cover so I know what to squeeze in before the tests. Or should I just work on getting them really good on what we've already covered and not stress about the area of circles and such? I just want to make sure they won't have 36 questions on probability or something like that we haven't gotten to yet ... Next, I'm *fried* with fractions. (Roberta)

On the test they took before break (March of Spring term) exactly half of my students got a C or better, and the other half got amazingly low F's. I don't know how to teach this any other way, but clearly I'm not being effective for half my students. But the other half has it, so what do I do? Barb, Could we have a phone conference, or could you pop into my class early next week? (Jessica)

After break we had the AIMS tests, then the SAT9 tests. When those were all said and done, the kids became real ugly. They were maxed out on testing. Honestly, I felt the same way. This whole year has been one big test. (Verna)

As district standardized tests were administered almost nine months into their first year, new TFA teachers were provided the time for internalization of tips, procedures, theoretical research, and strategies to boost student achievement and teaching for student engagement and understanding. These opportunities included university and district staff development, on-site observation of veteran mentors, tips from veteran educators who coached novice teachers and guest speakers brought in for TFA in-services; all of which were specifically designed to support novice TFAers in their teaching.

If we only did the TFA thing and never took any education courses, or observed teachers who knew what they were doing, we would be absolutely lost and so would our kids. (Carolena)

In districts where TFA were assigned, student scores on standardized tests were low to begin with. Teach For America teachers were dealing with a range of issues that surfaced in their classrooms: high percentages of English Language Learners, students with special needs mainstreamed into the regular classroom, inconsistent student attendance, and student mobility. So many corps members made it clear that efforts to improve the scores of their students—even during the first year—were not attributed to TFA's organization or one's districts, but their own tenacity, exhaustive efforts, extra coursework, and endless consultations with veterans whose modeling helped refine and, in some cases, define their practice. Nine months into the rookie-year teaching experience, TFAers developed a beginner's familiarity with their students, the grade-level content, and the complexities of learning how to teach. Yes, there were corps members who demonstrated almost two years' growth and achievement results, even in the first year. But so many participants discussed how TFA's organization was quick to "zero in" on corps members who were reaching high marks with respect to student achievement.

TFA was good at taking the credit. (Maura)

I worked my butt off this year because I didn't know what I was doing when I arrived. I found an outstanding mentor teaching in the room adjacent to mine. I was in her room every afternoon and picked her brain. I enrolled in university classes and completed eighteen credits my first year. I prepared all weekend, every weekend. I expected a lot from my students and more from myself. I lived for them; I had no other focus but my students.

Then when TFA's [regional] organization wanted to advertise the overall achievement of my students as a generic thing, like all TFA's achieve this and saying that it was TFA who made the difference in my students' 2-year growth from where they were previously, I had to laugh to myself. TFA had nothing to do with how my students performed. My students achieved because I believed in them and worked like a dog to make it happen. (Roberta)

Given the push for student achievement outcomes based upon TFA's corporate training model, would it not have been beneficial for TFA program planners to rely more on the aid of experts in the field of education? Could a benefit be had if content area specialization educators with more than a few years of teaching under their belts, modeled the integration of pedagogical technique, theory application, and practical "make-and-take" projects (adaptable to a range of grade levels) during the only foundational phase of a TFA trainee's opportunity to learn teaching? Year after year, however, TFA's Corps Training Institute relied heavily on trainers who were predominately former TFA corps members, not teacher educators. This programmatic policy of TFA appeared to be the mainstay of the organization's brand of training its own to become TFA teachers. But did it prove to be of value to TFA novices?

> I think that as dramatic as some of the things in the [TFA] national litera-
> ture that were sent out from the time that we were accepted and got to Insti-
> tute, it was kind of drilled into us that you have to set these outrageous goals
> and somehow achieve them. I say how do you achieve them?
>
> I don't think that TFA provides you with the tools to do that. I think that
> part of what they do also is create a misconception—and you [as a first year
> corps member] start to believe it. When they talk about challenging your
> kids by putting in those high standards saying, "Okay, every single child is
> going to be reading on grade level by the end of the year."
>
> I talked to another corps member about that and how we thought during
> our first year, we were challenging our kids. That's what we needed to do,
> [we were told] challenge them, challenge them, and challenge them! And
> she and I talked later and we said, a lot of the time we were just frustrating
> our kids. Because yes, you have to challenge them, but you have to chal-
> lenge them with something that's in their range. It doesn't help to set goals
> that are going to be flat out unreasonable! You can't just challenge them and
> say, yes, you can do this, this, this. You have to support them so much if
> you're going to give them huge challenges. You have to offer them lots of
> "stepping stones" to get there and you don't realize that at first. (Antonia)

POINTS TO CONSIDER: STUDENT ACHIEVEMENT

Novice TFAers were pushing themselves to push assessment, which seemed contrary to the literature on good teaching. Wouldn't pushing effective teaching make more sense in order to boost achievement? Bruner (1966) challenged this means-to-the-end reasoning: "The ability of problem solvers to use information correctly is known to vary as a func-tion of their internal state. One state in which information is least useful is that of strong drive and anxiety" (p. 52). Did imposing one more stress factor on novice teachers, namely the high expectations for reaching and surpassing student achievement goals, support those who were becoming Teach For America Teachers? How did the perceived organizational goals effect one's practice? Were TFA teachers in the same shoes as their stu-dents, or, as Antonia noted above, "In need of support, especially if given huge challenges and not provided 'stepping stones' to get there?"

In terms of assessment, Sanders and Rivers (1996) reported that stu-dent achievement is tied to the quality and know-how of their teachers. Darling-Hammond (2001) asserted, "Much of the differential in achieve-ment between Black and White students for example, is a function of the differences in the qualifications and expertise of the teachers to whom they have been assigned" (p. 758). Jordan, Mendro, and Weerasinghe's

(1997) research demonstrated the cumulative effects of ineffective teachers. Yet, according to Rice (2003),

> Empirical research has shown teachers to be the most influential institutional variables in producing student learning–students assigned to high-quality teachers learn more, all other variables being equal. Further, high quality teachers, as measured by the selectivity of the higher education institution they attended, degrees attained, and test scores, are most important for minority and disadvantaged students (p. 53).

Teach For America's novices *were* in the top 10% of their highly selective institutions (http://www.teachforamerica.com/about/index.htm). According to Decker, Mayer, and Glazerman (2004), "TFA recruits do stand out as high academic achievers. For example, the new corps members have an average SAT score of 1,310 and an average grade point average of 3.5" (p. 1). Teach For America novices' general academic abilities and intelligence was a major criteria for acceptance into the organization. Studies suggest that a teacher's verbal skills positively related to student achievement (Bowles & Levin, 1968; Hanushek, 1971). And, Decker et al. who authored The Mathematica Policy Research (2004) noted that "TFA teachers generated larger math achievement gains, which translated to an equivalent of roughly one additional month of math instruction" (p. xiv). Yet, that study compared TFA teachers with non-certified teachers or short-term substitutes. Other studies (cited on TFA's website) suggest that TFA teachers continue to meet or exceed the results of other teachers, both beginners and veterans alike:

> Principals regard TFA teachers as above average for their impact on student achievement compared to the overall teaching faculty. Teach For America corps members are smart, goal-oriented individuals, who have a proven track record of outstanding achievement and exceptional leadership skills. (www.TFAnet.org)

Other pro-TFA supporters proclaim their long-term effects on education. "TFA graduates often continue in the education world; two of its alumni, Michael Feinberg and David Levin, founded the wildly successful nationwide network of public charter schools called the Knowledge Is Power Program (KIPP)" (Mathews, 2009, back cover). CREDO, a research group based at Stanford University's Hoover Institute, noted that in Houston's Independent School District, the highest performing teachers were consistently TFA teachers for the period 1996-2000. That study also noted that the lowest performing teachers were consistently not the TFA teachers, but untrained emergency certified teachers.

But according to Dr. Glen Wilson (personal conversation, July 9, 2009), "TFA's record of improving student achievement is mixed. TFA strongly promotes studies that show student achievement gains under their corps members; however, few researchers consider the question of TFA teaching effectiveness as empirically settled or conclusive." Glass (2008) reviewed several of the studies and stated:

> Students of TFA teachers gained on average .15 standard deviation units more on the mathematics test than did the other students. This is equivalent to students having received one extra month of instruction. There was no difference between the average gain scores in Reading. Although the Mathematica group makes much of the fact that their study involved random assignment of students to teachers, the experimental unit in this case was an entire classroom and not individual students. Hence, the degrees of freedom, and consequently the degree of experimental control afforded by randomization, were exaggerated in the report of the study. As with so many issues in education research, the relative effectiveness of alternatively certified teachers dissolves into arguments about recondite matters of statistical methods. (pp. 13-14)

Ashton and Crocker (1987) reviewed studies of teachers' subject matter knowledge and student achievement and found that only 5 of 14 studies noted a positive relationship between subject matter knowledge of the teacher and their teaching performance. Rice (2003) also noted that some current teacher policies supported by the research are based on "thin evidence, or no evidence at all" (p. 53). While achievement qualifications related to teacher effectiveness seem to emphasize subject specific preparation, and a teacher's own test scores as criteria enough for generating student performance, Rice affirmed that most assessment reviews were gleaned from evidence related to high school teachers, most notably those teaching math and science: "The research on the elementary level of schooling and on subjects other than mathematics and science at the high school level is far more limited" (p. 53). Darling-Hammond, Holtzman, Gatlin, and Heilig (2005) analyzed data from Houston, Texas, which represented more than 132,000 students and 4,400 teachers in Grades 3-5 over 6 years on six achievement tests, and concluded:

> On 5 of the 6 tests, the negative effect of having an uncertified TFA teacher was greater than the negative effect of having another kind of uncertified teacher, depressing student achievement by between one-half month to 3 months annually, compared to a fully certified teacher with the same experience working in a similar school. Over the course of a year, students taught by uncertified TFA teachers could be expected to achieve at levels that are, in grade equivalent terms, one-half month to 3 months lower than students taught by teachers with standard certification. Although TFA teachers

appeared to improve when they became certified in their second or third year, few of them stayed in the district. On average, over the years studied, 69% of TFA teachers had left by the end of their second year of teaching, and 88% had left by the end of their third year. (pp. 18-21)

It seemed to me that Teach For America's achievement concerns contributed to corps members internal and external stress factors. Reaching and surpassing student achievement goals were expected, but corps members realized that attaining them was not as simplistic as the beliefs fueled by TFA's publicity that surrounded the gains of select corps members. When a relative few Teach For America teachers exceeded student achievement goals, then the pressure became intense on other corps members to achieve the same results. Novice corps members espoused what I term, *The Little Engine That Could* Theory, "I Think I Can, I Think I Can," which manifested in corps members who pushed, compared, and competed even in the midst of some very dire situations. But for most of the first- and second-year corps members that I met, it was not so. Teaching was damn hard work and stressors were involved with trying to keep up appearances, as well as test scores.

PART III

TEACH FOR AMERICA AND THE EDUCATION OF POOR CHILDREN

CHAPTER 9

TFA CORPS MEMBERS
AND THEIR STUDENTS

A VIEW FROM THE FIELD: "WHAT DID YOU LEARN THIS YEAR?"

Arnie was trained at TFA's Corps Training Institute in Atlanta. When I entered his sixth-grade math class one warm June morning, I noticed an array of triangular flags displaying academic pennants adorning the walls. He was positioned at the front of the whiteboard when he noticed me as I quietly moved to a seat in the back of the room. His sixth-grade students wore navy uniforms with white short-sleeved cotton shirts. The room appeared gender-balanced with equal numbers of male and female students, but all shared Hispanic roots.

Arnie was in the middle of teaching a math lesson from the looks of the notations on the board. But he paused and introduced me and then asked his students to tell me,

"What did you learn this year?"

Hands waved enthusiastically. Students were eager, smiling, and hoping to be called upon. Finally, Arnie selected one respondent from the array of willing volunteers.

"We learned a lot about colleges," Miguel remarked proudly.

A majority of Miguels' peers nodded in agreement.

"But, what about math?" prompted their teacher.

"Oh, yeah, we learned that, too," beamed Maria.

Learning on Other People's Kids: Becoming a Teach For America Teacher
pp. 159–163
Copyright © 2010 by Information Age Publishing
All rights of reproduction in any form reserved.

LEARNING ON OTHER PEOPLE'S KIDS

When asked to reflect upon their experiences of teaching in the region, corps members were passionate and rarely devoid of a position stance. Some looked at the question in general terms with respect to teacher shortages before discussing their own personal beliefs. They felt that TFA's expansion was an outgrowth of the need for new teachers in the next decade with the retirement of the Baby Boomers.

> Sania: Well what are the statistics in the next five years? How many teachers and administrators are going to be retiring from the educational system? Can you really attract that many new teachers in that short of a time? I mean, in a way, I think …
>
> Barb: So, in a way, there's a need for Teach For America? There are people who will say, "You're capable and have high cognitive ability."
>
> Sania: Yeah, but, they [the TFA organization] keep bringing them [TFA Corps members] in without support.

The reality of learning to teach on other people's kids offered numerous lessons to novice teachers. First and foremost, rookie teachers learned about themselves. Positive relationships developed as many of the TFA teachers attempted to execute student-centered lessons. Most TFA teachers saw glimpses of the school-based realities in high-needs communities. They may have read scenarios at TFA's Training Institute, but their experiences provided them with a realization that a low-quality education was not going to offer hope to kids who were poor and less privileged. Several corps members who had not intended to teach for more than a two-year stint before graduate school returned for a third year.

> I have talked to so many people in their second year who are right now thinking of throwing in the towel, calling it quits, not coming back for the third year. A lot of them had been very sure that they were going to come back for a third year and stay in the schools. I think part of it is disillusionment—it's a different kind of disillusionment though, because the second year gets hard for different reasons.
>
> You start to become so much more aware of the politics of so many things with TFA that are so completely beyond your control. You just feel like everything is stacked up against you. The ones who are not staying say that they are too tired of feeling helpless and they're too tired of the garbage that's going on. I know of three corps members who have dropped out of TFA but stayed teaching in their classrooms because their level of disillusionment with TFA has been that strong. The only reason that I'm still part of TFA is the stipend.

> The second thing that keeps me in it is—I don't want to keep doing this to corps members. I feel an obligation to speak up and try to get them [TFA and the organization's sponsors] thinking about what is really being done. (Roberta)

Others, who intended to pursue high-profile careers, remained in the profession—some even dedicated themselves to teaching and working for systemic change in urban education. But did the TFA experience really instigate a lifelong connection to the needs of urban and rural students impacted by poverty?

> Two years is far too short a time for stints with such things. I must admit that this leads me to question the Teach For America program in general. Can I really become an effective educator in such a short period of time? What is the actual quality of education I am providing to my students? Am I even affecting the inequity that infects our nation's educational system? Is it realistic to expect to come close to my original goals? (Marco)

> I feel like now that I am teaching into year six, I have an impact on my kids' learning. And while TFA brought me here, and I support the organization, it was me who decided to stay to work with the kids in the same community (different district) that I was placed in. And I know that most of the corps members go on to other things, and some of those other things are related to education. But, even though I hear about the salaries that those who with a degree in computer science, earn, I know that I'm making a difference and I love it! (Kyra)

The complexities of learning to teach on other people's kids offered eye-opening experiences for corps members. Relationships developed—with peers, mentors, school administrators, other teachers, parents and, most definitely, with their students. Many of the TFA teachers moved to a point of student-centered lessons. But each day teaching in their classrooms, offered a view of the teaching field in high poverty communities that left a lingering imprint on corps members' minds and hearts. Many participants were torn between feeling that their own involvement with TFA was well-intended, but the organization's (and their own) efforts fell short on its promises to urban and rural students who were impacted by poverty.

> It troubles me that, regardless of my good intentions, I am contributing to the cycle of inconsistency present in my school. I do firmly believe my presence at Jackson is a positive thing. I am working hard to get a hands-on science program in place. I love my students and will remain fully committed to them for the time I am at my school.

But, as I try to accomplish these goals, however, I am *learning to be a teacher*. Herein lies the struggle. My students need experienced teachers who know what works and can implement it effectively. Instead, they have me, and though I am learning quickly, *I am still learning on them,* experimenting on them, working on their time. (Marguerite)

As corps members reflected on their experiences, a pattern emerged— their discourse assumed a level of advocacy and agency. Corps members seemed to view their experiences from a different lens than the one that brought them to the region at the start of their TFA commitment.

And, when the question was posed, "Do you think that you succeeded in meeting the goal [both yours and the TFA organization's] of providing a quality education to all children?" participants' responses assumed a more passionate stance.

Not without the same vision from higher up. You know, there's only so much you can do in the classroom. I mean you can do a lot, but ... (Ali)

And those of us who *do* succeed, are we really in it for the long haul? I promised myself that I would stay for year four, so that I could actually say that I made up for the first year when I didn't know what I was doing. I made a commitment that I would move up two grades and once again teach those students who were my first class, so that I could really feel like they were receiving the best that I could give them. (Trudy)

I don't care how much research you do. I really feel like, with teaching, experience counts so much... I feel like Teach For America needs to do a better job in building relationships with districts and with universities and finding mentors—mentors who know what the situation is—and to not be afraid of exposing weaknesses within the program. Because, in the end, exposing weaknesses to the program will force people to come up with solutions and those solutions will inevitably impact students. And if that's truly the mission, you know, that one day all children, etc. ... then they need to start doing that, to take responsibility for what their corps members do in classes. (Antonia)

Curtis, a corps member who strongly advocated that young men of color join TFA, shared his suggestions for TFA's administration and voiced concerns that felt should be addressed:

Here, TFA is in schools where the population is 99% minority. They say 31% of the corps is minority. What is going on? Why do places like Philly have four Black men in the corps when you look at the demographics of the population you are working with? That's why to me, I tell my friends to do TFA. Not because of them [TFA], but, do it for the kids.

TFA says that they flood their pool with minorities, in hopes that when they [TFA] do the 'racially blind acceptance' they will accept more. No, if you flood it, take more! And recruit at places where you are going to get people to do it. And I think that's one of their [TFA's] faults. I have a lot of issues with their Diversity mission or their diversity initiatives.

Barb: Do they [TFA] listen?

Curtis: I have yet ... I've spoken to diversity people about that. I have brought my concerns about diversity and I will continue to speak my concerns about diversity to Teach For America because I think, as a Black male, I was insulted. I feel like a lot of my White counterparts felt the same way. It was too comfortable. You cannot stretch your limits unless you are uncomfortable. Lock people in a room, throw controversial topics out and deal with it for a day and then unpack it for the summer. That's my feeling about how it should be. Not, here's 15 minutes to talk with your group about this. And then we'll talk about something else.

And they try to relate everything to the classroom. But you cannot think about the classroom before you think about your self and what prejudices *you* are bringing to the classroom, what experiences *you* are bringing to the classroom, the concerns *you* have to the classrooms before you bring it in. So that's where I think their [TFA] approach is wrong.

I think they [TFA] have good intentions. I think they know their problems. But they haven't thought through the right way to do stuff. So, I feel like, for a lot of people, especially a lot of the minorities who do Teach For America feel like that also. A lot of us feel that TFA should be bringing in way more minorities and not the way they are doing it.

Barb: Now that you had this experience what do you think people should know?

Byron: [laughs out loud] There are so many things, like just everything. You can't just tell someone a lot of things. They [TFA] told me to have high expectations and be very strict. Okay. But I didn't really know what that looked like, so by telling me, that isn't the same as seeing it. So, it wouldn't do any good for me to give advice, it's like you really need to see for yourself what it's supposed to look like.

CHAPTER 10

FULL CIRCLE

A VIEW FROM THE FIELD: WHERE DO WE GO FROM HERE?

We sat cross-legged on the rug, enclosed by piles of corrugated cardboard boxes. All adornments had been stripped from the walls. In less than 12 hours, the apartment would be vacated. Meg, Roberta, Jackie, and Dana would be "moving on."

The former Teach For America Corps members greeted me with warm smiles, hearty hugs, and a familiarity that came from working, living, and supporting each other during a 3-year leg of life's journey. Small reminiscences gave way to unbridled laughter when the hostess hauled in over-stuffed shopping bags and placed them in the center of the worn carpet. "Door prizes," she called them. Gently used items, once treasured by their owner, were offered as gifts.

Roberta diverted everyone's attention to a red-and-white papier-mâché object that was less than three inches in diameter. Because of its rounded bottom, the trinket wobbled back and forth on the floor, but somehow, it managed to settle in an upright position. Roberta explained the symbolism of the Japanese *daruma*, named after the famous Chinese Buddhist priest, Dharma, who lived in the sixth century. Bonji-letter 'Dharma' means the rule, the truth, the law– the true form. Crafted into a miniature doll, the daruma offered a message of perseverance to its recipient: seven times down, eight times up. The onlookers were captivated.

Learning on Other People's Kids: Becoming a Teach For America Teacher
pp. 165–176

Roberta's daruma possessed a distinct history. She received her daruma with two blank white spaces where eyes would normally appear at the onset of her TFA teaching assignment. She honored the daruma's tradition:

> First of all, one eye (his right eye) is painted while praying for good luck (when you start to pray for good luck). And then, the daruma is given its other eye (his left) when the prayer is answered (when your prayer comes true).

Roberta established a goal, solidified it with a silent prayer, filled in the right eye space with a dark marker, and kept the left side conspicuously vacant until her goal was realized.

During her 4 years teaching middle-schoolers, Roberta bonded with her students, communicated with parents through home visits, achieved honors as the corps member whose students scored the highest on the state-mandated tests, and enriched her sixth-eighth graders by keeping the message of perseverance close at heart. She attended graduate classes, completed her master's degree with certification, borrowed curricula ideas, materials, and strategies from the veteran teachers on her grade level team, and taught beyond her 2-year TFA commitment.

The daruma rested upon her classroom desk throughout her challenges as a TFA novice teacher. She too, wobbled unsteadily, yet somehow managed to balance herself with the help of friends and mentors. Her daruma, now sporting matching eyes, per its legend, served as testimony of her commitment to herself and to her students. As corps members from a different cohort reflected on the tale of the daruma, Roberta's eyes met mine. She expressed her gratitude for this gift. My own daruma, also with matching eyes, rests comfortably perched on a shelf for safekeeping.

THE RESEARCHER'S JOURNEY: FULL CIRCLE

My interest in studying Teach For America teachers, stems from my own roots, almost three decades ago, as *an emergency-certified teacher.* Since I shared in some of the experiences as a participant observer, I reasoned, "Wouldn't it be beneficial to provide these tenacious, intelligent young teachers with what they needed more of … training, on-site experience, high-level support, and appropriate placements by districts, the TFA organization, and those who endorse this program?"

I encountered thousands of kids impacted by caring TFA teachers. I watched proudly as Teach For America teachers displayed their individual talents: coaching (soccer, basketball, softball, cheerleading), sponsoring clubs (drama, art, robotics, chess, and music), and tutoring before and after the school day and during the summer. Teach For America teachers, in this study, attended school board meetings, made home visits, wrote grants for classroom supplies and enrichment projects, and advocated for their students.

I defended their integrity and supported their efforts, as they taught in challenging urban classrooms. "Who else was going to go in there and do what they were doing?" I argued. "Who else was going to change the diapers of special education students? Who else was going to offer comfort to students during a school lockdown?"

Even when some in authority admonished them, "This is the way we do things around here," TFA corps members did not back down: they fit the prototype of high achievers and community leaders, starting clubs, teaching intercession classes, and recruiting guest speakers for their classes. Former First Lady Laura Bush traveled to the region at the request of a second-year corps member. Mrs. Bush spoke to an audience including Lydia's fifth graders, and her fellow TFA teachers at Arizona State University.

The data from this study confirmed that upwards of 60% of the TFA corps members committed to teach for a third year in their high-needs schools. "Wasn't this a good thing?" I reasoned, especially since I knew of other teachers who were both alternatively and traditionally certified who came into the inner-city district for less time and moved on to more desirable districts.

However, a professional colleague, who hailed from Ecuador and served as a principal in one of the central city school districts within the region, brought me to a reflective juncture. While she and I were talking one day she asked,

> So what's the big deal that they [TFA] stay for year three? How much do they really know after the second year? They are still learning, right? What do we call doctors who complete their second year of residency—an expert? All of the research on teacher education, and experts in general, make it clear that one is an advanced beginner when they enter year three of their professional work. And where does that leave the students in the high-needs districts if a revolving door escorts more novices annually, and offers a quick exit for those who have some experience to move on?

I persisted in spite of her questions. "But weren't Teach For America teachers better than the alternative?" I recalled classes with locked doors and shouting adult voices. Unqualified substitutes did not offer the consistency necessary for older-grade students, nor the patience for the young and impressionable 5- to 7-year-olds, whose views of schooling were shaped by their daily experiences with teachers. But Celia had seen the weaknesses of TFA in her school, year after year. She was quick to mention a few flaws in my reasoning.

> You were defending them, Barbara. I am glad to hear that you have looked at this organization. Do you realize now, that it is sending highly intelligent, young people into our communities, who *don't know how to teach*? I would ask the question.... Why is Teach For America learning on other people's kids? That is unconscionable.

At that point I began considering her question. The TFA organization never promised career educators for high poverty communities, but it is problematic when children face inconsistencies during their schooling. The "Where do we go from here?" dilemma of four former TFA teachers who were leaving not only their school, but, teaching, was instigated in part by TFA's 2-year teaching model that structurally builds-in teacher turnover. Teacher turnover adds to costs and inefficiency in educational settings. One study of teacher turnover in five school districts found the costs associated with teachers exiting the classroom at between $4,366 and $17,872 per teacher, depending on type of community (Barnes, Crowe, & Schaefer, 2007). Teach For America, along with its corporate and political sponsors seems to encourage corps mobility. Some TFA alumnae even espouse this belief, "The most significant work of Teach For America occurs when the corps members leave teaching after their two years and go into law, public policy and business," (Mr. Carino). That might bode well for corps members post TFA-career, but is that really what taxpayers, politicians, and school districts' paying finder's fees and AmeriCorps stipends want to hear, that one's "after teaching poor kids' career" matters most?

Yet, I too, initially asked the same questions posed in Teach For America's press releases, "Who else would be here if TFA weren't?" "Who else would arrive in poor, urban, rural school districts with mostly minority populations as having the collective ability to "Save Tough Schools?'"

When Roberta, Meg, Jackie, and Dana left the Jackson School, teaching, and the region, it dawned on me that educators who remain in the classroom, Mrs. Lauria, Mrs. Eagan, Mr. Porter, and Mrs. Shendis, are responsible for insuring that *no child is left behind*. I also realized that these effective veteran teachers continue to mentor current cohorts of TFA novices, who often require their support in: (a) preparing students for the state tests, (b) completing field trip request forms, (c) maintaining calm during a school lockdown, (d) modifying lesson content, and (e) effectively managing their classrooms.

Moreover, a good number of TFA teachers visited their own former teachers "back home" to seek teaching tips and advice during their first year. Why were corps members so confident that their own experienced teachers would still be teaching in their middle and affluent-professional school districts? Affluent districts experience minimal teacher turnover, value teacher experience, and seem to guarantee teacher consistency. Teach For America's emergency certified teachers are not hired in Scarsdale, New York; Greenwich, Connecticut; or Los Altos, California. In those affluent communities, children do not often learn from uncertified "intern" teachers.

TFA alums experienced this firsthand when they found it difficult to secure a teaching position outside of high poverty urban areas when they moved on from TFA. They were surprised that the recruitment and hiring processes were so competitive in the more affluent districts.

Hey Barb! Oh my gosh! The whole process was different! As a TFAer in the Randolph District, I was hired on good faith alone, as TFA had already "sold" me to them. Now, I'm in a school where 80% of the kids are meeting and/or exceeding the standardized reading tests (seriously, that's my school) yet I was interviewed by:

1. My principal,
2. A member of the school district,
3. A parent,
4. A veteran teacher, and
5. A veteran teacher who would be on my team.

That is the way I think it should be done. Each member of the interview team (above) took turns firing questions at me, and the mom was the most scrutinizing. It took all my energy to "win' her over. (Olivia)

According to the 34th Annual Gallup Poll, 84% of public school parents queried felt it "very important that teachers in the public schools in their community be licensed by the state in the subject areas in which they teach" (Rose & Gallup, 2002, p. 45). Further, the 38th annual poll noted that 84% of respondents attributed "lack of appropriate teacher training as a reason why public school teachers leave the profession within five years" (Rose & Gallup, 2006, p. 48). As the above polls suggest, Americans assume that certified teachers are providing quality education for their children, and that teacher preparation is regarded as a cause of teacher turnover.

The literature indicates that 80% of TFA corps members teach for two-three years in their assigned region and then, move on (Berliner, 2009; Boyd, Grossman, Lankford, Loeb, & Wyckoff, 2006). How might parents of students taught by TFAers, be insured that when corps members arrive to teach, they are prepared to do so when they get there? Katy Haycock (2004) of the Education Trust writes:

All parents want what's best for their kids, that's right and proper and to be expected. But our current education system— both in the practical reality of its relentless sorting of low-achieving, low-income, minority children into the classrooms of our least effective teachers, and in the underlying values and expectations for teachers in general—only responds to the desires of some parents, not to others. All children have the right to good teachers, but only the rights of some are being respected. This problem is so pervasive and so ingrained that we've stopped seeing it as a problem at all, and instead adjusted our values and beliefs to accommodate it. If we're ever going to truly make progress, we have to be honest with ourselves, and name injustice for what it is (p. 36).

Dr. Susan Mintz, of the University of Virginia School of Education, expresses a concern that is shared by others: "America needs Teachers, not Teach For America. In order to make a lasting difference on a child in the classroom, teachers need systematic opportunities to learn their profession and to perfect their craft" (Ness, 2004, p. 9). A former student and graduate of a 1200 hour teaching intern/residency program, compares his teacher preparation to that of Teach For America's:

> I would not be comfortable teaching had I not been in a real school getting real experience for fifteen weeks of student teaching. The fact that I studied at a Title 1 school (in the not-so-good part of town) made it even better; I gained a LOT of classroom management skills that I don't think I would have acquired otherwise. I gained insight into not only the "How" of teaching, but the school's culture, the student culture, how paper work is done, how working after school works, and how field trips are done. If you don't understand the students, the school, or the basic "paper-pushing" stuff, it doesn't matter how good you are at teaching—your life will be hell.
>
> After all I've gone through, I seriously think that 5 weeks of training is ridiculous. It isn't only bad for the new teachers (who will undoubtedly be having nervous breakdowns and information overload), but also for the students they have to "learn on," without direct help. After 5 weeks in the field, I barely had a handle on what was going on. Sending people out with a self-help book and a good luck wish is just setting the education system up for failure. They may be qualified as individuals, but I cannot say that they are "highly qualified" teachers … they just can't have had enough experience to be able to hit the ground running. I mean … a year of student teaching plus over a year of college coursework vs. 5 weeks. No brainer. It is unfair, and unethical, to give stipends to people for doing less work and being less qualified. That is "encouraging" less qualified teachers—which is exactly the opposite of what this country needs! (Nick, certified math/science teacher, Texas)

POINTS TO CONSIDER: WHERE DO WE GO FROM HERE?

Over the last decade, Teach For America has enjoyed a strong and positive image as a service organization that models itself on the Peace Corps (Zenilman, 2006; Sawchuck, 2009). Teach For America has assumed a proactive agenda in terms of its media relations and public image, and has been successful in its pursuit of continued financial assistance from the federal government, securing funding from both the U.S. Department of Education and AmeriCorps. Teach for America, incorporated as a 501(c)(3) nonprofit corporation in October 1989 with a mission of helping to eliminate educational inequity, asks its teachers to commit to teaching for two years in a TFA contracted placement. TFA's change model infers that after one's 2-year teaching commitment, some corps members will remain in education, while all TFA alumni will become lifelong education advocates.

Teach For America is hopeful that some number of its alumni will attain leadership or policymaking positions, inside or outside of education. In FY 2008, Teach For America launched a new, separate nonprofit organization entitled Leadership for Educational Equity, intended to support TFA alumni who run for elected office. In FY2008, 15 TFA alumni held elected political office (TFA 2008 Annual Report). Teach For America's strategic priority of building an enduring and sustainable institution is being pursued by efforts to maintain a positive brand image, strengthen the central organization, and grow and diversify their funding sources.

Laura Anderson (2009) suggests in her article titled, "Idealism, Inc.: Challenging the Conventional Wisdom on Nonprofits," published in The Columbia (University) *Daily Spectator*, that Teach For America has been criticized for failing to bridge the social divide between those serving and those served. Mallory Carr, a member of the current class of TFA (2009-2011) acknowledges this criticism, but notes that, "For those two years that TFA people are in the classroom, they are really bringing kids up to speed academically. Do you want to have kids who are coming up to grade level, or do you want teachers who are really understanding their kids' cultural background? It's hard to reconcile the two" (Carr as quoted in Anderson, 2009)

Teach For America has grown dramatically and, for the most part, met its growth goals. However it appears as if diversity initiatives have not been realized. Teach For America emphasizes the extra impact of corps members who share the racial and/or the socioeconomic background of the students they serve. While 90% of TFA students are African American or Latino/Hispanic, only 15.9% of new corps members in FY 2008 were African American or Latino/Hispanic (African American, 10%; Latino/Hispanic, 5.9%) (TFA, 2008 Annual Report).

Corps members in this study, noted frequently, that their own educational opportunities, family-of-origin, social class, and financial background, afforded them an advantage over the children they were teaching, and that contributed, in part, to their desire to teach through Teach For America.

> Well, I wanted to give back what I received: my years of education, my wonderful teacher, my insight, my understanding of myself and who I want to be, my excitement about learning and knowing. I wanted to give a piece of that back to the world. Remember Jonathan Kozol? Remember how incredibly unfair the world is? Remember W. E. B. Du Bois? Remember how you wanted to make the world right or at least better? Remember the March on Washington and the bus boycott? Those things did not just happen. It took persistence and hard work. (Tracy)

Newspaper headlines in every region tout the growing corps presence in the area's inner-city schools. But, Lisa Delpit (1995) notes how the offspring of the poor, working, and underclass from mostly racial minority populations, are marginalized in America's educational system. Is this the "America" that serves as training for unlicensed and inexperienced TFA "interns" through, Teach For America?

I learned that TFA's organization pressured minority corps members to recruit new members at universities and speak before local benefactors as TFA's expansion was prioritized. Some corps members and non-TFA participants in this study viewed this practice as tokenism, since the majority of corps members were and remain, middle class, Caucasian females.

> Maya is going to miss class tonight. She's speaking before the TFA Board of Directors Meeting to make it look like we have more minority corps members in here teaching the minority kids than we actually do. (Cassidy)

> They asked me to be on the TFA board, but I declined. You know what they do, don't you. They look to get the black and brown faces among us to do the TFA thing. But, I'm not in it for being the TFA poster child. I am here to try to teach my kids. Every time you go on a recruiting trip—which TFA pays for by the way—you are taking a day or two off from teaching your students. If I was coming here to have my kids have substitutes, why bother? It's just one more pressure on us and it's really just trying to make the organization look good. That's really what they think we are ultimately here for. (Rosa)

The majority of corps members with whom I met, believed that they were helping students simply by their presence in the community and their efforts. But, others were guilt-ridden that they were doing more harm, than good, by assuming the roles of social change agents for the larger organization. Who decides when one acts on behalf of "the other?" Do students who are impacted by poverty and targeted by TFA and its supporters in both political and corporate high places further the "service" agenda of TFA? Maribel Heredia, a California parent and one of the plaintiffs in the *Renee v. Spelling* case disagrees,

> Parents have the right to know the qualification of their children's teacher. My son's 1st grade teacher is still taking classes necessary to obtain her full teaching credential. I think it's wrong that she is called highly qualified. I feel like I am being lied to. (Honawar, 2007)

When cohorts of TFA teachers collectively venture into classrooms of predominately working and underclass populations, what image is at work? Does a "narrative" oversimplify issues inherent in poor urban and poor rural schools when TFAers seem to support not only the organization's "saving" scenario but corporate America's service agenda, too?

Teach For America argues that their operational methods make fiscal and social sense. But, questions persist. How does the Teach For America organization know what is good for other people's children in poor urban, rural, and nonmainstream linguistic populated schools? How does Teach For America know how to connect, relate, communicate, or provide the type of instructional methods necessary for diverse classroom populations? Corps members raised these questions annually:

> She [Wendy Kopp] always says ... she surrounds herself with people and "teachers" who know and that have a passion for education. She says that she doesn't see her role as a teacher. She sees her role as an organizer and an advocate for these children. Yet, I don't understand how they [Kopp and TFA] can organize and advocate for what's needed, if she's never really been in the classroom. And, she has never even taught in an urban district! How can she assess their needs? How can she have the final say? [But] she admits that she never really taught at all. If I see Wendy Kopp, I still want to ask her when she is going to teach the kids that she talks about. (Sabrina)

One of TFA's strategic priorities is to continue expanding geographically and numerically. Participants' exemplars raise questions for global teacher education policies as TFA exports its model to international regions. My visit with a lifelong ministry of education director, who happened to be open to my drop-in visit at one school on the outskirts of Puerto Vallarta, Jalisco, Mexico posits interesting points to consider.

When I commented that my work at the university included supporting students whose parents were Mexican and Central American natives, Señora Castro was very interested in speaking with me. But when I told her that teachers with only 5 weeks [cinco semanas] of training were teaching poor children, she questioned my statement. Thinking that perhaps I confused Spanish vocabulary, she asked for clarification.

"No semanas. Meses?"

Señora Castro then inquired again, this time in English, "Not weeks. Months?"

I confirmed that it was, in fact, 5 *weeks* of training. Her smile faded into seriousness.

"How can this be possible?" she lamented in English, with hands folded across her chest.

She elaborated, "In Mexico teachers are trained for 4 years, especially the ones who teach the elementary children." She expressed concern that this American program not be exported to her country. "We don't need this kind of education that you speak of" (personal conversation, in Puerto Vallarta, Jalisco Province, Mexico).

Over the years, I came to acknowledge that this study was not limited in scope to the academic confines of curriculum and instruction, alternative pathways to the classroom, or even teacher or educational policy. In reflecting upon my experiences in the high-poverty classrooms of TFA teachers, my exposure to site-based realities uncovered how the hidden curriculum of economics, social class, and public policies, perpetuate particular processes and paradigms, privileging some programs over others.

As this study was discussed with close friends and family, issues of our social class structure entered into the conversation. It was acknowledged that education's ripple effect assumes an integral part in the range of opportunities offered to children. This work hit home on a personal level because my own mother is the daughter of non-English-speaking, immigrant parents, who worked in factories. My mother noted how she and her four siblings (and other poor children in her neighborhood) relied on public schools and experienced teachers to provide a quality education for all. From these discussions, I began to question whether Teach For America was really beneficial for the kids it was designed to serve.

Through mass media accounts, and TFA's own lobbying efforts, messages continue to be disseminated to the public that TFA is meeting its goals in leveling the educational playing field. When intelligent TFAers sign on to teach in high-poverty classrooms, the public perception that poor kids are being well educated is promoted. But is this really true? Are *all* students of TFAers receiving a quality education, according to participants' accounts? A larger question emerged from examination of the lived realities of TFA participants, whose experiences as underprepared beginning teachers, gelled, in part, with my own "rookie year."

My professional journey had led me full circle into TFA classrooms in two regions, where corps members admitted that they were *learning to teach on other peoples' kids*—just as I had, decades ago.

But, as I reflected upon my career transition—from teaching in an overcrowded classroom in the Bronx, New York, to teaching the sons of the "corporate elite" at an independent boys' school in Greenwich, Connecticut, where I had been provided a view of a winning playing field—I wondered why the short-term solution for educational reform in poor communities was different than the excellent education that is the expectation, in more affluent communities.

> TFA's model got me here. Was it enough to get by? Well, it was not enough to get me to teach well! And there's a big difference between getting by and providing kids a quality education, which is what I would want for my own kids. Right? (Kaylie)

A good number of study participants and I realized that top graduates arrive in impoverished regions in a cyclical stream. When 80% of corps members, like Roberta, go on to other careers after receiving training and experience in the classroom, is there, in fact, a leveling of the playing field, or merely an *appearance* of one?

> I don't know what it is about this quick road to the classroom. Maybe people just think, "Well there's a shortage of teachers and I need to work, *so maybe I ought to be a teacher.*" Each year my six-school K-8 district faces the task of replacing one third of its staff. One-third of the new hires are young Teach For America teachers who arrive after a five-week summer training session. I don't know if it's the shortened preparation. I don't know if it's lack of student teaching. I don't know if it's the fact that maybe teachers aren't looking to really be teachers for their career anymore. (Mrs. Lauria)

As corps members moved on after the completion of their TFA commitment, both participants and researcher traveled full circle. Prompted by flashbacks that instigated reminiscences of my own baptism-by-fire-first-year-in-the-classroom experience, I questioned the impact of the TFA Corps Revolving Door. When districts hire TFA corps members they are guaranteeing that teaching "interns" will always be coming in and eventually, going elsewhere.

In the next decade, many experienced teachers will also move on from teaching, through retirement. This poses serious implications for educational equity and teacher quality.

I reflected on Mrs. Lauria's heartfelt remarks, "Maybe teachers aren't looking to really be teachers for their career anymore." I wondered, if this is true, where do we *really* go from here, and how will America's children be affected?

CHAPTER 11

THE MASTER NARRATIVE AND TEACH FOR AMERICA'S MISSION

A VIEW FROM THE FIELD:
CORPORATE DONATIONS TO A CHARITY

My retired mother received a letter dated June 12, 2009 from Wachovia Securities/Wells Fargo Advisors, LLC. The financial firm requested her input on a customer service questionnaire. The letter, signed by Daniel J. Ludeman, president and CEO, noted:

> Enclosed is the survey that I told you about in a recent letter. It should take no more than 10 minutes of your time. We've included a postage-paid return envelope for your convenience. For each survey received, we will make a donation to your choice of one of the following charities: American Red Cross, Teach For America or the National Council On Aging. Please mail back your survey by July 13.

"Why would donations be solicited by Wachovia Securities/Wells Fargo Advisors for Teach for America?" my mother wondered. "Is Teach For America a long-established organization like the American Red Cross? And since when is teaching some kind of charity? When I went to school, teachers were looked upon as professionals and they were respected as

Learning on Other People's Kids: Becoming a Teach For America Teacher
pp. 177–193
Copyright © 2010 by Information Age Publishing
177

such," she continued. "This letter bothers me because it is demeaning to real teachers who dedicate their lives to being teachers. I doubt anyone is collecting funds for them.

By distributing this letter out to its clients, Wachovia/Wells Fargo is sending a message to its customers that Teach For America is an organization on par with other reputable and already proven American nonprofits and is, therefore, worthy of donations. To me, TFA is a rather new organization and it has far to go to reach the reputation of the American Red Cross and The National Council On Aging."

THE MASTER NARRATIVE AND TEACH FOR AMERICA

Teach For America, boasting a 20-year track record, has emerged as an agency to procure, train, and place teachers in high-needs public schools. President Bush and President Clinton both endorsed the organization during their terms in office, and President Obama's service agenda signals a message that Teach For America is a worthy option for college seniors.

> From my observations at Princeton and Duke, people are keeping their ears open a little bit. What we've seen more of is that, as a nation, there is a new investment in service, from grassroots efforts to the messaging of our commander-in-chief to reinvest in social justice and service work. (Shamma, 2009)

Teach For America appears to be effective, efficient, and noble in the minds of its supporters. These include American corporations, high-profile individuals, media outlets, and politicians. President Bush's 2002 State of the Union Address featured a Teach For America banner displayed prominently behind his podium as he introduced TFA's founder and president, Wendy Kopp, seated in the Congressional balcony next to the former first lady, Laura Bush.

> Out of an idea came the desire to convince folks to teach in schools having trouble getting teachers. There are 8,000 Teach For America teachers and alumni around the country. I am proud to stand up and talk about the best of America and Wendy Kopp. (President George W. Bush, January 31, 2002)

Good Housekeeping profiled Teach For America teachers in an article entitled "Teaching Hope." Its subtitle, "Meet four dedicated young women helping needy kids across America," offered readers a glimpse into the organization and its "mission":

Overcrowded classrooms. Parental disinterest. Textbooks and maps in desperate need of updating. This is the grim landscape that greets the newly minted recruits of Teach For America. Since its inception in 1990, Teach For America has built a corps of 10,000 outstanding college graduates who commit two years to serving in the nation's most despairing urban and rural public schools. The program currently faces funding problems; for now, though, 3,100 dedicated teachers continue to reach out to forgotten children. (Rubin, 2004, p. 84)

Reader's Digest (October, 2003) presented its 15.6 million American subscribers with an account of a Teach For America teacher's experience in a South Bronx kindergarten classroom. Editorial license changed the article's title for its cover blurb from "Class Action" to "Saving America's Toughest Schools" (Wolfman, 2003, p. 75). It appears problematic when well-respected national publications present messages to the public that "America's Toughest Schools Need Saving," especially when the teachers it touts are portrayed as "rescuers" of poor, urban, and mostly minority children.

Persuasive messages in mainstream publications, as well as images from the presidential podium, send citizens the message that Teach For America is an outstanding American program. Teach For America's story is believable and compelling when it is presented in the media and in political speeches. Teach For America's press is viewed favorably when it is continuously associated with prominent people, companies, organizations, and institutions. Teach For America's funding requests are often honored without question because the name, Teach For America, sounds patriotic and noble. Who would disagree that we need teachers for America? And, if we can recruit young, enthusiastic graduates of prestigious universities to work in poor schools, that sounds even better. Moreover, mass media accounts suggest that TFA is meeting its goals in leveling the playing field, by highlighting student achievement outcomes garnered by smart TFA corps members who teach in high-poverty classrooms.

In *The Postmodern Condition: A Report on Knowledge*, Jean-François Lyotard (1984) posed the question, "Who has the right to decide for society? Who is the subject whose prescriptions are norms for those they obligate?" (p. 30). Lyotard discussed the term, "master narrative," a belief system meant for average citizens to espouse. A "master narrative" is supported by powerful sectors of society that promote a particular set of assumptions that are rarely questioned. A "master narrative" furthers a dominant group's message and appears believable when circulated through the media, policy briefs, and corporate sponsorships as the viewpoint. Additionally, a "master narrative" contains unexamined assumptions in discourse that are pervasive and embedded in cultural contexts, signs, mission statements, advertisements, slogans, trademarks, graphic design, color schemes, and rhetoric. A "master narrative" is at work when the populace embraces the messages endorsed by policymakers, as their own, without interrogating them. Barone (2001) suggests, "meta-narratives are those grand stories with seemingly awesome power to bring final meaning to cultural phenomena, and ones we cling to for comfort and familiarity" (p. 89).

Media messages fuel the "master narrative" and impact educational policy by suggesting to the public, that educational reform will occur through the support of "no-education school," short-term teacher placement, business-type programs. As a result, the public endorses this program for public education and financially supports the entrepreneurial organization that has spawned it, because the name sounds credible and corporations advertise their support. When mass media promotes these messages, it influences the public viewpoint toward education, public schools, and teaching as a profession. Darling-Hammond (2001) notes how the public perception shifts:

> The public views teaching as a relatively simple, straightforward work. If teaching can be routinized, teachers need only the modest training required to apply the procedures indicated by a textbook, curriculum guide, or management technique. Because the public has no guarantee about what teachers can be expected to know and be able to do, the need to regulate practice against the prospect of incompetence has created a highly regulated occupation. (p. 761)

Apple (2004) notes a public distrust of teachers that results in their "deskilling" (p. 190). Darling-Hammond (2001) views these messages as ones that undermine the value of teaching as a profession and contrasts this belief system with how other professional fields are viewed.

> In professions like medicine, nursing, architecture, accounting, and law, professional standards boards composed of expert members of the profession, establish standards for education and entry. In the bureaucratic conception of teaching work, little rationale exists for substantial teacher education, or ongoing opportunities for learning. (p. 760)

The *Reader's Digest* title, "Saving America's Toughest Schools," presents a highly charged message. It registers as a "danger signal." Alarmist in nature, the title alerts readers to a situation that needs attention and public action. Namely, there are tough schools in America, and it is in the country's best interest to save them. Perhaps Teach For America, supported by American corporations and taxpayer dollars, is the one organization equipped to tackle and act upon this worthy goal. Teach For America's own "master narrative" espouses the belief that TFA teachers are prepared to take up that challenge and the organization's mission. While Teach For America has been hailed as a "proven innovation that gets results" and "a good thing for kids" (Toppo, 2004; Gammill, 2009), scholars are not convinced.

Regents' Professor David Berliner's editorial, published in the *Sydney Morning Herald* (New South Wales, Australia) on August 17, 2009, entitled, "The View from America: what on earth are you thinking?" challenges the notion that TFA is benefitting poor kids.

> Simply put, you are being conned. Teach For America (TFA), the model for your national program is not effective in helping students in poverty learn more, though it is very effective at raising large amounts of money. The facts are much tougher to dismiss than the feel-good announcements made by the corporate supporters and those who derive their income from the program. Professor Donald Easton-Brooks concluded that students in the early grades taught by fully certified teachers scored higher than students of teachers trained in the way that Teach For Australia proposes. Further, full university certification was associated with a narrowing of the achievement gap between African American and European American students. To become an expert at teaching requires five to seven years. So, if you want to increase inequality in Australian education, just import the hype.

Teach For America's rescuer role in urban and rural communities enables TFA's "master narrative," and plays into the organization's "saving" paradigm. When school administrators cite community isolation, limited opportunities for social interaction, and teachers' low morale as restricting the districts' ability to attract qualified teachers, TFA responds, as do their supporters, by sending more corps members and raising more money.

The missionary discourse of saving and rescuing the urban/rural child emerged through researcher Thomas Popkewitz's (1998) interviews and observations in the schools where Teach For America placed its corps members.

> It seemed to me that the languages of "helping" children embodied ways of reasoning about teaching and children and that the reasoning itself was the problem. "Mission" was an operative word for the corps members. The sense of mission did not form around abstract principles, but instead, coalesced in the pedagogical distinctions and a grid of ideas to classify the capabilities and achievement of the children. (1998, p. 2)

Popkewitz (1998) also noted,

> The redemptive focus of Teach For America was to have a social effect on the nation as a whole. Teach For America symbolically articulated a societal

"feeling" about the needs and deficiencies of urban and rural schooling. Furthermore, the establishment of a social mission was considered crucial in establishing TFA's organizational integrity, and in establishing its credibility with the educational community, the news media and potential corporate funding sources. (pp. 59-60)

A "master narrative" attempts to lead the populace to accept a position as "truth." It is systematically, yet subtly, reinforced in the public mind as something to believe in and embrace.

Teach For America fuels a public "master narrative" that a remedy to failing schools is in place and cost effective. Teach For America engages the support of the mainstream media who assist in spreading that message, which supports the organization's expansion plans. Dave Eggers (2003) wrote:

> The power of Teach For America can redirect lives. It can make bright young people aware of where they're most needed and where they'll find the most rewarding work. This is why we need Teach For America teachers in hundreds of schools from New Mexico's Navajo Nation to the District of Columbia. (p. A15)

Cameron McCarthy (1998) argues that images presented by the mass media and/or corporate communication reflect a middle-class notion of urban youth perpetuated through what he terms,

> The discourse of bourgeois social voluntarism which is exemplified by TFA's highly ideologically motivated intervention in the education of the inner-city child. This voluntarism is backed by the leading corporations in the country such as Xerox, IBM and Union Carbide. (p. 142)

Either subtly or through pervasive acknowledgment, critical societal issues are often minimized or dismissed when a belief is simplified and disseminated in the public mindset. For example, the public hears that underprivileged public schools are not working in the way the general populace expects them to work. The "master narrative" heightens the average citizen's awareness that "America's tough schools need saving," and the citizen dismisses the systemic societal issues that contribute to the problem. A heightened perception alerts the public that not only do tough schools need saving, but, the citizen infers that the students in those schools are somehow less successful, educated, or intelligent than others. Sometimes, they are perceived as less deserving, less loved, or "forgotten."

> My school was across the street from a housing complex. Every child in my school lived there. It literally was the school that belonged to the complex.

You would call them, I don't know, something else [projects]. The kids just walked across the street and that is where they went to school. We had roaches in our school and the worst part though, was that we didn't have toilet paper in the bathroom because it would get stolen. So, you had to carry it with you. So, if a kid wanted to go to the bathroom, you had to give them toilet paper to take with them. I never heard of such a thing. I mean it was that low. (Irene)

In a just society, should children who grow up poor be considered less than other children? Should they be bound to sub-par conditions and offered teachers-in-training? These questions suggest that a "master narrative" has infiltrated the popular mindset with respect to how one perceives education. If pervasive images in the popular media suggest that schools in high-poverty communities are failing, that is problematic. But perhaps more problematic is the proposed solution, which accepts, promotes, and funds the idea that merely recruiting and minimally training intelligent individuals from highly competitive universities will equate to hiring highly effective teachers for impoverished schools, even in the absence of support and professional development.

Lyotard (1991) wrote:

It is understood that the work, (a law, a policy, a film, etc.) induces a feeling–before inducing an understanding–which constitutively and therefore immediately is universally communicable, by definition. And it cannot be said of a feeling that it must gather everyone's agreement without mediation, immediately, without presupposing a sort of community of feeling such that every one of the individuals placed before the same situation, can at least dispose of an identical judgment. (pp. 109-110)

When media headlines alert readers to the "service" element of teaching children from high-poverty communities, is a "master narrative" positioning its policy into the public mindset? The readership of the newspapers listed, might accept without interrogation, the viewpoint of the writers, especially as the publications listed boast a long-standing journalistic reputation: *The Washington Post* noted, "Education 'Peace Corps' Expanding Area Presence" (Pressley-Montes, 2007); *The Arizona Republic* stated, "By 2008, 400 Corps Members Will Aid Poor Kids" (Carver, 2007); *The New York Times* alerts readers, "Top Grads Line Up to Teach the Poor" (Lewin, 2005). Do these articles send a message to the American public that teaching poor, urban, minority children is equated to a form of national community service that requires minimal training for intelligent noneducation college graduates?

If they [TFA, its sponsors and policymakers] can show that the poor kids are being taken care of, by just putting TFA in there, saying, "Get TFAers, they're at the top of their class," then they don't have to go and take money from the wealthy districts. It's shocking that I thought I joined Teach For America, an organization that was going to help, and now I realize that I was just sleeping with the enemy. (Nan)

Ogbu (1990), Dilworth and Brown (2001), and Pope (2001) note the differences in how school is "done." The elements that constitute success, methods of discourse, consequences, and "ways of being" in school settings, varies from place to place, and is often privileged based on academic standing, teachers' perceptions, and social class. "Doing service" for a finite commitment is *not* "Doing School." Corps members and others, myself included, questioned whether Teach For America prepares *teachers* for high-needs areas, or if they prepare *TFA teachers* to teach in poor schools (Darling-Hammond, Hammerness, Grossman, Rust, & Shulman, 2005; Laczko-Kerr & Berliner, 2002; Lipka, 2007). Since when is teaching poor children in America's public schools, a form of community service?

Corps members arrive in high-poverty areas and make it their goal to demonstrate to the public that without any education course work and with minimal pre-service training, they can get the job done—and will successfully boost student achievement. This perpetuates what one participant noted as "The Myth of Teach For America," or the organization's ancillary "master narrative." Corps members, surrounded by their smiling, predominately brown-faced students, look good in photographs. The images and success statements heighten TFA's reputation, expansion efforts, and financial goals (Zelilman, 2006).

These issues, essentially problematic, spawn further questions, which are deeply embedded in our frame of reference and our collective belief system.

The questions not only interact with how we view the information presented in this book, but are steeped in the notion of "truth" as outlined by how the "master narrative" views education for other people's children.

The majority of participants in this study challenge the "master narrative" that relates to TFA's "mission" and suggest that all is not well with the model and mindset of rescuing students under the guise of teaching for America.

Why am I doing this? When I have time to breathe sometimes on the drive home, I ask myself this very question. My frustration comes in that I don't know if I am helping. I feel like someone else should be here. I don't see the injustice that Kozol was talking about except in the fact that I am teaching these kids. Why isn't someone more qualified in my position? I keep hearing the TFA line over and over in my head, "You will be qualified; you are qualified." I need to remember that this is not for me. This is for the kids. I am dedicating at least two years of my life, and I knew that before I came. It is my job to teach these kids and show them that education is important. This is to give back. (Jeannie)

If one is "giving back" or "dedicating two years of my life," does that sound like community service or a teaching career? If one engages in or supports charities that target poor children, should you call that teaching or charity work? Cameron McCarthy (1998) notes,

> It is striking how TFA's representation of the inner-city child seems to be skimmed directly from the surface of the television set and the anti-teacher education pamphlets of Teach For America—the voluntaristic, Ross Perot-inspired youth organization that has as its goal, "saving" the American inner-city schoolchild. (pp. 19, 143)

Teach For America offers what appears to be a feasible solution to public school educational reform in poor minority communities. Popkewitz (1998) asserts that "urban and rural education" is a term historically constructed.

> It is not surprising then that the discourses about teaching and school improvement in Teach For America carried a redemptive concern. In the promotional literature of Teach For America during its formative period, a sense of something special was portrayed. That something would enable the participants to go beyond what was seen as normal and everyday about teaching. Teach for America symbolically articulated a societal "feeling" about the need and deficiencies of urban and rural schooling. (p. 59)

Some of the issues that are oversimplified or hidden by the "rescue" mentality stem from a "master narrative" that leads the populace to accept a position that teaching poor children is somehow equated with performing community service. This "truth" appears systematically yet, subtly, reinforced in the minds of the public, as a good thing, without much in the way of critical examination or query. Barone (2001) writes, "those who are long distanced from the specific contingencies of school life, rely on a "master narrative" for guidance, virtually participating in that world through the descriptive powers of the author" (pp. 95-96).

Teach For America, through its own "master narrative," successfully communicates through public press and corporate communication, such as the Wachovia/Wells Fargo Financial Advisors letter suggesting to clients, that Teach For America is a charity worthy of corporate funding. In politicizing education through a "mission" model, Teach For America has, in a sense, commodified the urban and rural students whom they "serve" by citing data in an almost fast food-like fashion to both longtime and prospective donors. Teach For America *uses* student demographics to solicit

Table 11.1.   TFA Outreach Data for the 2009-2010 School Year

Years	Corps Members	Students Reached	Operating Budget
2005-2006	4,700	297,500	$39,500,000
2009-2010	7,300	450,000	$160,000,000

Source: Adapted from data supplied at http://www.teachforamerica.org/history

funds with targeted public appeals, "In order to reach our ambitious goals we must continue to grow our revenue base significantly" (2008 Annual Report)

Teach For America's expansion includes reaching an increasing number of poor students each year, as noted in Table 11.1.

It appears that TFA is focused on four strategic organizational priorities—growing its operations while increasing diversity, improving student achievement, placing alumni into leadership or policymaking positions, and building an enduring American institution (TFA 2008 Annual Report).

Teach For America's association with prominent people, from film industry executive, Sherry Lansing, who sits on the board of Teach For America, to National Public Radio host, Diane Rehm, who interviewed Teach For America's founder and CEO, Wendy Kopp, signals to the public that TFA is a credible and effective teaching organization. When multinational foundations and corporations such as Visa, Inc., HSBC Global Education Trust, The Michael & Susan Dell Foundation, The Broad Foundation, McKinsey & Company, the Google Foundation, Credit Suisse, and hundreds of other Fortune 500 companies suggest that TFA is worthy of financial and in-kind support, people take notice.

When corporations solicit support from their customers for designated charities, the "master narrative" expands into the public domain. Average citizens do not often question the organizations that target their donations. It is not uncommon, therefore, for an agency with a perceived track record in a certain domain, to appear worthy of and validate one's contribution through its association with recognized companies, soliciting on their behalf. In writing the check to TFA, most donors do not fully examine the explicit and implicit agendas of both the recipient and the corporation advocating on their behalf.

Corporations make these donations at the end of the year. It's a tax deduction for them. TFA is touted as a charity worthy of its contributions, so they support the organization without doing any research to see where the money actually goes. Their main concern is writing *that* check because it lets them "off the hook." They should question, "How will my check be used and will it, indeed, help a child in need get a quality education?" Donors should give more thought to the true worthiness of a charity when making their donations and not just go with the hype. (Mr. Green)

The Teach For America's website states that their national operating budget is $160 million dollars for the 2010-2011 year. Additional monetary support comes from school districts, regional fundraising, individual, and corporate support. *Worth* magazine included Teach For America in its list of "America's Best Charities," which identified non-profits that put donors' money to work most efficiently. Selected as one of a dozen organizations that effectively utilize charitable gifts for programs, TFA is listed as an organization that puts $42 of every $100 into programs (Yaqub, 2002, p. 91). Study participants, however, often wondered, "Where *does* the money go?"

Many TFA members made personal and financial contributions to their travel and teaching expenses and felt the hardship of needing classroom supplies. If TFA is capable of procuring federal and state grants, charitable donations, and corporate funding, why did so many TFA teachers feel financially depleted?

> Money! I spent at least $2,000. I kept receipts. And Teach For America is going to expand and they want us to spend our own money doing this? (Antonia)

> And you had to get yourself there [to the region] then to training [in Atlanta] and you had to get yourself back. This is all out of your own pocket. (Luz)

> I didn't have the money even to move my belongings and I had to take out a $1,000 loan from TFA, which I will have to pay back. So, I don't know where $8,000 for each of us goes. It's not for tuition, staff development, mentors to help you, or supplies for the classroom. I don't even have pencils for my kids. (Victoria)

> We had to get ourselves from our college commencement to our regional site. That's a plane ticket. We had to find our own transportation to the schools and find an apartment. Then we had a week to get to Institute (Houston). That was another plane ticket, which I couldn't afford, so I drove. We [all who were accepted to the TFA program from every U.S. region] were then housed in dorms, two to a room, with community-style showers, that you had to wait on line for hours to use, for 5 weeks. The food was cafeteria stuff, not that healthy, and we had some supplies provided. After training, we had to get ourselves back to our region, another plane ticket, and get ready to begin to get our classroom ready. I can't tell you how much money I spent out of pocket on all of that. (JT)

TY 2006 Special Events Schedule

Name: Teach For America Inc
EIN: 13-3541913

Event Name	Gross Receipts	Contributions	Gross Revenue	Direct Expense	Net Income (Loss)
DC GOLF TOURNAMENT	13,085		13,085	5,713	7,372
HOUSTON 2007 BENEFIT DINNER	495,224		495,224	71,618	423,606
CHICAGO ARETE HONORS	178,500		178,500	5,000	173,500
NEW YORK 2007 BENEFIT DINNER	2,419,767		2,419,767	356,481	2,063,286
PHOENIX 2007 BENEFIT DINNER	182,300		182,300	64,766	117,534

Figure 11.1.   Teach For America Form 990 TY 2006 special events schedule.

How is it possible that I have no textbooks or have to ration pencils and charge kids for them? (Martina)

Kate, Valerie, and I are all going to form a site collaborative to ensure [that] beginning teachers and TFAers at Sully get materials needed so they do not go through the same issues as we had to. (Tina)

Corps members also questioned funds that TFA allocated for fund-raising galas and events that most couldn't afford to attend, such as the regional benefits dinner which generated significant income as noted in Figure 11.1.

Teach For America directs significant efforts to influence "national, state, or local legislation and public opinion on a legislative matter or referendum," as noted in the organization's U.S. Treasury Form 990, 2006, Schedule A, Part III, p. 2. Teach For America Inc. reported $129,177.00 in total expenses paid or incurred in connection with its lobbying activities (U.S. Treasury Form 990, 2006). Teach For America appears to continually forego the opportunity to strengthen the educational foundations and support that corps members' request. According to Teach For America's U.S. Treasury Form 990 (Appendix B), filed over the period 1997-2005, Teach For America, Inc. spends *three times as much* on marketing and expansion, as it does on training. This pattern of expenditures seems curious given the persistent criticism that TFA corps members are not sufficiently prepared when they begin their teaching assignments and, in effect, corps members actually learn to teach when they arrive at their TFA contracted placements. The non-profit consistently expends more funds on recruiting corps members than on their preservice training.

Instead of reviewing the data from critics and acting upon the suggestions from consecutive cohorts of corps members with the intent of improving TFA's model of teacher preparation, support, and professional development, Teach For America's leadership, and their sponsors chose instead to prioritize the long-range goals that "bolstered image, finances, and management" (Kopp, 2003, pp. 112-113).

Corporate executives and even select college deans use their influence to further Teach For America's stronghold by encouraging the newly hired and recent graduates to apply to TFA prior to the onset of their intended careers.

In spite of the fact that corps members' efforts are regarded highly by some administrators, colleagues, and even academics whose own children are TFA alumnae (Koerner,[1] Lynch, & Martin, 2008; Xu, Hannaway,[2] & Taylor, 2008), by what criteria or instrument is their effectiveness in the classroom truly measured? How many TFA catastrophes are buried? Is Teach For America concerned about protecting an image or does it want to examine and improve the program's existing structure? Does it appear that an automatic buffer shields TFA from criticism?

Dr. Glen Wilson, argues, "Corps members are giving up their personal and career life to do this [teach for 2 years]. It's a noble commitment that is part of the myth and the narrative that people buy into. Because TFA is now even more selective than Harvard, those accepted into TFA are showcased by districts and TFA supporters" (personal conversation, July 11, 2009).

Those familiar with the process of becoming a Teach For America teacher, noted how it was less problematic to move on from TFA, than to advocate for the systemic changes that are really needed in Teach For America and in the districts that hired them to teach their kids. Beginning corps members appeared initially compliant as they embrace the organization's strategic goals, but over their 2-year commitment, TFAers wondered about the answers to persistent questions that concerned them.

> So like yes, we're supposed to keep it, "Education Reform," in the forefront and no matter what you do after the 2 years are up, you're supposed to stay focused on education because you've been there. So you can take any influence you may have in your future and use that towards education reform. But I don't know. I think a lot of people end up moving on and are just glad to have it, not necessarily glad, but to have it [TFA] behind them. I know I'll be glad that I did this, and if I hadn't done it, I would have always asked myself, "What if?" But, what can you really do? Really! I mean like No Child Left Behind. Yeah, it has a great name attached to it. Yeah, I don't want to leave any children behind. Let's really look at it though. It's such BULL! I don't think it [No Child Left Behind] is going to help. It's just bureaucratic nonsense! We're still looking at test scores. We're still not increasing any funding. Education's the first thing that's cut. So the kids, who have the least, are getting whatever's left over. I see that now completely. (Kaylie)

Some of the people I am meeting out here, architects, lawyers and other professionals in their 20's from Harvard and Yale say that they've heard about TFA and they're confused. Why? I ask. What is there to be confused about? It's *not* a good thing. (Sania)

Dr. Ronald Lewis is among the researchers and scholars who dedicated their careers to education in high-needs communities. As a former associate superintendent, Atlanta Public Schools; former commissioner of education for the State of Pennsylvania and former director of Urban Education, New Jersey Dept. of Education and consultant to the NAACP, he argues that Teach For America's goal of "providing a quality education to all children" falls short:

African American and Latino communities desperately need experienced, committed teachers who understand the teaching/learning process from the onset. For highly committed and highly motivated young people to use our children to learn/experiment on is potentially dangerous because of what they don't know. Teaching is an art form that must be practiced. No artist would be proficient without practice. I think it is a disservice and an insult to think that unprepared young people can be sent into urban areas and properly instruct our students. If this process is so good, why isn't it practiced in suburban areas? Why is it that the young people who need the most [urban youth impacted by poverty] receive marginal young professionals?

Teach For America is publicized as an organization that policymakers support, but will that support continue if this model of teacher preparedness produces long-term ill effects on the children who are provided with "instant" teachers? Are poor children a fitting constituency for underprepared graduates from top colleges to be hired as teaching "interns" in the most problem-plagued school districts for 2-year teaching commitments? How is this programmatic strategy equitable? These and other questions related to Teach For America are essentially problematic and raise issues that are deeply embedded in our collective frame of reference and belief system. How do we respond to the notion of a "master narrative" and the perception it creates around education for other people's kids?

Teach For America perpetuates the stereotype where anybody could walk into a classroom and make it a successful classroom. When really, like now, as a teacher, as a real teacher, [into my fifth year], I feel like it takes so much more than a quiet classroom or like laughing kids to know whether or not you're successful...or test scores even. I mean, in any other profession, we would never have doctors, you know pretend to be a doctor for two years. It's just unbelievable to me. And, it's so offensive now. It really is. I mean, not anyone can do it and yet that is what the public is now hearing. Anybody can come in and do it, so sooner or later, I mean maybe we won't even need a teacher education program. We would just need TFA to place everyone. How long can this continue? (Sania)

A noticeable disparity exists between what counts as a quality education in mostly affluent community schools, and what corps members seem to be delivering to their students during their rookie year in the classroom.

I'll tell you what I have seen. Some corps members would not fly in any other district. Just because we are an underresourced school, with no one really supervising you does not mean that you should be able to do whatever you want to do in your classroom to fill time. (Trudy)

When I was interviewed for a position in a middle-to-affluent professional school district on the East Coast, after I left TFA, I completed a master's degree and two years of teaching with TFA. As you know, Barb, I was a long-term substitute for two years before I was hired. The schools looked down upon my TFA teaching experience because they felt that I never really worked as a student teacher to learn how to teach with feedback from a mentor who could fine-tune the areas that I needed to work on. They felt that I was learning how to teach when I was teaching fourth-grade students, and they were right. (Stephanie)

Is unintended damage being done to kids when underprepared rookie TFAers are offered as solutions to the shortage of qualified teachers in poor urban and rural school districts? Do students require more than what intelligent and tenacious individuals with a content-based degree and idealism can provide? When some TFA teachers surpass the organization's expectations through personal dedication, hard work, and learning as much as they can through course work and observing effective and experienced educators, is it "truth in advertising" to hold *them* up, as the models for all corps members?

Lisa Delpit (1995) uses the term, "Other People's Children," in her book of the same name and offers these enduring questions:

What are we really doing to better educate poor children and children of color? What should we be doing? I have come to understand that power plays a critical role in our society and in our educational system. The world-views of those with privileged positions are taken as the only reality, while the world-views of those less powerful are dismissed as inconsequential. Indeed it is others who determine how they should act, how they are to be judged (p. xiv–xv).

Learning how to teach on other people's kids appears highly problematic and morally unconscionable, especially when we learn that certain American students are assigned novice TFA teachers every year. The 55th anniversary of the landmark Supreme Court Decision handed down in *Brown v. The Board of Education* was recently celebrated, but are we, as a nation, adhering to its principles? Are we willing to look at the true costs involved in ensuring that all children receive a quality education?

The constructs of "qualified," "highly qualified," "highly effective," "intern," and "content-knowledge proficient," appear to be part of a confusing 'spin,' directed toward the public mindset as it affects those who are hired to teach, as a result of The No Child Left Behind Act (U.S. Congress, P.L. 107-110 2001). Members of Congress, presidential administrations, and the Department of Education "shift attention from merely 'highly qualified' to 'highly effective' by means of identifying such teachers and paying them for their performance, and for teaching in the neediest schools" (Keller, 2007 p. 1).

Education Secretary Arne Duncan's remarks, critical of teachers' colleges, was delivered in a speech at the Curry School of Education in Charlottesville, Virginia, on October 8, 2009 (Sawchuck, 2009):

> In far too many universities, education schools are the neglected stepchild. Often they don't attract the best students or faculty. The programs are heavy on educational theory—and light on developing core area knowledge and clinical training under the supervision of master teachers. (Retrieved from http://blogs.edweek.org/edweek/teacherbeat/2009/10/ duncan_has_harsh_words_for_tea.html)

If the education secretary, who was neither a teacher, nor an education school graduate, speaks to audiences about the limitations of an education school teacher-training model, what image is presented?

John Affeldt, the lead attorney representing parents of children assigned "intern" teachers in the *Renee v. Duncan* case, argues:

> The Department is blurring NCLB's definition, which requires all highly qualified teachers to be fully certified, which means they've completed all their training. Their regulation is calling underprepared, provisionally certified TFA teachers and other interns fully certified. Districts don't want to send parents letters that admit, "Hey, your student is getting a not 'highly qualified' TFA teacher." Parents don't get those letters because of the regulation's loophole calling teachers still in training "highly qualified." Many would not even think to question the policies of the schools, and are most likely unaware of the fact, that underprepared interns including TFA teachers are disproportionately allocated in California and nationally to poor kids and kids of color.

How can all parties involved in America's collective educational reform agenda collaboratively recruit, train, support, equip, and sustain those who are not just ready reserves, but those who are committed to the important work of teaching? John Affeldt shared his view of the Federal Law's intent, in a phone interview on June 22, 2009:

> TFA teachers still in training fall under the "intern" teacher designation. There are higher allocations of "interns," teaching poor kids of color. Will we passively accept continuing to fill classrooms with teachers who are still in training, or be proactive? Two-year TFA teachers are an important stop-gap, but what we ultimately need in classrooms in high-poverty schools is not the Peace Corps. What we need is the Marine Corps—highly trained individuals who are not in teaching for a 2-year commitment, but for the long haul, and who know what they are doing when they arrive.

I suggest that because of reasoning based on (a) "'The Tinkerbell Tenet of Teaching," where teachers and others "believe that something will occur solely on the strength of that belief" (Hamilton, 1993, p. 206), and (b) the "TINA Thesis: There Is No Alternative" (Saltman & Gabbard, 2003, p. 6) stakeholders, policymakers, donors, and citizens, consider the TFA press to be the truth.

But, teaching in poor communities takes commitment. It is not an 'in the meantime' job, nor a resume booster. It is not service, rather, it is a calling. Teach For America *seems* to be acceptable public and corporate policy; yet, nearly two decades after the organization's founding, questions persist. Has the time come for a closer examination of Teach For America's "master narrative" and the ripple effect it appears to have on our society?

The larger issues surround what constitutes quality education for "other people's kids." Should it not be the same for all, regardless of circumstance, ethnicity, social class, or geographical location? All children deserve qualified teachers to educate them, not just learn on them. The ultimate question remains: how *do* we achieve true equality in our educational system?

NOTES

1. Dr. Mari Koerner, dean of the College of Teacher Education and Leadership at Arizona State University, is the mother of a Teach For America Alumna.
2. Dr. Jane Hannaway, principal researcher at the Urban Institute, is the mother of a Teach For America alumna.

CHAPTER 12

PROBLEMATICS AND PERSISTENT QUESTIONS

We entrust the education of our children to teachers without adequate licensure. Such a lack of quality control would be considered criminally negligent in any other profession. (Bob Chase, president of the National Education Association)

From ancient civilizations to the present, newcomers were expected to practice their skills as a prerequisite for entrée into a profession. A novice was usually required to complete an apprenticeship with a master in order to learn their craft. Medieval craftspeople spent years as an apprentice, or beginner on the job, working under an accomplished and experienced "teacher" before they could become a journeyman, let alone a master. As a nation, we rest easy knowing that our workforce is prepared and well-trained. The scope of that training process and its subsequent licensing and accreditation looks different for a range of occupations.

Major League baseball players are even considered "rookies" during their first year, in spite of their progression through an extensive tiered-system of pre-service training. This consists of graduated levels (Single-A, Double-A, Triple-A) under the watchful eyes of coaches and mentors who evaluate and hone a player's skills for years (Burns, 1994). Likewise, cosmetologists are required to complete nine months of full-time study and clinical experiences through an accredited program before the state board in Arizona will issue an individual license to practice. Still, Arizona's high-

Learning on Other People's Kids: Becoming a Teach For America Teacher
pp. 195–196
Copyright © 2010 by Information Age Publishing

est educational policymaker advocated an "Instant Teacher" certification after only 30 days of preparation for those holding a college degree in any discipline (Todd, 2004, pp. 1-2). When teacher training is compressed like a microwaveable meal and field experience is deemed unnecessary or a waste of time by those in public policy positions, a message is sent that "other people's kids" are able to withstand someone learning how to teach, on them.

QUESTIONS PERSIST REGARDING TEACH FOR AMERICA'S TRAINING

Questions persist with respect to Teach For America's 5-week Corps Training Institute. It is the only opportunity for teaching and learning that corps members receive prior to their placement in high-needs public school classrooms. How does it function as an Institute when high percentages of former TFAers are *the* main instructional staff? Is *that* programmatic policy effective in preparing Teach For America's first-year teachers?

> Quite frankly, I think the TFA training is a joke. Granted, [why] I may have gotten less out of it than others, simply because I did already have the background, but regardless, I don't think it did *or* would have helped prepare me for teaching. My understanding of the intention of the TFA summer training is to introduce corps members to being a teacher ... actually standing in front of a class and being "in charge," and second to that is a brief introduction to some theory and teaching strategies. Personally, I would have preferred 6 weeks of becoming familiar with my district, the adopted curriculum, and the state standards under the guidance of veteran teachers who know more about teaching than TFA alums.
>
> I don't believe that 5 weeks of team-teaching summer school prepares anyone for their first year of teaching. It would be much more beneficial to spend six quality weeks of long-term planning *specific to my school and grade level*. There is just too much going on for corps members their first year (TFA meetings and university classes) not to give new TFA teachers as big a head start as possible. I think I would have been a much more effective teacher if I had been given the time and the guidance to plan my year. In fact, I don't think training needs to be and maybe *shouldn't* be, out of state. None of the planning I did in Houston was relevant to my first year of teaching. Why waste my time creating a long-term plan when it's fictitious? I would gladly forego mingling with other state's corps members, whom I'll probably never see again, to stay in my placement city TEAM planning, learning what resources I have available to me within my school, district, city, and becoming familiar with the textbooks I'll be expected to use. (Rebecca)

QUESTIONS PERSIST REGARDING
TEACH FOR AMERICA'S SUPPORT OF CORPS MEMBERS

Persistent questions regarding TFA's training, district hiring and placement, the organization's expansion, and the levels of financial and programmatic support remain consistent over the years, and are reminiscent of what every previous cohort noted. If each year's corps members asked the same questions, what answers do *we* have for them? If each year's students receive the same underprepared TFA teacher, what solutions do *we* have for them? "Who will pay for the mentors?" was a question raised by a superintendent and echoed by corps members:

Can somebody pay our mentors so we can have them? I don't have one. (Gina)

There is a lack of quality mentors who can guide without exerting additional expectant pressures on the new teachers. (Pam)

Well, from what I know of the Randolph district, there's no way that I'd want to have a first-year person who didn't know anything at the mercy of some of the people I met here who are running things. That could really mess someone up. Maybe if it was someone who was really good at each school, that might work. (Joel)

These accounts led to an inquiry about how the first-year TFA teachers were actually supported and what that support entailed. Teach For America's organization placed a heavy responsibility on the regional team, especially the Executive and Program Directors, to carry out its corporate work, which prioritized fundraising, recruitment, publicity, and organizational duties. Regional administrators were also responsible for maintaining a positive image for TFA within the community. With such a busy schedule, when and under what conditions did the first- and second-year teachers receive support? Participants were left jaded by unfulfilled promises of support and professional development.

We heard they were bringing in 82 new corps members next year with no support. We just shook our heads. (Katherine)

Yeah, they're bringing them in, but without support. (Gilda)

When our executive director spoke proudly about how TFA was growing, we were all angry. We asked about SUPPORT. "Will that mean more Program Directors?" someone questioned. "No," was the response, "other sites operate with the same numbers of staff and have higher numbers." (Rich)

QUESTIONS PERSIST REGARDING
TEACH FOR AMERICA'S EXPANSION

Public education is usually the largest expenditure for state and local municipalities nationally. Approximately 90% of total K-12 public education funding comes from state and local budgets, 46% state, 44% local, (Roza, 2009). In the current economic climate, it is expected that the education sector will endure significant budget cuts. Roza (2009) projects that as many as 9% of the total jobs in public K-12 education may have to be eliminated during the 3-year period from FY2009 through FY2012. In an effort to close an estimated $600 million budget deficit, The Los Angeles School Board voted in April 2009, to authorize thousands of job layoffs (Retrieved from http://www.google.com/hostednews/afp/article/ALeqM5h 3mFy5eGsaWJONJ84hPUh7NSorKQ). Yet, the Los Angeles School district hired Teach For America corps members in the region (www.teachforamerica.org/regions). Similar findings are noted from accounts of both veteran and new-to-the-profession credentialed teachers who applied for positions in the public schools in: Atlanta, Washington, DC, Dallas, and Oakland, California. Does the tenuous economic climate warrant examination of the perks, fees, teacher turnover, and economies of scale related to recruiting, training and supporting uncredentialed TFA intern teachers, in light of tightened government and philanthropic resources and—a force of unemployed, credentialed teachers?

Should districts hire TFA rookies when more experienced corps members (who have completed their two years of service with TFA) wish to remain teaching in their urban school district, but fall a few credits short of certification? How is it that certification barriers are removed for first-year TFAers but held firm when third-year TFA alumni wish to stay in their familiar school and grade level? Some participants suggested that districts were holding slots for TFA, yet "pink-slipping" teachers who were experienced in their schools.

> How is it that districts like mine are laying off certified teachers yet TFA is still there? How is it that TFA is expanding in districts that are laying off teachers? Are districts making deals with TFA? Absolutely, it happened to me last year in the Bay Area. The Steven Fishers (of THE GAP) are putting money into the KIPP academies run by former TFA (Sania).

QUESTIONS PERSIST REGARDING DISTRICTS' HIRING POLICIES

District hiring policies in urban K-8 schools come under scrutiny as one ponders whether a) TFAers should determine which grade level they [or TFA newcomers] teach in, or b) if TFAers are "highly qualified" [with only content based degrees] to teach kindergarten, first grade, reading, or special education.

> Did you know that our district rep for special education has no classroom experience? Did you know that they asked me … to be the special education rep next year? I am a first year teacher! I don't even know what I'm doing in special education this year. Who would believe it? (Ashanti)

Should districts place a first year TFA teacher in a special education or kindergarten /first grade class without prior experience?

> I didn't understand why both of our school's special education teachers were TFA teachers. What do they know about regular teaching, let alone special education? I wanted to be sure that teachers tried other strategies instead of just dropping kids they don't know anything about into special education. I told my principal that I didn't want to have my kids go to their resource [special education classes] for anything. I also said that I was going to get involved with the Child Study Team (CST) and be sure that I was an advocate for our Native-American students. (Sam, certified teacher, enrolled member of the Hopi Nation)

ENDURING QUESTIONS

Questions lingered in my mind long after data were gathered and analyzed. The questions spoke to a moral consciousness. Questions persisted as to whether the "mission" of Teach For America falls short. Does the program leave participants feeling jaded by promised support and unrealistic initial training? Is TFA's corporate-like policy of only recruiting young recent college grads who will not challenge the organization during their first 2 years while they "learn the ropes" in order to reap the benefits of "being a good corps member," an intentional strategy?

The problematics and questions that persisted throughout this study were ones that I reflected upon along with my TFA study participants. How did all of this—messages from the media, research from policy institutes, corporate advertisements that highlight Teach For America, boxes of data, my own reflections and observer's notes—filter into this study on *becoming a TFA teacher*? The national push to hire those with a content-based degree and minimal training for abbreviated teaching periods for populations of mostly poor children was illuminated by what participants were saying and asking, and what I was seeing. This caught my attention. More significant was the realization that each Teach For America cohort was experiencing similar concerns. Why was that?

If Teach For America is to live up to its perceived reputation of being a positive force in the education of mostly poor students, should they not be held accountable for delaying implementation of the necessary changes its corps members and critics repeatedly ask for: more training, mentors, and support?

We collectively wondered, "What feels suspect about the notion that anyone can teach with a content-based degree, and no experience is necessary, as long as under-prepared intern teachers with good intentions are sent into certain schools in other people's neighborhoods? What feels wrong about the alignment between TFA's organization and its complicit partners, the districts who hire corps members, and the corporations and policy makers who sponsor them, that obscures the real issues from public view? What feels improper about an automatic buffer that appears to shield TFA from criticism?"

Learning how to teach on other people's kids seems, at the very least, unfair in a democracy such as ours. The situation is significantly worsened when we learn that some of those students, the ones who comprise our greatest educational concerns, receive a novice TFA teacher *almost every year*.

> Teach For America is still a system that brings middle- and upper class white college grads to poor areas to teach black and brown kids, who are then used as resume-builders. (Lee)

This work is not merely another study of first-year teachers. It is a study that is contextualized within the broader issues of social and economic inequities inherent in, not only education, but in health, housing, human services, and employment opportunities. It is also a study that hinges on privilege. What kinds of assumptions allow TFAers to be privileged over credentialed beginning teachers with respect to hiring, certification standards, and ongoing professional development? Does a double standard appear to offer corps members an advantage over traditionally prepared and certified teachers by districts who hire corps members to teach, even special education and primary grades, and, in some cases, pick the grade they wanted to "try?"

Is TFA a program that should be offered as a solution to the shortage of qualified teachers in high-poverty urban and rural school districts, and is it a program that warrants taxpayer support? Can policy makers, corporate sponsors, funding sources, government agencies, the media, potential TFA corps members, their families, school districts, average citizens (uninformed about TFA), and the TFA organization, review this study's questions and problematics *and* make improvements to the existing program?

I wondered, "*Whose* America is Teach For America really teaching for? Why is it tolerable for education to be *less-than* for other peoples' kids? And, what are we, as a nation, *really* prepared to do about it?"

APPENDIX A

District Contract

Learning on Other People's Kids: Becoming a Teach For America Teacher
pp. 201–207
Copyright © 2010 by Information Age Publishing

MEMORANDUM OF UNDERSTANDING
BETWEEN
THE BOARD OF EDUCATION OF THE CITY OF
AND TEACH FOR AMERICA, INC.
For School Years 2007-8, 2008-9, 2009-10, and 2010-11

The purpose of this Memorandum of Understanding is to memorialize the terms of an agreement between the The Board of Education of the City of   ("District") and Teach For America, Inc. for a four-year period beginning with the commencement of the 2007-08 school year.

WHEREAS, the District seeks to recruit qualified new teachers and to equip them with the ongoing support and professional development necessary to ensure that they succeed in the classroom;

WHEREAS, Teach For America has a proven history of successfully recruiting and training high quality teachers who are specifically equipped to positively impact student achievement in under-resourced communities and developing a pipeline of people with the potential to serve as future leaders, exceptional teachers, school principals, staff and community leaders in an array of capacities; and

BOTH PARTIES HEREBY RESOLVE to enter into this Memorandum of Understanding (also referred to as "Agreement") to carry out the goals and activities of the District and Teach For America set out herein.

I.   **Responsibilities of the District:**

A.   <u>Hiring and Placement Process</u>

    1.   Commit to hiring, as provided herein, Teach For America teachers each year of this Memorandum of Understanding. The District, subject to its needs and available resources, hereby commits to hire an incoming corps of at least 50 teachers for the 2007-2008 school year, 50 for the 2008-2009 school year, and 50 for the 2009-2010 school year, and 50 for the 2010-2011 school year with the possibility of increases as determined by District for District growth. This hiring commitment includes the following:

        A.   Teach For America teachers will be hired across the full range of grade levels and subject matters, including non-critical shortage areas. The goal is 25-50 percent elementary and 50-75 percent secondary, including, depending upon District needs and available resources, 20-25 percent Math/Science, 30-35 percent Communication Arts, and 20 percent special education.

        B.   Teach For America teachers will be "clustered" in groups of two or more at individual schools.

C. Teach For America teachers will receive the same salary and benefits as other full-time certified first-year teachers. Teach For America teachers returning for their second year of service will have the same seniority rights and salary as other full-time certified second-year teachers.

D. Teach For America teachers will be considered for vacant teaching positions within the District on an equal basis as other alternatively certified teachers, and traditionally certified teachers, as permitted by, and to the extent not inconsistent with, each District Policy Statement and District policies and regulations.

2. Commit, to the extent reasonable and feasible to facilitating the hiring of Teach For America teachers by June 30th each year. District further commits, to the extent feasible, to the following:

A. By April 30th of each year, the District will inform Teach For America, in writing, of the number of new Teach For America teachers the District will hire for the upcoming school year (this is in addition to Teach For America teachers returning for their second year of service) including general subject matter and grade level assignment.

B. After new Teach For America teachers join Teach For America, District will work with Teach For America to attempt to ensure that Teach For America teachers complete the new teacher selection process, e.g., interview with individual schools, and receive a final classroom assignment by June 30th of each year.

B. Financial Obligations

1. Commit to pay Teach For America $2,000.00 per year per teacher during each of the two years of their Teach For America commitment. The amount payable to Teach For America will be determined by the number of first and second year teachers who begin teaching on the first day of school of the current school year. Payment will be made to Teach For America within thirty (30) days of receipt by District of satisfactory invoice.

2. Provide assistance, if deemed appropriate, possible and practicable, in District's sole discretion, to Teach For America's fundraising objectives with private foundations, corporations and other government agencies in and around

C. Professional Credentialing/Development

1. To the extent, appropriate, possible and necessary, work with Teach For America staff and, if applicable the staff of an approved alternative certification program to ensure the smooth enrollment and matriculation of Teach For America teachers.

2.   Communicate with Teach For America regional staff and individual Teach For America teachers regarding any changes in certification requirements, renewal requirements and the certification status of individual teachers that may impact hiring or placement.

3.   To the extent permitted by, and not inconsistent with, each District Policy Statement and District employment policies and regulations, allow Teach For America teachers, as part of their regular paid time off leave, to take up to 12 hours of paid leave per year for professional development activities sponsored by Teach For America, the District or another credible source of professional development for teachers.

II.   Responsibilities of Teach For America:

A.   Recruitment and Selection of New Teachers

1.   Recruit and select applicants from diverse ethnic and racial backgrounds with a proven track record of personal and academic achievement and a commitment to work relentlessly to close the achievement gap between their students and students in more affluent school districts.

2.   Select individuals for hiring and placement within the District who meet federal, state and District requirements for new teacher hires.

B.   Pre-Service Training and Professional Development

1.   Require all Teach For America teachers to participate in an intensive five-week summer institute designed to prepare new teachers to enter the classroom. During the institute, teachers will work in teams of 3-4 to assume full responsibility for teaching a class of students in morning summer schools run by Teach For America under the supervision of a faculty of experienced teachers. Simultaneously, teachers will also participate in a full schedule of professional development activities in the morning and afternoons centered upon Teach For America's training curriculum.

2.   Hold a weeklong induction for teachers assigned to the District to orient them to the city and the District. Teach For America regional staff will organize activities designed to introduce new teachers to the resources and history of the communities in which they will teach.

3.   Provide access to ongoing professional development for all Teach For America teachers throughout the school year, including occasional classroom observations by regional program staff, one-on-one reflective discussions twice yearly, monthly content-area/grade level meetings facilitated by veteran teachers, regular small group dinners and discussions with Teach For America teachers to discuss/share best practices and other corps-building activities. Teach For

America regional staff will also work to ensure that Teach For America teachers have access to local teaching resources and professional development opportunities available in the District and the surrounding areas.

C.   <u>Hiring and Placement Process</u>

    1.   Communicate to the District the estimated number of entering teachers for the upcoming school year. Note: Because the numbers of teachers who will matriculate and complete the summer institute cannot be determined with complete certainty, Teach For America may place fewer teachers in the fall than originally estimated.

    2.   Provide accurate and timely information about new teachers that the District requests to facilitate hiring and placement process. Work with the District to identify specific schools within the District and to develop relationships with school leadership to meet "clustering" objectives of placing two or more Teach For America teachers in each such school.

    3.   Provide the District with a list of all of the new teachers assigned to the District, including the grade level preference and subject matter background of each candidate by May 15th. Teach For America staff will work with District staff to meet District needs regarding subject matter and grade level assignments for new teachers to the extent possible. NOTE: Because new teachers must meet state and federal certification requirements, Teach For America cannot guarantee that a specific teacher will be found eligible by the alternative certification program to teach a particular subject.

III.   Term and Termination:

A.   <u>Term</u>

The term of this Memorandum of Understanding is a four-year period beginning with the commencement of the 2007-08 school year.

B.   <u>Termination for Cause</u>

If either party breaches a material provision hereof ("Cause"), the non-breaching party shall give the other party notice of such Cause. The Cause must be remedied within ten (10) days in the case of failure to make payment when due or within sixty (60) days in the case of any other Cause. If such Cause is not remedied within the specified periods, the party giving notice shall have the right to terminate the Agreement upon expiration of such remedy period. The rights of termination referred to in the Agreement are not intended to be exclusive and are in addition to any other rights available to either party at law or in equity.

C.   <u>Termination for Convenience</u>

Either party may terminate this Agreement at any time upon thirty (30) days' prior written notice to the other party.

D.   Fiscal Funding

While the parties intend for the term of this Memorandum of Understanding to be four (4) years, the term is subject to, and conditioned on, the appropriation, availability and budgeting of sufficient funds. For any fiscal year of the District during the term hereof, in the event that sufficient funds are not available to the District, are not able to be appropriated by the District or cannot be budgeted by the District for the services hereunder, the District shall have the right to terminate this Memorandum of Understanding upon sixty (60) days prior written notice to Teach for America. In the event of any such termination, the District shall pay Teach for America for the services performed up to the date of termination. Thereafter, neither party shall have any further liability or responsibility, except as may be otherwise provided in this Memorandum of Understanding.

IV.   Miscellaneous:

A.   Governing Law – Jurisdiction

This Agreement shall be governed, construed and interpreted under Missouri law, and shall be deemed to be executed and performed in the City of   Any legal action arising out of, or relating to this Agreement shall be governed by the laws of the State of Missouri, and the parties agree to the exclusive exercise of jurisdiction and venue over them by a court of competent jurisdiction located in the City of   Missouri.

B.   Notice

Any notice or communication required or permitted to be given hereunder shall be in writing and served personally, delivered by courier or sent by United States certified mail, postage prepaid with return receipt requested, addressed to the other party as follows:

To District: Superintendent, Legal Notice Enclosed
Public Schools

Teach For America:

and/or to such other persons or places as either of the parties may hereafter designate in writing. All such notices shall be effective when received

C.   Construction and Effect

A waiver of any failure to perform under the Agreement shall neither be construed as nor constitute a waiver of any subsequent failure. The article and section headings used herein are used solely for convenience and shall not be deemed to limit the subject of the articles and sections or be considered in their interpretation. The Agreement may be executed in several counterparts, each of which shall be deemed an original.

D.   Severability

If any term or provision of the Agreement or the application thereof to any person or circumstance shall, to any extent or for any reason be invalid or unenforceable, the remainder of the Agreement and the application of such term or provision to any person or circumstance other than those as to which it is held invalid or unenforceable shall not be affected thereby, and each remaining term and provision of the Agreement shall be valid and enforceable to the fullest extent permitted by law.

E.   Entire Agreement

This Agreement contains the entire understanding and agreement of the parties concerning the matters contained herein, and supersedes and replaces any prior or contemporaneous oral or written contracts or communications concerning the matters contained herein, and may not be changed other than by an agreement in writing signed by the parties hereto.

F.   Binding Effect

This Agreement shall not be binding and effective unless and until it is fully executed by both parties.

The Board of Education of the City of   and Teach For America, Inc. have approved this
Memorandum of Understanding.

THE BOARD OF EDUCATION   **TEACH FOR AMERICA, INC.**
OF THE

By:_____   By:_____

Title:_____*Supt.*_____   Title:__*Executive Director*__

Date:_____*11-13-07*_____   Date:__*11/1/07*_____

APPENDIX B

TFA Form 990

Learning on Other People's Kids: Becoming a Teach For America Teacher
pp. 209–242
Copyright © 2010 by Information Age Publishing

efile GRAPHIC print - DO NOT PROCESS	As Filed Data -		DLN: 93490150001108

Form 990

Department of the Treasury
Internal Revenue Service

Return of Organization Exempt From Income Tax

Under section 501(c), 527, or 4947(a)(1) of the Internal Revenue Code (except black lung benefit trust or private foundation)

▶ The organization may have to use a copy of this return to satisfy state reporting requirements

OMB No 1545-0047

2006

Open to Public Inspection

A For the 2006 calendar year, or tax year beginning 10-01-2006 and ending 09-30-2007

B Check if applicable
☐ Address change
☐ Name change
☐ Initial return
☐ Final return
☐ Amended return
☐ Application pending

Please use IRS label or print or type. See Specific Instructions.

C Name of organization
Teach For America Inc

Number and street (or P O box if mail is not delivered to street address) | Room/suite
315 WEST 36TH STREET

City or town, state or country, and ZIP + 4
NEW YORK, NY 10018

D Employer identification number
13-3541913

E Telephone number
(212) 279-2080

F Accounting method ☐ Cash ☑ Accrual
☐ Other (specify) ▶

● Section 501(c)(3) organizations and 4947(a)(1) nonexempt charitable trusts must attach a completed Schedule A (Form 990 or 990-EZ).

G Web site: ▶ WWW TEACHFORAMERICA ORG

J Organization type (check only one) ▶ ☑ 501(c) (3) ◀ (insert no) ☐ 4947(a)(1) or ☐ 527

K Check here ▶ ☐ if the organization is not a 509(a)(3) supporting organization and its gross receipts are normally **not** more than 25,000 A return is not required, but if the organization chooses to file a return, be sure to file a complete return

L Gross receipts Add lines 6b, 8b, 9b, and 10b to line 12 ▶ 107,009,010

H and **I** are not applicable to section 527 organizations
H(a) Is this a group return for affiliates? ☐ Yes ☑ No
H(b) If "Yes" enter number of affiliates ▶
H(c) Are all affiliates included? ☐ Yes ☐ No
(If "No," attach a list See instructions)
H(d) Is this a separate return filed by an organization covered by a group ruling? ☐ Yes ☑ No
I Group Exemption Number ▶
M Check ▶ ☐ if the organization is **not** required to attach Sch B (Form 990, 990-EZ, or 990-PF)

Part I   Revenue, Expenses, and Changes in Net Assets or Fund Balances (See the instructions.)

1	Contributions, gifts, grants, and similar amounts received			
a	Contributions to donor advised funds	1a		
b	Direct public support (not included on line 1a)	1b	59,681,859	
c	Indirect public support (not included on line 1a)	1c	195,146	
d	Government contributions (grants) (not included on line 1a)	1d	17,062,078	
e	Total (add lines 1a through 1d) (cash $ 74,584,724 noncash $ 2,354,359)		1e	76,939,083
2	Program service revenue including government fees and contracts (from Part VII, line 93)		2	9,319,218
3	Membership dues and assessments		3	
4	Interest on savings and temporary cash investments		4	1,288,046
5	Dividends and interest from securities		5	194,437
6a	Gross rents	6a	12,274	
b	Less rental expenses	6b		
c	Net rental income or (loss) subtract line 6b from line 6a		6c	12,274
7	Other investment income (describe ▶)		7	
8a	Gross amount from sales of assets other than inventory	(A) Securities 15,827,252	(B) Other	8a
b	Less cost or other basis and sales expenses	15,573,858		8b
c	Gain or (loss) (attach schedule)	253,394		8c
d	Net gain or (loss) Combine line 8c, columns (A) and (B)		8d	253,394
9	Special events and activities (attach schedule) If any amount is from **gaming**, check here ▶☐			
a	Gross revenue (not including $ of contributions reported on line 1b)	9a	3,317,329	
b	Less direct expenses other than fundraising expenses	9b	526,855	
c	Net income or (loss) from special events Subtract line 9b from line 9a		9c	2,790,474
10a	Gross sales of inventory, less returns and allowances	10a		
b	Less cost of goods sold	10b		
c	Gross profit or (loss) from sales of inventory (attach schedule) Subtract line 10b from line 10a		10c	
11	Other revenue (from Part VII, line 103)		11	111,371
12	**Total revenue** Add lines 1e, 2, 3, 4, 5, 6c, 7, 8d, 9c, 10c, and 11		12	90,908,297
13	Program services (from line 44, column (B))		13	68,659,102
14	Management and general (from line 44, column (C))		14	8,113,182
15	Fundraising (from line 44, column (D))		15	6,620,014
16	Payments to affiliates (attach schedule)		16	
17	**Total expenses** Add lines 16 and 44, column (A)		17	83,392,298
18	Excess or (deficit) for the year Subtract line 17 from line 12		18	7,515,999

Form 990 (2006)   Page :

Part II	Statement of Functional Expenses	All organizations must complete column (A) Columns (B), (C), and (D) are required for section 501(c)(3) and (4) organizations and section 4947(a)(1) nonexempt charitable trusts but optional for others *(See the instructions.)*

Do not include amounts reported on line 6b, 8b, 9b, 10b, or 16 of Part I.		**(A)** Total	**(B)** Program services	**(C)** Management and general	**(D)** Fundraising
22a Grants paid from donor advised funds (attach Schedule) (cash $0 noncash $0) If this amount includes foreign grants, check here ► ⌐	**22a**				
22b Other grants and allocations (attach schedule) 🖼 (cash $3,859,799 noncash $0) If this amount includes foreign grants, check here ► ⌐	**22b**	3,859,799	3,859,799		
23 Specific assistance to individuals (attach schedule)	**23**				
24 Benefits paid to or for members (attach schedule)	**24**				
25a Compensation of current officers, directors, key employees etc Listed in Part V-A (attach schedule)	**25a**	1,459,763	1,203,429	140,721	115,61:
b Compensation of former officers, directors, key employees etc listed in Part V-B (attach schedule)	**25b**				
c Compensation and other distributions not icluded above to disqualified persons (as defined under section 4958(f)(1)) and persons described in section 4958(c)(3)(B) (attach schedule)	**25c**				
26 Salaries and wages of employees not included on lines 25a, b and c	**26**	40,607,672	33,106,720	3,341,921	4,159,03:
27 Pension plan contributions not included on lines 25a, b and c	**27**	1,237,214	1,019,960	119,267	97,98:
28 Employee benefits not included on lines 25a - 27	**28**	3,245,143	2,460,208	257,337	527,59!
29 Payroll taxes	**29**	3,396,195	2,799,823	327,393	268,97!
30 Professional fundraising fees	**30**				
31 Accounting fees	**31**	265,675		265,675	
32 Legal fees	**32**	35,771	29,490	3,448	2,83:
33 Supplies	**33**	1,000,401	826,192	96,610	77,59!
34 Telephone	**34**	1,302,650	1,088,145	163,251	51,254
35 Postage and shipping	**35**	500,507	447,047	37,684	15,77(
36 Occupancy	**36**	3,165,475	2,560,657	474,428	130,39(
37 Equipment rental and maintenance	**37**	1,245,136	1,107,083	138,053	
38 Printing and publications	**38**	2,305,452	2,090,233	70,399	144,82(
39 Travel	**39**	8,600,581	7,652,931	508,631	439,01!
40 Conferences, conventions, and meetings . .	**40**	300,967	235,975	51,309	13,68:
41 Interest	**41**				
42 Depreciation, depletion, etc (attach schedule)	**42**	1,718,754	1,378,290	147,336	193,12!
43 Other expenses not covered above (itemize)					
a See Additional Data Table	**43a**				
b _____	**43b**				
c _____	**43c**				
d _____	**43d**				
e _____	**43e**				
f _____	**43f**				
g _____	**43g**				
44 **Total functional expenses.** Add lines 22a through 43g (Organizations completing columns (B)-(D), carry these totals to lines 13-15)	**44**	83,392,298	68,659,102	8,113,182	6,620,01:

Joint Costs. Check ► ⌐ if you are following SOP 98-2
Are any joint costs from a combined educational campaign and fundraising solicitation reported in **(B)** Program services?   ► ⌐ **Yes** ☑ **N:**
If "Yes," enter **(i)** the aggregate amount of these joint costs $0_____ , **(ii)** the amount allocated to Program services $0_____
(iii) the amount allocated to Management and general $0_____ , and **(iv)** the amount allocated to Fundraising $0_____

Form **990** (2006

Part III   **Statement of Program Service Accomplishments** *(See the instructions.)*

Form 990 is available for public inspection and, for some people, serves as the primary or sole source of information about a particular organization How the public perceives an organization in such cases may be determined by the information presented on its return Therefore, please make sure the return is complete and accurate and fully describes, in Part III, the organization's programs and accomplishments

What is the organization's primary exempt purpose? ▶ Teach For America, Inc is the national teacher corps of outstanding recent college graduates who commit two years to teach in public schools in low-income urban and rural areas, and who become lifelong leaders in pursuit of educational excellence and equity Teach for America, Inc recruits top graduates of all academic majors from campuses across the country, selects corps members through an intensive application process, trains them in an intensive pre-service institute, places them in schools as regular beginning teachers, coordinates an ongoing support network among them, and builds a network among its alumni to foster their ongoing leadership and collaboration

Program Service Expenses
(Required for 501(c)(3) and (4) orgs , and 4947(a)(1) trusts, but optional for others)

All organizations must describe their exempt purpose achievements in a clear and concise manner State the number of clients served, publications issued, etc Discuss achievements that are not measurable (Section 501(c)(3) and (4) organizations and 4947(a)(1) nonexempt charitable trusts must also enter the amount of grants and allocations to others)

a PLACEMENT, PROFESSIONAL DEVELOPMENT, EDUCATION AWARDS, AND OTHER TFA PLACES CORPS MEMBERS IN VARIOUS URBAN AND RURAL REGIONS OF THE UNITED STATES IN EACH REGION, TFA HAS REGIONAL OFFICES, WHICH ARE RESPONSIBLE FOR PLACING CORPS MEMBERS IN SCHOOLS, MONITORING THEIR PROGRESS THROUGHOUT THE TWO YEAR COMMITMENT, PROVIDING OPPORTUNITIES FOR ONGOING PROFESSIONAL DEVELOPMENT, AND HELPING CORPS MEMBERS TO FEEL PART OF A NATIONAL CORPS IN 2007 AND 2006, TFA PLACED CORPS MEMBERS IN 27 AND 25 REGIONS RESPECTIVELY

(Grants and allocations $ 3,952,473)   If this amount includes foreign grants, check here ▶ ☐   30,481,855

b TEACHER RECRUITMENT AND SELECTION TFA RECRUITS AND SELECTS A TEACHING CORPS OF OUTSTANDING COLLEGE GRADUATES TO TEACH THE NATION'S MOST UNDERSERVED STUDENTS THE RECRUITMENT AND SELECTION PROCESS CONSISTS OF SCHEDULING AND ATTENDING ON AND OFF CAMPUS RECRUITMENT EVENTS, PROCESSING APPLICATIONS (APPROXIMATELY 18,000 IN 2007 AND 19,000 IN 2006) AND CONDUCTING DAYLONG INTERVIEW SESSIONS IN MULTIPLE SITES ACROSS THE COUNTRY TFA HAD APPROXIMATELY 2,900 AND MORE THAN 2,400 NEW CORPS MEMBERS BEGIN THEIR FALL TEACHING ASSIGNMENTS IN 2007 AND 2006 RESPECTIVELY

(Grants and allocations $)   If this amount includes foreign grants, check here ▶ ☐   18,192,947

c Pre-Service Institute For incoming corps members, TFA conducts intensive summer training institutes held on university campuses and in conjunction with local public school districts In 2007, approximately 2,900 corps members were trained at one of our five institute campuses University of Houston, Temple University, California State University - Long Beach, St John's University, and Georgia Institute of Technology As a part of TFA's ongoing relationship with the Houston Independent School District, the School District of Philadelphia, the Los Angeles Unified School District, the New York City Department of Education, and the Atlanta Public Schools, corps members taught students who enrolled in Houston's, Philadelphia's, Los Angeles', New York's, and Atlanta's public summer school programs

(Grants and allocations $)   If this amount includes foreign grants, check here ▶ ☐   16,200,250

d Alumni TFA has over 12,000 alumni across the country In FY2007, TFA focused on fostering the leadership of our alumni as a force for social change and engaging alumni with the work of TFA Specifically, we * Achieved goals of 285 School Leaders, 7 Elected Officials, and 25% of alumni donating time or money back to TFA * Produced two alumni magazines called "One Day" that was mailed out to over 17,000 people * Launched the Alumni Career and Leadership center The Alumni Career and Leadership Center guides alumni through their career cycles from assessing their skills, talents and interests, exploring careers and learning how to leverage their experience to best position themselves to transition into the field, and connect them to resources to be successful in the outreach and securing of a job

(Grants and allocations $)   If this amount includes foreign grants, check here ▶ ☐   3,784,050

e Other program services (attach schedule)
(Grants and allocations $) If this amount includes foreign grants, check here ▶ ☐

f   Total of Program Service Expenses (should equal line 44, column (B), Program services) . . . . ▶   68,659,102

Form 990 (2006)   Page **4**

Part IV   **Balance Sheets** *(See the instructions.)*

Note:	Where required, attached schedules and amounts within the description column should be for end-of-year amounts only.			**(A)** Beginning of year		**(B)** End of year
	45	Cash—non-interest-bearing		2,023,835	**45**	3,152,812
	46	Savings and temporary cash investments		11,715,218	**46**	13,513,884
	47a	Accounts receivable	**47a**	6,360,283		
	b	Less allowance for doubtful accounts	**47b**	0	4,705,079	**47c**	6,360,283
	48a	Pledges receivable	**48a**	64,061,917		
	b	Less allowance for doubtful accounts	**48b**	0	61,214,726	**48c**	64,061,917
	49	Grants receivable		6,323,743	**49**	4,510,997
	50a	Receivables from current and former officers, directors, trustees, and key employees (attach schedule)			**50a**	
	b	Receivables from other disqualified persons (as defined under section 4958(c)(3)(B) (attach schedule)			**50b**	
	51a	Other notes and loans receivable (attach schedule)	**51a**	4,166,025		
	b	Less allowance for doubtful accounts	**51b**	419,302	4,037,229	**51c** 🔧	3,746,723
	52	Inventories for sale or use			**52**	
	53	Prepaid expenses and deferred charges		168,135	**53**	505,738
	54a	Investments—publicly-traded securities . ▶ ☐ Cost ☑ FMV		16,524,490	**54a**	17,166,395
	b	Investments—other securities (attach schedule) ▶ ☐ Cost ☐ FMV			**54b**	
	55a	Investments—land, buildings, and equipment basis	**55a**			
	b	Less accumulated depreciation (attach schedule)	**55b**			**55c**	
	56	Investments—other (attach schedule)			**56**	
	57a	Land, buildings, and equipment basis	**57a**	14,097,152		
	b	Less accumulated depreciation (attach schedule)	**57b**	5,257,922	5,038,056	**57c**	8,839,230
	58	Other assets, including program-related investments (describe ▶ _____)		330,735	**58** 🔧	489,166
	59	**Total assets** (must equal line 74) Add lines 45 through 58 . . .		112,081,246	**59**	122,347,145
	60	Accounts payable and accrued expenses		4,641,746	**60**	6,396,978
	61	Grants payable		2,006,199	**61**	1,788,852
	62	Deferred revenue			**62**	
	63	Loans from officers, directors, trustees, and key employees (attach schedule)			**63**	
	64a	Tax-exempt bond liabilities (attach schedule)			**64a**	
	b	Mortgages and other notes payable (attach schedule)			**64b**	
	65	Other liabilities (describe ▶ _____)		661,663	**65** 🔧	1,018,211
	66	**Total liabilities** Add lines 60 through 65		7,309,608	**66**	9,204,041
		Organizations that follow SFAS 117, check here ▶ ☑ **and complete lines 67 through 69 and lines 73 and 74**				
	67	Unrestricted		39,321,474	**67**	45,559,207
	68	Temporarily restricted		61,288,331	**68**	63,422,064
	69	Permanently restricted		4,161,833	**69**	4,161,833
		Organizations that do not follow SFAS 117, check here ▶ ☐ **and complete lines 70 through 74**				
	70	Capital stock, trust principal, or current funds			**70**	
	71	Paid-in or capital surplus, or land, building, and equipment fund . .			**71**	
	72	Retained earnings, endowment, accumulated income, or other funds .			**72**	
	73	**Total net assets or fund balances** Add lines 67 through 69 **or** lines 70 through 72 (Column (A) **must** equal line 19 and column (B) **must** equal line 21)		104,771,638	**73**	113,143,104
	74	**Total liabilities and net assets / fund balances** Add lines 66 and 73 . .		112,081,246	**74**	122,347,145

Form **990** (2006)

Form 990 (2006)   Page **5**

Part IV-A	**Reconciliation of Revenue per Audited Financial Statements With Revenue per Return** *(See the instructions.)*			
a	Total revenue, gains, and other support per audited financial statements		**a**	92,958,125
b	Amounts included on line **a** but not on Part I, line 12			
1	Net unrealized gains on investments	**b1**	855,467	
2	Donated services and use of facilities	**b2**	1,245,905	
3	Recoveries of prior year grants	**b3**		
4	Other (specify) _____	**b4**		
	Add lines **b1** through **b4**		**b**	2,101,372
c	Subtract line **b** from line **a**		**c**	90,856,753
d	Amounts included on Part I, line 12, but not on line **a**			
1	Investment expenses not included on Part I, line 6b	**d1**	39,270	
2	Other (specify) 🖉 _____	**d2**	12,274	
	Add lines **d1** and **d2**		**d**	2,101,372
e	**Total revenue** (Part I, line 12) Add lines **c** and **d** . . . . ▶		**e**	90,908,297

Part IV-B	**Reconciliation of Expenses per Audited Financial Statements With Expenses per Return**			
a	Total expenses and losses per audited financial statements		**a**	84,586,659
b	Amounts included on line **a** but not on Part I, line 17			
1	Donated services and use of facilities	**b1**	1,245,905	
2	Prior year adjustments reported on Part I, line 20	**b2**		
3	Losses reported on Part I, line 20	**b3**		
4	Other (specify) _____	**b4**		
	Add lines **b1** through **b4**		**b**	1,245,905
c	Subtract line **b** from line **a**		**c**	83,340,754
d	Amounts included on Part I, line 17, but not on line **a:**			
1	Investment expenses not included on Part I, line 6b	**d1**	39,270	
2	Other (specify) _____	**d2**	12,274	
	Add lines **d1** and **d2**		**d**	51,544
e	**Total expenses** (Part I, line 17) Add lines **c** and **d** . . . . ▶		**e**	83,392,298

Part V-A	**Current Officers, Directors, Trustees, and Key Employees** (List each person who was an officer, director, trustee, or key employee at any time during the year even if they were not compensated.) *(See the instructions.)*			
(A) Name and address	**(B)** Title and average hours per week devoted to position	**(C)** Compensation (If not paid, enter -0-.)	**(D)** Contributions to employee benefit plans & deferred compensation plans	**(E)** Expense account and other allowances
See Additional Data Table				

Form 990 (2006)   Page **6**

Part V-A	Current Officers, Directors, Trustees, and Key Employees *(continued)*					Yes	No

75a Enter the total number of officers, directors, and trustees permitted to vote on organization business at board

    meetings . . . . ▶25

  b Are any officers, directors, trustees, or key employees listed in Form 990, Part V-A, or highest compensated

    employees listed in Schedule A, Part I, or highest compensated professional and other independent

    contractors listed in Schedule A, Part II-A or II-B, related to each other through family or business

    relationships? If "Yes," attach a statement that identifies the individuals and explains the relationship(s) .   **75b**   No

  c Do any officers, directors, trustees, or key employees listed in Form 990, Part V-A, or highest compensated

    employees listed in Schedule A, Part I, or highest compensated professional and other independent

    contractors listed in Schedule A, Part II-A or II-B, receive compensation from any other organizations, whether

    tax exempt or taxable, that are related to the organization? See the instructions for the definition of "related

    organization" . . . . ▶   **75c**   No

    If "Yes," attach a statement that includes the information described in the instructions

  d Does the organization have a written conflict of interest policy? . . . .   **75d**   Yes

Part V-B	Former Officers, Directors, Trustees, and Key Employees That Received Compensation or Other

Benefits (If any former officer, director, trustee, or key employee received compensation or other benefits (described below) during the year, list that person below and enter the amount of compensation or other benefits in the appropriate column. See the instructions.)

(A) Name and address	**(B)** Loans and Advances	**(C)** Compensation (If not paid enter -0-)	**(D)** Contributions to employee benefit plans and deferred compensation plans	**(E)** Expense account and other allowances

Part VI	Other Information *(See the instructions.)*		Yes	No

76 Did the organization make a change in its activities or methods of conducting activities? If "Yes," attach a

  detailed statement of each change . . . .   **76**   No

77 Were any changes made in the organizing or governing documents but not reported to the IRS? . . .   **77**   No

  If "Yes," attach a conformed copy of the changes

78a Did the organization have unrelated business gross income of $1,000 or more during the year covered by this return? . . .   **78a**   No

  b If "Yes," has it filed a tax return on **Form 990-T** for this year? **78b**

79 Was there a liquidation, dissolution, termination, or substantial contraction during the year? If "Yes," attach

  a statement . . . .   **79**   No

80a Is the organization related (other than by association with a statewide or nationwide organization) through common membership,

  governing bodies, trustees, officers, etc , to any other exempt or nonexempt organization? . . . . . .   **80a**   No

  b If "Yes," enter the name of the organization ▶ _____

  _____ and check whether it is ⌐ exempt **or** ⌐ nonexempt

81a Enter direct or indirect political expenditures (See line 81 instructions) . . . | **81a** | 0

  b Did the organization file **Form 1120-POL** for this year? . . . .   **81b**   No

Form **990** (2006)

Part VI	**Other Information** *(continued)*		Yes	No

82a Did the organization receive donated services or the use of materials, equipment, or facilities at no charge or at substantially less than fair rental value? . . . . **82a** | Yes |

  b If "Yes," you may indicate the value of these items here Do not include this amount as revenue
in Part I or as an expense in Part II (See instructions in Part III) . . . . | **82b** | 1,245,905

83a Did the organization comply with the public inspection requirements for returns and exemption applications? | **83a** | Yes |

  b Did the organization comply with the disclosure requirements relating to quid pro quo contributions? . . . | **83b** | Yes |

84a Did the organization solicit any contributions or gifts that were not tax deductible? . . . . | **84a** | | No

  b If "Yes," did the organization include with every solicitation an express statement that such contributions or gifts were not tax deductible? . . . . | **84b** |

85 *501(c)(4), (5), or (6) organizations.* **a** Were substantially all dues nondeductible by members? . . . . | **85a** |

  b Did the organization make only in-house lobbying expenditures of $2,000 or less? . . . . | **85b** |

  If "Yes," was answered to either 85a or 85b, **do not** complete 85c through 85h below unless the organization received a waiver for proxy tax owed the prior year

  c Dues assessments, and similar amounts from members . . . . | **85c** |

  d Section 162(e) lobbying and political expenditures . . . . | **85d** |

  e Aggregate nondeductible amount of section 6033(e)(1)(A) dues notices . . | **85e** |

  f Taxable amount of lobbying and political expenditures (line 85d less 85e) . . | **85f** |

  g Does the organization elect to pay the section 6033(e) tax on the amount on line 85f? . . . . | **85g** |

  h If section 6033(e)(1)(A) dues notices were sent, does the organization agree to add the amount on line 85f to its reasonable estimate of dues allocable to nondeductible lobbying and political expenditures for the following tax year? . . . . | **85h** |

86 *501(c)(7) orgs.* Enter **a** Initiation fees and capital contributions included on line 12 | **86a** | 0

  b Gross receipts, included on line 12, for public use of club facilities . . . . | **86b** | 0

87 *501(c)(12) orgs.* Enter **a** Gross income from members or shareholders . . . | **87a** | 0

  b Gross income from other sources (Do not net amounts due or paid to other sources against amounts due or received from them) . . . . | **87b** | 0

88a At any time during the year, did the organization own a 50% or greater interest in a taxable corporation or partnership, or an entity disregarded as separate from the organization under Regulations sections 301 7701-2 and 301 7701-3? If "Yes," complete Part IX . . . . | **88a** | | No

  b At any time during the year, did the organization directly or indirectly own a controlled entity within the meaning of section 512(b)(13)? If yes complete Part XI . . . . | **88b** | | No

89a *501(c)(3) organizations* Enter Amount of tax imposed on the organization during the year under
section 4911 ▶ _____ 0 , section 4912 ▶ _____ 0 , section 4955 ▶ _____ 0

  b *501(c)(3) and 501(c)(4) orgs.* Did the organization engage in any section 4958 excess benefit transaction during the year or did it become aware of an excess benefit transaction from a prior year? If "Yes," attach a statement explaining each transaction . . . . | **89b** | | No

  c Enter Amount of tax imposed on the organization managers or disqualified persons during the year under sections 4912, 4955, and 4958 . . . . ▶ _____ 0

  d Enter Amount of tax on line 89c, above, reimbursed by the organization . . . ▶ _____ 0

  e *All organizations.* At any time during the tax year was the organization a party to a prohibited tax shelter transaction? . . . . | **89e** | | No

  f *All organizations.* Did the organization acquire direct or indirect interest in any applicable insurance contract? | **89f** | | No

  g *For supporting organizations and sponsoring organizations maintaining donor advised funds.* Did the supporting organization, or a fund maintained by a sponsoring organization, have excess business holdings at any time during the year? . . . . | **89g** | | No

90a List the states with which a copy of this return is filed ▶ See Additional Data Table

  b Number of employees employed in the pay period that includes March 12, 2006 (See instructions) . . . . | **90b** | 461

91a The books are in care of ▶ MIGUEL ROSSY   Telephone no ▶ (212) 279-2080
315 WEST 36TH STREET 5TH FLOOR
Located at ▶ NEW YORK, NY   ZIP + 4 ▶ 10018

  b At any time during the calendar year, did the organization have an interest in or a signature or other authority over a financial account in a foreign country (such as a bank account, securities account, or other financial account)? . . . . | Yes | No |
| | | | **91b** | | No

  If "Yes," enter the name of the foreign country ▶_____

  See the instructions for exceptions and filing requirements for **Form TD F 90-22.1,** Report of Foreign Bank and Financial Accounts

Form 990 (2006)   Page **8**

Part VI	**Other Information** *(continued)*					**Yes**	**No**
c	At any time during the calendar year, did the organization maintain an office outside of the United States?				**91c**		No

If "Yes," enter the name of the foreign country ▶_____

92   Section 4947(a)(1) nonexempt charitable trusts filing Form 990 in lieu of **Form 1041**—Check here . . . . ▶ ☐

and enter the amount of tax-exempt interest received or accrued during the tax year . . . . ▶ | **92** |

Part VII   Analysis of Income-Producing Activities *(See the instructions.)*

Note: *Enter gross amounts unless otherwise indicated.*

		Unrelated business income		Excluded by section 512, 513, or 514		(E)
		(A) Business code	**(B)** Amount	**(C)** Exclusion code	**(D)** Amount	Related or exempt function income
93	Program service revenue					
a	FEE FOR SERVICE REVENUE					9,319,218
b						
c						
d						
e						
f	Medicare/Medicaid payments					
g	Fees and contracts from government agencies					
94	Membership dues and assessments . . .					
95	Interest on savings and temporary cash investments			14	1,288,046	
96	Dividends and interest from securities . . .			14	194,437	
97	Net rental income or (loss) from real estate					
a	debt-financed property					
b	non debt-financed property			16	12,274	
98	Net rental income or (loss) from personal property					
99	Other investment income					
100	Gain or (loss) from sales of assets other than inventory			18	253,394	
101	Net income or (loss) from special events . .			01	2,790,474	
102	Gross profit or (loss) from sales of inventory					
103	Other revenue a MISCELLANEOUS			01	111,371	
b						
c						
d						
e						
104	Subtotal (add columns (B), (D), and (E)) . .				4,649,996	9,319,218

105   **Total** (add line 104, columns (B), (D), and (E)) . . . . ▶ _____   13,969,214

Note: *Line 105 plus line 1e, Part I, should equal the amount on line 12, Part I.*

Part VIII   Relationship of Activities to the Accomplishment of Exempt Purposes *(See the instructions.)*

Line No. ▼	Explain how each activity for which income is reported in column (E) of Part VII contributed importantly to the accomplishment of the organization's exempt purposes (other than by providing funds for such purposes)
93A	FEES FROM CONTRACTUAL AGREEMENTS WITH VARIOUS SCHOOL
0	DISTRICTS ACROSS THE UNITED STATES TO RECRUIT, SELECT,
0	TRAIN, AND PLACE CORPS MEMBERS TO WORK IN THEIR SCHOOL
0	DISTRICTS

Part IX   Information Regarding Taxable Subsidiaries and Disregarded Entities *(See the instructions.)*

(A) Name, address, and EIN of corporation, partnership, or disregarded entity	(B) Percentage of ownership interest	(C) Nature of activities	(D) Total income	(E) End-of-year assets
	%			
	%			
	%			
	%			

Part X   Information Regarding Transfers Associated with Personal Benefit Contracts *(See the instructions.)*

(a)   Did the organization, during the year, receive any funds, directly or indirectly, to pay premiums on a personal benefit contract? . . . . ☐ **Yes** ☑ **No**

(b)   Did the organization, during the year, pay premiums, directly or indirectly, on a personal benefit contract? . . . . ☐ **Yes** ☑ **No**

NOTE: *If "Yes" to **(b)**, file Form 8870 **and** Form 4720 (see instructions).*

Form **990** (2006)

218   B. T. VELTRI

Form 990 (2006)   Page **9**

Part XI   **Information Regarding Transfers To and From Controlled Entities** *Complete only if the organization is a controlling organization as defined in section 512(b)(13)*

| | | | Yes | No |
| **106** | Did the reporting organization **make** any transfers **to** a controlled entity as defined in section 512(b)(13) of the Code? If "Yes," complete the schedule below for each controlled entity | | | No |

| **(A)** Name and address of each controlled entity | **(B)** Employer Identification Number | **(C)** Description of transfer | **(D)** Amount of transfer |
| Totals | | | |

| | | | Yes | No |
| **107** | Did the reporting organization **receive** any transfers **from** a controlled entity as defined in section 512(b)(13) of the Code? If "Yes," complete the schedule below for each controlled entity | | | No |

| **(A)** Name and address of each controlled entity | **(B)** Employer Identification Number | **(C)** Description of transfer | **(D)** Amount of transfer |
| Totals | | | |

| | | | Yes | No |
| **108** | Did the organization have a binding written contract in effect on August 17, 2006 covering the interests, rents, royalties and annuities described in question 107 above? | | | No |

Under penalties of perjury, I declare that I have examined this return, including accompanying schedules and statements, and to the best of my knowledge and belief, it is true, correct, and complete. Declaration of preparer (other than officer) is based on all information of which preparer has any knowledge

Please Sign Here

······   2008-05-28
Signature of officer   Date

MIGUEL ROSSY CHIEF FINANCE & INFRASTRUCTURE OFF
Type or print name and title

Paid Preparer's Use Only

Preparer's signature ▶	Date	Check if self-employed ▶ ⌐	Preparer's SSN or PTIN (See Gen Inst W)
Firm's name (or yours if self-employed), address, and ZIP + 4 GRANT THORNTON LLP		EIN ▶	
666 THIRD AVENUE NEW YORK, NY 10017		Phone no ▶	

Form **990** (2006)

efile GRAPHIC print - DO NOT PROCESS	As Filed Data -	DLN: 93490150001108

SCHEDULE A (Form 990 or 990EZ) 🖅 Department of the Treasury Internal Revenue Service	**Organization Exempt Under Section 501(c)(3)** (Except Private Foundation) and Section 501(e), 501(f), 501(k), 501(n), or 4947(a)(1) Nonexempt Charitable Trust **Supplementary Information—(See separate instructions.)** ▶ MUST be completed by the above organizations and attached to their Form 990 or 990-EZ	OMB No 1545-0047 **2006**

Name of the organization
Teach For America Inc

Employer identification number
13-3541913

Part I   **Compensation of the Five Highest Paid Employees Other Than Officers, Directors, and Trustees**
(See page 2 of the instructions. List each one. If there are none, enter "None.")

(a) Name and address of each employee paid more than $50,000	**(b)** Title and average hours per week devoted to position	**(c)** Compensation	**(d)** Contributions to employee benefit plans & deferred compensation	**(e)** Expense account and other allowances
JEFFREY WETZLER 315 WEST 36TH STREET NEW YORK, NY 10018	SR VP- TEACHER PREP 60 0	180,800	20,799	0
ELISSA CLAPP 315 WEST 36TH STREET NEW YORK, NY 10018	SR VP- RECRUIT MGMT 60 0	174,985	15,875	0
SUSAN ASIYANBI 315 WEST 36TH STREET NEW YORK, NY 10018	VP INSTITUTES 60 0	170,405	8,002	0
MELISSA GOLDEN 315 WEST 36TH STREET NEW YORK, NY 10018	VP- NATIONAL MARK 60 0	137,042	10,435	0
AYLON SAMOUHA 315 WEST 36TH STREET NEW YORK, NY 10018	SVP- TEACHER SUPPORT 60 0	131,174	10,539	0
Total number of other employees paid over $50,000 ▶	282			

Part II-A   **Compensation of the Five Highest Paid Independent Contractors for Professional Services**
(See page 2 of the instructions. List each one (whether individuals or firms). If there are none, enter "None.")

(a) Name and address of each independent contractor paid more than $50,000	**(b)** Type of service	**(c)** Compensation
MONITOR COMPANY GROUP LP 2 CANAL PARK CAMBRIDGE, MA 02141	CONSULTING	258,226
VML PO BOX 14229 COLLECTIONS CENTER DRI CHICAGO, IL 60693	RENDERED DESIGN	162,700
KPMG LLP PO BOX 120001 DALLAS, TX 753120511	AUDITING	104,550
JAMES S BECKER III 262 TAFFE PLACE 515 BROOKLYN, NY 11205	TECH CONSULTANT	102,400
LYNN DOUPSAS 104 WEST 70TH STREET APT 3GH NEW YORK, NY 10023	TECH CONSULTANT	85,346
Total number of others receiving over $50,000 for professional services ▶	4	

Part II-B   **Compensation of the Five Highest Paid Independent Contractors for Other Services**
(List each contractor who performed services other than professional services, whether individuals or firms. If there are none, enter "None". See page 2 for instructions.)

(a) Name and address of each independent contractor paid more than $50,000	**(b)** Type of service	**(c)** Compensation
PITNEY BOWES MANAGEMENT SERVICES PO BOX 845801 DALLAS, TX 752845801	PRINTING PACKAGES	616,026
COWBOY CARPENTRY 260 W 36TH STREET ROOM 502 NEW YORK, NY 10018	CONSTRUCTION	453,197
FED EX PO BOX 371461 PITTSBURGH, PA 152507461	SHIPPING	271,594
FED EX KINKO'S PO BOX 672085 DALLAS, TX 752672085	PRINTING	233,048
RIT PRINTING		

220   B. T. VELTRI

Part III   Statements About Activities (See page 2 of the instructions.)

		Yes	No
1	During the year, has the organization attempted to influence national, state, or local legislation, include any attempt to influence public opinion on a legislative matter or referendum? If "Yes," enter the total expenses paid or incurred in connection with the lobbying activities ▶$ 120,177 _____ (Must equal amounts on line 38, Part VI-A, or line i of Part VI-B)		
	Organizations that made an election under section 501(h) by filing Form 5768 must complete Part VI-A Other organizations checking "Yes" must complete Part VI-B AND attach a statement giving a detailed description of the lobbying activities	**1**	Yes	
2	During the year, has the organization, either directly or indirectly, engaged in any of the following acts with any substantial contributors, trustees, directors, officers, creators, key employees, or members of their families, or with any taxable organization with which any such person is affiliated as an officer, director, trustee, majority owner, or principal beneficiary? *(If the answer to any question is "Yes," attach a detailed statement explaining the transactions.)*			
a	Sale, exchange, or leasing property?	**2a**		No
b	Lending of money or other extension of credit?	**2b**		No
c	Furnishing of goods, services, or facilities?	**2c**		No
d	Payment of compensation (or payment or reimbursement of expenses if more than $1,000)?	**2d**	Yes	
e	Transfer of any part of its income or assets?	**2e**		No
3a	Did the organization make grants for scholarships, fellowships, student loans, etc ? (If "Yes," attach an explanation of how the organization determines that recipients qualify to receive payments)	**3a**	Yes	
b	Did the organization have a section 403(b) annuity plan for its employees?	**3b**	Yes	
c	Did the organization receive or hold an easement for conservation purposes, including easements to preserve open space, the environment , historic land areas or structures? If "Yes" attach a detailed statement	**3c**		No
d	Did the organization provide credit counseling, debt management, credit repair, or debt negotiation services?	**3d**		No
4a	Did the organization maintain any donor advised funds? If "Yes," complete lines 4b through 4g If "No," complete lines 4f and 4g	**4a**	Yes	
b	Did the organization make any taxable distributions under section 4966?	**4b**		No
c	Did the organization make a distribution to a donor, donor advisor, or related person?	**4c**		No
d	Enter the total number of donor advised funds owned at the end of the tax year ▶ _____			
e	Enter the aggregate value of assets held in all donor advised funds owned at the end of the tax year ▶ _____			
f	Enter the total number of separate funds or accounts owned at the end of the tax year (excluding donor advised funds included on line 4d) where donors have the right to provide advice on the distribution or investment of amounts in such funds or accounts ▶0 _____			
g	Enter the aggregate value of assets held in all funds or accounts included on line 4f at the end of the tax year ▶0 _____			

Part IV   **Reason for Non-Private Foundation Status** (See pages 4 through 7 of the instructions.)

I certify that the organization is not a private foundation because it is (Please check only **ONE** applicable box)

5   ☐   A church, convention of churches, or association of churches Section 170(b)(1)(A)(i)

6   ☐   A school Section 170(b)(1)(A)(ii) (Also complete Part V)

7   ☐   A hospital or a cooperative hospital service organization Section 170(b)(1)(A)(iii)

8   ☐   A federal, state, or local government or governmental unit Section 170(b)(1)(A)(v)

9   ☐   A medical research organization operated in conjunction with a hospital Section 170(b)(1)(A)(iii) **Enter the hospital's name, city, and state ▶**

10   ☐   An organization operated for the benefit of a college or university owned or operated by a governmental unit
Section 170(b)(1)(A)(iv) (Also complete the **Support Schedule** in Part IV-A)

11a ☑   An organization that normally receives a substantial part of its support from a governmental unit or from the general public
Section 170(b)(1)(A)(vi) (Also complete the **Support Schedule** in Part IV-A)

11b ☐   A community trust Section 170(b)(1)(A)(vi) (Also complete the **Support Schedule** in Part IV-A)

12   ☐   An organization that normally receives **(1) more than 33 1/3%** of its support from contributions, membership fees, and gross
receipts from activities related to its charitable, etc , functions—subject to certain exceptions, and **(2) no more than 33 1/3%** of
its support from gross investment income and unrelated business taxable income (less section 511 tax) from businesses
acquired by the organization after June 30, 1975 See section 509(a)(2) (Also complete the **Support Schedule** in Part IV-A)

13   ☐   An organization that is not controlled by any disqualified persons (other than foundation managers) and otherwise meets the
requirements of section 509(a)(3) Check the box that describes the type of supporting organization

☐ Type I   ☐ Type II   ☐ Type III - Functionally Integrated   ☐ Type III - Other

Provide the following information about the supported organizations. (see page 7 of the instructions.)

(a) Name(s) of supported organization(s)	(b) Employer identification number	(c) Type of organization (described in lines 5 through 12 above or IRC section)	(d) Is the supported organization listed in the supporting organization's governing documents?		(e) Amount of support?
			Yes	No	
Total				▶	

14   ☐   An organization organized and operated to test for public safety Section 509(a)(4) (See page 7 of the instructions)

Part IV-A   **Support Schedule** (Complete only if you checked a box on line 10, 11, or 12) *Use cash method of accounting.*
Note: *You may use the worksheet in the instructions for converting from the accrual to the cash method of accounting.*

Calendar year (or fiscal year beginning in) ▶	(a) 2005	(b) 2004	(c) 2003	(d) 2002	(e) Total
15 Gifts, grants, and contributions received (Do not include unusual grants See line 28)	60,571,268	53,722,125	37,218,104	38,753,991	190,265,488
16 Membership fees received					0
17 Gross receipts from admissions, merchandise sold or services performed, or furnishing of facilities in any activity that is related to the organization's charitable, etc , purpose					0
18 Gross income from interest, dividends, amounts received from payments on securities loans (section 512(a)(5)), rents, royalties, and unrelated business taxable income (less section 511 taxes) from businesses acquired by the organization after June 30, 1975	408,068	804,617	586,531	528,303	2,327,519
19 Net income from unrelated business activities not included in line 18					0
20 Tax revenues levied for the organization's benefit and either paid to it or expended on its behalf					0
21 The value of services or facilities furnished to the organization by a governmental unit without charge Do not include the value of services or facilities generally furnished to the public without charge					0
22 Other income Attach a schedule Do not include gain or (loss) from sale of capital assets					806,907
23 Total of lines 15 through 22	61,190,013	54,817,636	37,946,674	39,445,591	193,399,914
24 Line 23 minus line 17	61,190,013	54,817,636	37,946,674	39,445,591	193,399,914
25 Enter 1% of line 23	611,900	548,176	379,467	394,456	

26 Organizations described on lines 10 or 11: **a** Enter 2% of amount in column (e), line 24 ▶		**26a**	3,867,998
b Prepare a list for your records to show the name of and amount contributed by each person (other than a governmental unit or publicly supported organization) whose total gifts for 2002 through 2005 exceeded the amount shown in line 26a **Do not file this list with your return.** Enter the total of all these excess amounts ▶		**26b**	23,695,020
c Total support for section 509(a)(1) test Enter amount in line 24, column (e) ▶		**26c**	193,399,914
d Add Amounts from column (e) for lines 18 2,327,519 19 0			
22 26b 23,695,020		**26d**	26,829,446
e Public support (line 26c minus line 26d total) ▶		**26e**	166,570,468
f Public support percentage (line 26e (numerator) divided by line 26c (denominator)) ▶		**26f**	86 13 %

27 Organizations described on line 12: **a** For amounts included in lines 15, 16, and 17 that were received from a "disqualified person," prepare a list for your records to show the name of, and total amounts received in each year from, each "disqualified person " **Do not file this list with your return.** Enter the sum of such amounts for each year	
(2005) (2004) (2003) (2002)	
b For any amount included in line 17 that was received from each person (other than "disqualified persons"), prepare a list for your records to show the name of, and amount received for each year, that was more than the **larger** of **(1)** the amount on line 25 for the year or **(2)** $5,000 (Include in the list organizations described in lines 5 through 11b, as well as individuals) **Do not file this list with your return.** After computing the difference between the amount received and the larger amount described in **(1)** or **(2)**, enter the sum of these differences (the excess amounts) for each year	
(2005) (2004) (2003) (2002)	

c Add Amounts from column (e) for lines 15 16		
17 20 21 ▶	**27c**	
d Add Line 27a total and line 27b total ▶	**27d**	
e Public support (line 27c total minus line 27d total) ▶	**27e**	
f Total support for section 509(a)(2) test Enter amount from line 23, column (e) ▶ 27f		
g Public support percentage (line 27e (numerator) divided by line 27f (denominator)) ▶	**27g**	
h Investment income percentage (line 18, column (e) (numerator) divided by line 27f (denominator)) ▶	**27h**	

28 **Unusual Grants:** For an organization described in line 10, 11, or 12 that received any unusual grants during 2002 through 2005, prepare a list for your records to show, for each year, the name of the contributor, the date and amount of the grant, and a brief description of the nature of the grant **Do not file this list with your return.** Do not include these grants in line 15

Schedule A (Form 990 or 990-EZ) 2006   Page **4**

Part V   **Private School Questionnaire** (See page 7 of the instructions.)
(To be completed ONLY by schools that checked the box on line 6 in Part IV)

			Yes	No
29	Does the organization have a racially nondiscriminatory policy toward students by statement in its charter, bylaws, other governing instrument, or in a resolution of its governing body?	29		
30	Does the organization include a statement of its racially nondiscriminatory policy toward students in all its brochures, catalogues, and other written communications with the public dealing with student admissions, programs, and scholarships?	30		
31	Has the organization publicized its racially nondiscriminatory policy through newspaper or broadcast media during the period of solicitation for students, or during the registration period if it has no solicitation program, in a way that makes the policy known to all parts of the general community it serves?	31		
	If "Yes," please describe, if "No," please explain (If you need more space, attach a separate statement)			
32	Does the organization maintain the following			
a	Records indicating the racial composition of the student body, faculty, and administrative staff?	32a		
b	Records documenting that scholarships and other financial assistance are awarded on racially nondiscriminatory basis?	32b		
c	Copies of all catalogues, brochures, announcements, and other written communications to the public dealing with student admissions, programs, and scholarships?	32c		
d	Copies of all material used by the organization or on its behalf to solicit contributions?	32d		
	If you answered "No" to any of the above, please explain (If you need more space, attach a separate statement)			
33	Does the organization discriminate by race in any way with respect to			
a	Students' rights or privileges?	33a		
b	Admissions policies?	33b		
c	Employment of faculty or administrative staff?	33c		
d	Scholarships or other financial assistance?	33d		
e	Educational policies?	33e		
f	Use of facilities?	33f		
g	Athletic programs?	33g		
h	Other extracurricular activities?	33h		
	If you answered "Yes" to any of the above, please explain (If you need more space, attach a separate statement)			
34a	Does the organization receive any financial aid or assistance from a governmental agency?	34a		
b	Has the organization's right to such aid ever been revoked or suspended?	34b		
	If you answered "Yes" to either 34a or b, please explain using an attached statement			
35	Does the organization certify that it has complied with the applicable requirements of sections 4 01 through 4 05 of Rev Proc 75-50, 1975-2 C B 587, covering racial nondiscrimination? If "No," attach an explanation	35		

Schedule A (Form 990 or 990-EZ) 2006   Page **5**

Part VI-A **Lobbying Expenditures by Electing Public Charities** (See page 10 of the instructions.)
(To be completed **ONLY** by an eligible organization that filed Form 5768)

Check ► **a** ⌐ if the organization belongs to an affiliated group   Check ► **b** ⌐ if you checked "a" and "limited control" provisions apply

	Limits on Lobbying Expenditures (The term "expenditures" means amounts paid or incurred)		**(a)** Affiliated group totals	**(b)** To be completed for all electing organizations
36	Total lobbying expenditures to influence public opinion (grassroots lobbying)	**36**		
37	Total lobbying expenditures to influence a legislative body (direct lobbying)	**37**		120,177
38	Total lobbying expenditures (add lines 36 and 37)	**38**		120,177
39	Other exempt purpose expenditures	**39**		83,272,121
40	Total exempt purpose expenditures (add lines 38 and 39)	**40**		83,392,298
41	Lobbying nontaxable amount Enter the amount from the following table—	**41**		1,000,000
42	Grassroots nontaxable amount (enter 25% of line 41)	**42**		250,000
43	Subtract line 42 from line 36 Enter -0- if line 42 is more than line 36	**43**		0
44	Subtract line 41 from line 38 Enter -0- if line 41 is more than line 38	**44**		0

Line 41 table:

If the amount on line 40 is—	The lobbying nontaxable amount is—
Not over $500,000	20% of the amount on line 40
Over $500,000 but not over $1,000,000	$100,000 plus 15% of the excess over $500,000
Over $1,000,000 but not over $1,500,000	$175,000 plus 10% of the excess over $1,000,000
Over $1,500,000 but not over $17,000,000	$225,000 plus 5% of the excess over $1,500,000
Over $17,000,000	$1,000,000

Caution: If there is an amount on either line 43 or line 44, you must file Form 4720.

4-Year Averaging Period Under Section 501(h)
(Some organizations that made a section 501(h) election do not have to complete all of the five columns below
See the instructions for lines 45 through 50 on page 13 of the instructions)

	Calendar year (or fiscal year beginning in) ►	**Lobbying Expenditures During 4-Year Averaging Period**				
		(a) 2006	**(b)** 2005	**(c)** 2004	**(d)** 2003	**(e)** Total
45	Lobbying nontaxable amount	1,000,000				1,000,000
46	Lobbying ceiling amount (150% of line 45(e))					1,500,000
47	Total lobbying expenditures	120,177				120,177
48	Grassroots nontaxable amount	250,000				250,000
49	Grassroots ceiling amount (150% of line 48(e))					375,000
50	Grassroots lobbying expenditures					

Part VI-B **Lobbying Activity by Nonelecting Public Charities**
(For reporting only by organizations that did not complete Part VI-A) (See page 13 of the instructions.)

During the year, did the organization attempt to influence national, state or local legislation, including any attempt to influence public opinion on a legislative matter or referendum, through the use of	Yes	No	Amount
a Volunteers		No	
b Paid staff or management (Include compensation in expenses reported on lines **c** through **h.**)			
c Media advertisements			
d Mailings to members, legislators, or the public			
e Publications, or published or broadcast statements			
f Grants to other organizations for lobbying purposes			
g Direct contact with legislators, their staffs, government officials, or a legislative body			
h Rallies, demonstrations, seminars, conventions, speeches, lectures, or any other means			
i Total lobbying expenditures (Add lines **c** through **h.**)			

If "Yes" to any of the above, also attach a statement giving a detailed description of the lobbying activities

Schedule A (Form 990 or 990-EZ) 2006

Part VII	Information Regarding Transfers To and Transactions and Relationships With Noncharitable Exempt Organizations (See page 13 of the instructions.)

51 Did the reporting organization directly or indirectly engage in any of the following with any other organization described in section 501(c) of the Code (other than section 501(c)(3) organizations) or in section 527, relating to political organizations?

			Yes	No
a	Transfers from the reporting organization to a noncharitable exempt organization of			
	(i) Cash	**51a(i)**		No
	(ii) Other assets	**a(ii)**		No
b	Other transactions			
	(i) Sales or exchanges of assets with a noncharitable exempt organization	**b(i)**		No
	(ii) Purchases of assets from a noncharitable exempt organization	**b(ii)**		No
	(iii) Rental of facilities, equipment, or other assets	**b(iii)**		No
	(iv) Reimbursement arrangements	**b(iv)**		No
	(v) Loans or loan guarantees	**b(v)**		No
	(vi) Performance of services or membership or fundraising solicitations	**b(vi)**		No
c	Sharing of facilities, equipment, mailing lists, other assets, or paid employees	**c**		No

d If the answer to any of the above is "Yes," complete the following schedule Column (b) should always show the fair market value of the goods, other assets, or services given by the reporting organization If the organization received less than fair market value in any transaction or sharing arrangement, show in column (d) the value of the goods, other assets, or services received

(a) Line no	(b) Amount involved	(c) Name of noncharitable exempt organization	(d) Description of transfers, transactions, and sharing arrangements

52a Is the organization directly or indirectly affiliated with, or related to, one or more tax-exempt organizations described in section 501(c) of the Code (other than section 501(c)(3)) or in section 527? ▶ ☐ Yes ☑ No

b If "Yes," complete the following schedule

(a) Name of organization	(b) Type of organization	(c) Description of relationship

Additional Data

Software ID:
Software Version:
EIN: 13-3541913
Name: Teach For America Inc

Form 990, Part II, Line 43 - Other expenses not covered above (itemize):

Do not include amounts reported on line 6b, 8b, 9b, 10b, or 16 of Part I.		(A) Total	(B) Program services	(C) Management and general	(D) Fundraising
a INVESTMENT EXPENSES	43a	39,270		39,270	
b STUDENT LODGING AND MEALS	43b	4,673,910	4,673,304	437	169
c INSURANCE	43c	159,644	89,401	62,261	7,982
d REGIONAL COSTS	43d	143,685	106,558	10,439	26,688
e BAD DEBT	43e	264,153	85,905		178,248
f FEES AND OTHER EXPENSES	43f	85,703	10,273	13,816	61,614
g OTHER PROFESSIONAL FEES	43g	3,749,218	1,827,679	1,813,936	107,603
h LOSS ON DISP OF FIXED ASSETS	43h	29,560		29,560	

Form 990, Part V-A - Current Officers, Directors, Trustees, and Key Employees:

(A) Name and address	(B) Title and average hours per week devoted to position	(C) Compensation (If not paid, enter -0-.)	(D) Contributions to employee benefit plans & deferred compensation plans	(E) Expense account and other allowances
Wendy Kopp 315 West 36 St New York, NY 10018	CEO & Founder 60 0	275,500	23,952	0
Matthew Kramer 315 West 36 St New York, NY 10018	President 60 0	222,735	13,097	0
Kevin Huffman 315 West 36 St New York, NY 10018	Exec VP Strategy 60 0	222,340	21,294	0
Miguel Rossy 315 West 36 St New York, NY 10018	EVP & CFO 60 0	190,095	8,137	0
Aimee Davis 315 West 36 St New York, NY 10018	Chief People Officer 60 0	162,564	16,265	0
Elisa Beard 315 West 36 St New York, NY 10018	Chief Operating Officer 60 0	139,275	15,101	0
Gillian C Smith 315 West 36 St New York, NY 10018	Chief Marketing Officer 60 0	134,827	14,581	0
Walter Isaacson 315 West 36 St New York, NY 10018	Chair 1 0	0	0	0
Paula A Sneed 315 West 36 St New York, NY 10018	Vice Chair 1 0	0	0	0
Jide Zeitlin 315 West 36 St New York, NY 10018	Treasurer 1 0	0	0	0

Form 990, Part V-A - Current Officers, Directors, Trustees, and Key Employees:

(A) Name and address	(B) Title and average hours per week devoted to position	(C) Compensation (If not paid, enter -0-.)	(D) Contributions to employee benefit plans & deferred compensation plans	(E) Expense account and other allowances
Stephen F Bollenbach 315 West 36 St New York, NY 10018	Director 1 0	0	0	0
Donald G Fisher 315 West 36 St New York, NY 10018	Director 1 0	0	0	0
Lew Frankfort 315 West 36 St New York, NY 10018	Director 1 0	0	0	0
David Gergen 315 West 36 St New York, NY 10018	Director 1 0	0	0	0
Leo Hindery Jr 315 West 36 St New York, NY 10018	Director 1 0	0	0	0
David W Kenny 315 West 36 St New York, NY 10018	Director 1 0	0	0	0
Sherry Lansing 315 West 36 St New York, NY 10018	Director 1 0	0	0	0
Sue Lehmann 315 West 36 St New York, NY 10018	Director 1 0	0	0	0
Michael L Lomax PHD 315 West 36 St New York, NY 10018	Director 1 0	0	0	0
Stephen F Mandel Jr 315 West 36 St New York, NY 10018	Director 1 0	0	0	0

Form 990, Part V-A - Current Officers, Directors, Trustees, and Key Employees:

(A) Name and address	(B) Title and average hours per week devoted to position	(C) Compensation (If not paid, enter -0-.)	(D) Contributions to employee benefit plans & deferred compensation plans	(E) Expense account and other allowances
Anthony W Marx 315 West 36 St New York, NY 10018	Director 1 0	0	0	0
James M McCormick 315 West 36 St New York, NY 10018	Director 1 0	0	0	0
Richard S Pechter 315 West 36 St New York, NY 10018	Director 1 0	0	0	0
Nancy Peretsman 315 West 36 St New York, NY 10018	Director 1 0	0	0	0
Sir Howard Stringer 315 West 36 St New York, NY 10018	Director 1 0	0	0	0
Lawrence J Stupski 315 West 36 St New York, NY 10018	Director 1 0	0	0	0
Lawrence H Summers 315 West 36 St New York, NY 10018	Director 1 0	0	0	0
G Kennedy Thompson 315 West 36 St New York, NY 10018	Director 1 0	0	0	0
John Thompson 315 West 36 St New York, NY 10018	Director 1 0	0	0	0
Gregory W Wendt 315 West 36 St New York, NY 10018	Director 1 0	0	0	0

Form 990, Part VI, Line 90a - List the states with which a copy of this return is filed:

List the states with which a copy of this return is filed	AL, AK, AZ, AR, CA, CO, CT, FL, GA, IL, KS, KY, LA, ME, MD, MA, MI, MN, MS, NJ, NM, NY, NC, OH, OK, OR, PA, SC, TN, UT, VA, WA, WV

efile GRAPHIC print - DO NOT PROCESS	As Filed Data -		DLN: 93490150001108

TY 2006 Cash Grants Paid Schedule

Name: Teach For America Inc
EIN: 13-3541913

Class of Activity	Recipient's name	Address	Amount	Relationship
	FINANCIAL AIDSUPPORT	315 WEST 36TH STREET NEW YORK, NY 10018	3,859,799	NONE

| efile GRAPHIC print - DO NOT PROCESS | As Filed Data - | | DLN: 9349015000108 |

TY 2006 General Explanation Attachment

Name: Teach For America Inc

EIN: 13-3541913

Identifier	Return Reference	Explanation
ACCUMULATED DEPRECIATION	LINES 42 AND 57B	BEGINNING CURRENT YEAR ENDING BALANCE EXPENSE BALANCE LEASEHOLD $ 615,652 425,283 1,040,93 5 IMPROVEMENTS FURNITURE 321,604 165,414 487,018 FIXTURES & EQUIPMENT COMPUTER 2,601,912 1,128,057 3,729,969 TOTALS $ 3,539,168 1,718,754 5,257,922

efile GRAPHIC print - DO NOT PROCESS	As Filed Data -	DLN: 93490150001108

TY 2006 Other Assets Schedule

Name: Teach For Amenca Inc

EIN: 13-3541913

Description	Beginning of Year Amount	End of Year Amount
ACCRUED INTEREST RECEIVABLE		113,330
SECURITY DEPOSITS		338,418
MISCELLANEOUS		37,418

TY 2006 Other Changes in Net Assets Schedule

Name: Teach For America Inc
EIN: 13-3541913

Description	Amount
UNREALIZED APPRECIATION IN INVESTMENTS	855,467

TY 2006 Other Expenses
Not Included Schedule

Name: Teach For America Inc
EIN: 13-3541913

Description	Amount
GROSS RENT REVENUE	12,274

TY 2006 Other Liabilities Schedule

Name: Teach For America Inc
EIN: 13-3541913

Description	Beginning of Year Amount	End of Year Amount
DEFERRED RENT PAYABLE		1,018,211

**TY 2006 Other Notes/Loans
Receivable Short Schedule**

Name: Teach For America Inc
EIN: 13-3541913

Category/Name	Amount
LOANS RECEIVABLE FROM CORPS MEMBERS	3,746,723

TY 2006 Other Revenues
Not Included Schedule

Name: Teach For Amenca Inc
EIN: 13-3541913

Description	Amount
GROSS RENT REVENUE	12,274

TY 2006 Special Events Schedule

Name: Teach For America Inc
EIN: 13-3541913

Event Name	Gross Receipts	Contributions	Gross Revenue	Direct Expense	Net Income (Loss)
DC GOLF TOURNAMENT	13,085		13,085	5,713	7,372
HOUSTON 2007 BENEFIT DINNER	495,224		495,224	71,618	423,606
CHICAGO ARETE HONORS	178,500		178,500	5,000	173,500
NEW YORK 2007 BENEFIT DINNER	2,419,767		2,419,767	356,481	2,063,286
PHOENIX 2007 BENEFIT DINNER	182,300		182,300	64,766	117,534

TY 2006 Scholarship Award Statement

Name: Teach For America Inc

EIN: 13-3541913

Statement: FINANCIAL AID AND STUDENT LOANS TEACH FOR AMERICA, INC. OFFERS GRANTS AND INTEREST-FREE LOANS TO HELP CORP MEMBERS TRANSITION INTO THE CORPS. PACKAGES RANGE FROM APPROXIMATELY $1,000 TO $6,000 AND ARE BASED ON AN APPLICANT'S DEMONSTRATED NEED AND THE COST OF TRANSITIONING TO THEIR ASSIGNED REGION. APPROXIMATELY 55% OF OUR INCOMING CORPS MEMBERS APPLY FOR AWARDS. EDUCATION AWARDS THE EDUCATION AWARD IS A CREDIT IN VARYING AMOUNTS UP TO $4,725 PER YEAR OF SERVICE THAT CORPS MEMBERS CAN USE TO PAY BACK UNDERGRADUATE DEBT ON QUALIFIED LOANS AND/OR PAY FUTURE EDUCATIONAL EXPENSES.

TY 2006 Self Dealing Statement

Name: Teach For America Inc

EIN: 13-3541913

Line Number	Explanation
2d	CERTAIN OFFICERS, DIRECTORS AND KEY EMPLOYEES RECEIVE COMPENSATION AND BENEFITS. SEE FORM 990 PART V. UNDER THE ACCOUNTABLE PLAN RULES, THE ORGANIZATION ALSO PROVIDES REIMBURSEMENTS FOR REASONABLE AND NECESSARY BUSINESS EXPENSES INCURRED BY ITS OFFICERS, DIRECTORS AND KEY EMPLOYEES.

DLN: 93490150001108

Note: To capture the full content of this document, please select landscape mode (11" x 8.5") when printing.

TY 2006 Supplemental Support Schedule

Name: Teach For America Inc

EIN: 13-3541913

Year	Gifts, Grants and Contributions Received	Membership Fees Received	Gross Receipts From Admissions, Etc.	Gross Investment Income And Post 1975UBI	Net UBI Pre 1975	Tax Revenues Levied For Organization's Benefit	Value Of Services, Facilities Furnished By Government	Other Income	Total
2006	60,571,268			408,068				210,677	61,190,013
2004	53,722,125			804,617				290,894	54,817,636
2003	37,218,104			586,531				142,039	37,946,674
2002	38,753,991			528,303				163,297	39,445,591

APPENDIX C

TFA 501(c)(3) Letter

Internal Revenue Service

Date: September 24, 2003

Teach For America, Inc.
TFA, Inc.
315 W 36th St 6th Floor
New York, NY 10018-6404

Department of the Treasury
P. O. Box 2508
Cincinnati, OH 45201

Person to Contact:
  Richard E. Owens 31-07974
  Customer Service Representative
Toll Free Telephone Number:
  8:00 a.m. to 6:30 p.m. EST
  877-829-5500
Fax Number:
  513-263-3756
Federal Identification Number:
  13-3541913

Dear Sir or Madam:

This is in response to your request of September 24, 2003, regarding your organization's tax-exempt status.

In June 1993 we issued a determination letter that recognized your organization as exempt from federal income tax. Our records indicate that your organization is currently exempt under section 501(c)(3) of the Internal Revenue Code.

Based on information subsequently submitted, we classified your organization as one that is not a private foundation within the meaning of section 509(a) of the Code because it is an organization described in sections 509(a)(1) and 170(b)(1)(A)(vi).

This classification was based on the assumption that your organization's operations would continue as stated in the application. If your organization's sources of support, or its character, method of operations, or purpose: have changed, please let us know so we can consider the effect of the change on the exempt status and foundation status of your organization.

Your organization is required to file Form 990, Return of Organization Exempt from Income Tax, only if its gross receipts each year are normally more than $25,000. If a return is required, it must be filed by the 15th day of the fifth month after the end of the organization's annual accounting period. The law imposes a penalty of $20 a day, up to a maximum of $10,000, when a return is filed late, unless there is reasonable cause for the delay.

All exempt organizations (unless specifically excluded) are liable for taxes under the Federal Insurance Contributions Act (social security taxes) on remuneration of $100 or more paid to each employee during a calendar year. Your organization is not liable for the tax imposed under the Federal Unemployment Tax Act (FUTA).

Organizations that are not private foundations are not subject to the excise taxes under Chapter 42 of the Code. However, these organizations are not automatically exempt from other federal excise taxes.

Donors may deduct contributions to your organization as provided in section 170 of the Code. Bequests, legacies, devises, transfers, or gifts to your organization or for its use are deductible for federal estate and gift tax purposes if they meet the applicable provisions of sections 2055, 2106, and 2522 of the Code.

-2-

Teach For America, Inc.
13-3541913

Your organization is not required to file federal income tax returns unless it is subject to the tax on unrelated business income under section 511 of the Code. If your organization is subject to this tax, it must file an income tax return on the Form 990-T, Exempt Organization Business Income Tax Return. In this letter, we are not determining whether any of your organization's present or proposed activities are unrelated trade or business as defined in section 513 of the Code.

Section 6104 of the Internal Revenue Code requires you to make your organization's annual return available for public inspection without charge for three years after the due date of the return. The law also requires organizations that received recognition of exemption on July 15, 1987, or later, to make available for public inspection a copy of the exemption application, any supporting documents and the exemption letter to any individual who requests such documents in person or in writing. Organizations that received recognition of exemption before July 15, 1987, and had a copy of their exemption application on July 15, 1987, are also required to make available for public inspection a copy of the exemption application, any supporting documents and the exemption letter to any individual who requests such documents in person or in writing. For additional information on disclosure requirements, please refer to Internal Revenue Bulletin 1999 - 17.

Because this letter could help resolve any questions about your organization's exempt status and foundation status, you should keep it with the organization's permanent records.

If you have any questions, please call us at the telephone number shown in the heading of this letter.

This letter affirms your organization's exempt status.

Sincerely,

John E. Ricketts, Director, TE/GE
Customer Account Services

APPENDIX D

Letter from Alison Stachniak

Learning on Other People's Kids: Becoming a Teach For America Teacher
pp. 247–249
Copyright © 2010 by Information Age Publishing

From: Alison Stachniak [astachniak@gmail.com]
Sent: Saturday, August 01, 2009 4:03 PM
To: Barbara T. Veltri
Subject: Teach For America experience

Dear Ms. Veltri,

I recently read your article "Teaching or Service? The Site-Based Realities of Teach For America Teachers in Poor, Urban Schools" and was both impressed and intrigued by your research. Thank you so much for investigating this important issue! I have recently become an advocate of questioning the policies of Teach For America and wanted to share my personal experience with you.

In May of this year, I graduated from Valparaiso University with a double major in elementary education and Spanish. My search for a job, however, began in March when I visited urban, heavily Hispanic schools in the Atlanta area to scope out possible positions. Although I met with several principals, I connected the most with a principal of a school in the Atlanta Public Schools district. She and I shared the same vision for education and were troubled by the same modern issues in our field. The principal urged me to immediately apply to APS via the online system, because she intended to hire me as soon as one of her teachers officially took educational leave. I was delighted at the thought of working at an urban school with a mostly-Hispanic population, because I studied Spanish in college so I could do just that. Moreover, this school seemed like an ideal environment for teaching and learning. I eagerly awaited her phone call.

Unfortunately, that phone call never came. I visited the school later in the spring only to have the dismayed principal tell me that she had just found out she could not hire me because she had to accept a Teach for America graduate forced upon her by the district. Only several weeks earlier, the principal had informed the human resources department that she intended to hire me, but HR still required her to accept a TFA grad so that the candidates could all be placed.

I was very upset by the situation and also confused. Earlier that year, TFA representatives had visited my university and informed us that teaching with TFA meant going into low-income schools where no one wanted to teach. This certainly was not the case with the aforementioned school, since the principal had already requested that a certified teacher be given the position. I was so surprised by the apparent deception of TFA that I began to study the system. I realized that APS was only posting positions for the high-income schools in a heavily-Caucasian part of Atlanta, where TFA grads could not teach because the schools were not Title I. I realized then that experienced, highly-qualified teachers were being placed into the already-successful schools, while the lower-income schools didn't even receive an opportunity to hire experienced teachers who might have applied, had those positions been posted. To me, this seemed as though the cycle of inequality in education was only being perpetuated. I was very disturbed by this realization.

I was soon after hired to teach for a different high-need, heavily Hispanic school in a district that does not accept TFA grads. Still, it bothers me that although I graduated with a 4.0 GPA, double majored in Spanish, took a course in educating diverse populations, completed hundreds of hours of field experience, and student taught in a diverse elementary school, an uncertified individual was hired in my place at that school. I am extremely committed to my profession, while I overheard TFA teachers at the aforementioned school make comments such as, "I have no idea what I want to do with my life" and "I'm going to law school as soon as my 2 years are up here."

Again, I want to thank you for doing this much-needed research. TFA gets so much positive press, but I think the American public needs to hear more about its flaws so that its policies can be questioned and changed for the better. If you have any suggestions as to how I can further this cause in the Atlanta area, please feel free to let me know. Thank you for writing about such an important issue!

Sincerely,
Alison Stachniak

APPENDIX E

Public Advocates
Parents' Right-to-Know Letter

Learning on Other People's Kids: Becoming a Teach For America Teacher
pp. 251–252

Date

Dear [Insert Name and Address of District Superintendent],

I am writing to exercise my rights as a parent under the federal No Child Left Behind Act (NCLBA) to know the qualifications of my child's teacher(s). *See 20* U.S.C. § 6311(h)(2)(A)(6). My child, [insert name of child,] is in the [insert grade level] at [insert name of school]. His/Her teacher is [insert name(s) of teacher(s) and, where applicable, the subject each teacher teaches].

As you know, the NCLBA provides that any school district receiving Title I funds must notify the parents of children at any school that receives Title I funding that the parents may request and receive from the district information about the professional qualifications of their child's teachers, including, at a minimum, the following:

- the type of state credential that the teacher holds,
- whether the teacher is teaching on an emergency permit or other provisional status,
- the educational level and subject area of the teacher's college degree(s), and
- whether the child is receiving services from a paraprofessional, and, if so, the paraprofessional's qualifications.

This information must be provided "in a timely manner." In addition, the NCLBA provides that schools receiving Title I funding must notify parents whenever their child has been taught for four or more consecutive weeks by a teacher who is not "highly qualified" pursuant to the NCLBA definition of this term.

Please provide me with the information requested above for my child's teacher. Thank you for your prompt attention to this matter.

Sincerely,

[Your name and contact information]

cc: Name and Address of Principal of Your Child's School

Source: © Public Advocates, Inc. (Tara Kini, author, March 2007, p. 35).

REFERENCES

Anchors, S. (2003, March 20). Teach For America wants districts to pay per teacher. *Arizona Republic.* Retrieved from http://www.azcentral.com/news/ education/0320phx teachAmerica20.html

Anderson, J. (2003). Managing the impossible. *Inc. Magazine, 24*(4), 79.

Anderson, L. (2009, April 30). Idealism, Inc.: Challenging the wisdom on nonprofits. *The Eye: The Weekly Features and Arts Magazine of The Columbia Daily Spectator, 6*(12) pp. 7-10.

Anyon, J. (1980). Social class and the hidden curriculum of work. *Journal of Education, 162*(1), 67-92.

Apple, M. (2004). *Ideology and curriculum.* New York, NY: Routledge-Falmer.

Ashforth, B. E., & Mael, F. (1989, January). Social identity theory and the organization. *The Academy of Management Review, 14*(1), 20-39.

Ashton, P., & Crocker, L. (1987). Systematic study of planned variations: the essential focus of teacher education reform. *Florida Journal of Teacher Education, 38*(3), 2-8.

Ballou, D., & Podgursky, M. (1996). Do public schools hire the best applicants? *Quarterly Journal of Economics, 111*(1), 97-133.

Bandura, A. (1997). *Self-efficacy: The exercise of control.* New York, NY: W. H. Freeman.

Barnes, G., Crowe, E., & Schaefer, B. (2007). *The cost of teacher turnover in five school districts: A pilot study.* Washington, DC: National Commission on Teaching and America's Future. Retrieved from http://nctaf.org.zeus.silvertech.net/resources/demonstration_projects/turnover/documentsCTTPolicyBrief-FINAL.pdf

Barone, T. (2001). The end of the terror: On disclosing the complexities of teaching [Review]. *Curriculum Inquiry, 31*(1), 89-103.

Barr, R. (2001). Research on the teaching of reading. In V. Richardson (Ed.), *Handbook of research on teaching* (pp. 390-415). Washington, DC: American Educational Research Association.

Bartiromo, M. (2006, June). Money makers: The problem solver. *Reader's Digest,* pp. 69-72.

Bereiter, C. (1995). *A dispositional view of transfer: Fostering generalization in learning.* Mahwah, NJ: Erlbaum.

Berliner, D. C. (1986) In pursuit of the expert pedagogue. *Educational Researcher, 15*(7), 5-13.

Berliner, D. C. (1990). The place of process-product research in developing the agenda for research on teacher thinking. *Educational Psychologist, 24*(4), 325-344.

Berliner, D. C. (1992). The nature of expertise in teaching. In F. K. Oser, A. Dick, & J. -L. Patry (Eds.), *Effective and responsible teaching: The new synthesis* (pp. 227-248). San Francisco, CA: Jossey-Bass.

Berliner, D. C. (1994) Expertise: The wonder of exemplary performances. In J. N. Mangiere & C. C. Block (Eds.), *Creating powerful thinking in teachers and students: Diverse perspectives* (pp. 161-186). Fort Worth, TX: Harcourt Brace College.

Berliner, D. C. (2009, August 17). The view from America: What on Earth are you thinking? *Sydney Morning Herald,* New South Wales, Australia. Retrieved from http://www.smh.com.au/national/the-view-from-america-what-on-earth-are-you-thinking-20090816-eme4.html

Berry, B. (2001). No shortcuts to preparing good teachers. *Educational Leadership, 58*(8), 32-36.

Berry, B. (2002). *What it means to be a "highly qualified teacher."* Hillsborough, NC: Southeast Center for Teaching Quality. Retrieved from http://www.teachingquality.org/resources/pdfs/definingHQ.pdf

Bowles, S., & Levin, H. M. (1968). The determinants of scholastic achievements—An appraisal of some recent evidence. *The Journal of Human Resources, 3*(1), 1-24.

Boyd, D., Grossman, P., Lankford, H., Loeb, S., & Wyckoff, J. (2006). How changes in entry requirements alter the teacher workforce and affect student achievement. *Education Finance and Policy, 1*(2), 176-216.

Breaux, A. L. & Wong, H. K. (2003). *New teacher induction: How to train, support, and retain new teachers.* Mountain View, CA: Harry K. Wong Publications.

Britzman, D. (1991). *Practice makes practice: A critical study of learning to teach.* Albany, NY: State University of New York Press.

Broadbent, F., & Cruickshank, D. (1965). *The identification and analysis of problems of first year teachers*. Brockport, NY: State University of New York.

Bruner, J. (1966). *Toward a theory of instruction*. Cambridge, MA: Harvard University.

Bruner, J. (1978). The role of dialogue in language acquisition. In A. Sinclair, R. J. Jarvella, & W. Levelt (Eds.), *The child's concept of language* (pp. 241-255). New York, NY: SpringerVerlag.

Burns, K. (1994). *Baseball*. New York, NY: Alfred Knopf & Sons.

Carter, G. (2003, January). *They pass the test, but can they teach?* Retrieved from http://www.edforfemocrac past_the_test.htm

Carter, K. (1990). Teachers' knowledge and learning to teach. In W. R. Houston (Ed.), *Handbook of research on teacher education* (pp. 291-310). New York, NY: Macmillan.

Carter, K., & Gonzalez, L. (1993). Beginning teachers' knowledge of classroom events. *Journal of Teacher Education, 44,* 223-232.

Carter, K., Cushing, K., Sabers, D., Stein, P., & Berliner, D. C. (1988). Expert–novice differences in perceiving and processing visual information. *Journal of Teacher Education, 39*(3), 25-31.

Carver, C. (2007, May 23). Teach For America grows in Arizona: By 2008, 400 corps members will aid poor kids. *Arizona Republic*, p. B3.

Children's Defense Fund. (2003). *The state of America's children: Yearbook 2003*. Retrieved from http://www.childrensdefensefund.org

Clandinin, J., & Connelly, M. (2000). *Narrative inquiry: Experience and story in qualitative research*. San Francisco, CA: Jossey-Bass.

Clark, C. M., & Peterson, P. L. (1986a). Teacher knowledge and learning to teach. In W. R. Houston (Ed.), *Handbook of research on teacher education* (pp. 291-310). New York, NY: Macmillan.

Clark, C. M., & Peterson, P. L. (1986b). Teachers' thought processes. In M. C. Wittrock (Ed.), *Handbook of research on teaching* (3rd ed., pp. 155-296). New York, NY: Macmillan.

Cochran, K. F., & Jones, L. L. (1998). The subject matter knowledge of pre-service science teachers. In B. Fraser & K. Tobin (Eds.), *International handbook of science education* (pp. 707-718). Dordrecht, The Netherlands: Kluwer.

Cochran-Smith, M., & Lytle, S. L. (Eds.). (1993). *Inside/outside: Teacher research and knowledge*. New York, NY: Teachers College Press.

Codell, E. (1999). *Educating Esme: Diary of a teacher's first year*. Chapel Hill, NC: Algonquin Books.

Connelly, F. M., & Clandinin, D. J. (1985). Personal practical knowledge and the modes of knowing: Relevance for teaching and learning. In E. Eisner (Ed.), *Learning and teaching the ways of knowing* (84th Yearbook of the National Society for the Study of Education, Part II, pp. 174-198). Chicago, IL: University of Chicago Press.

Connelly, F. M., & Clandinin, D.J. (1998). *Teachers as curriculum planners: Narratives of experience*. New York, NY: Teachers College Press.

Crosby, B. (2002). *The $100,000 teacher: A teacher's solution to America's declining public school system*. Herndon, VA: Capital Books.

Darling-Hammond, L. (1997a). Doing what matters most: Investing in quality teaching. New York, NY: National Commission on Teaching and America's Future.

Darling-Hammond, L. (1997b). *The right to learn: A blueprint for creating schools that work*. San Francisco, CA: Jossey-Bass.

Darling-Hammond, L. (2000). Reforming teacher education and licensing: Debating the evidence. *Teacher College Record, 102*(1), 28-56.

Darling-Hammond, L. (2001). Standard setting in teaching: Changes in licensing, certification, and assessment. In V. Richardson (Ed.), *Handbook of research on teaching* (4th ed., pp. 751-776). Washington, DC: American Educational Research Association.

Darling-Hammond, L., Hammerness, K., Grossman, P., Rust, F., & Shulman, L. (2005). The design of teacher education programs. In L. Darling-Hammond & J. Bransford (Eds.), *Preparing teachers for a changing world: What teachers should learn and be able to do* (pp. 390-441). San Francisco, CA: Jossey-Bass.

Darling-Hammond, L., Holtzman, D., Gatlin, S. J., & Heilig, J. V. (2005). Does teacher preparation matter? Evidence about teacher certification, Teach For America, and teacher effectiveness. *Education Policy Analysis Archives, 13*(42). Retrieved from http://epaa.asu.edu/epa//v13n42/

Darling-Hammond, L., & Sykes, G. (Eds.). (1999). *Teaching as the learning profession: Handbook of policy and practice*. San Francisco, CA: Jossey-Bass.

Decker, P. T., Mayer, D. P., & Glazerman, S. (2004). *The effects of Teach For America on students: Findings from a national evaluation*. Princeton, NJ: Mathematica.

Delpit, L. (1995). *Other people's children: Cultural conflict in the classroom*. New York, NY: New Press.

Dewey, J. (1938). *Experience and education*. New York, NY: Collier.

DeWitz, R., Carr, E. M., & Patberg, J. P. (1987). Effects of inference training on comprehension and comprehension monitoring. *Reading Research Quarterly, 22*, 99-121.

Dilworth, M. E., & Brown, C. (2001). Consider the difference: Teaching and learning in culturally rich schools. In V. Richardson (Ed.), *Handbook of research on teaching* (pp. 643-667). Washington, DC: American Educational Research Association.

Duffee, L., & Aikenhead, G. S. (1992). Curriculum change, student evaluation, and teacher practical knowledge. *Science Education, 76*, 493-506.

Eggers, D. (2003, August 2). Muting the call to service. *The New York Times*, p. A15.

Eisner, E. (1983). The art and craft of teaching. *Educational Leadership, 40*(4), 4-13.

Eisner, E. (1998). *The enlightened eye.* Upper Saddle River, NJ: Prentice Hall.

Elbaz, F. (1983). *Teacher thinking: A study of practical knowledge.* London: Croom Helm.

Estes, M. (Ed.). (1999, August). Teach For America enriches Valley schools. *SRP Learning Circuit, 4*(3), 125-129.

Feiman-Nemser, S., & Remillard, J. (1996) Perspectives on learning to teach. In F. B. Murray (Ed.), *The teacher educator's handbook: Building a knowledge base for the preparation of teachers* (pp. 63-91). San Francisco, CA: Jossey-Bass.

Feistritzer, C. E., & Chester, D. C. (1998-1999). *Alternative teacher certification: A state-by-state analysis (1998-1999).* Washington, DC: National Center for Education Information.

Freire, P. (1998). *Teachers as cultural workers: Letters to those who dare to teach.* Boulder, CO: Westview.

Gammill, A. (October 4, 2009). *Untraditionally trained teachers getting mixed reviews. Indystar.com.* Retrieved from http://www.indystar.com/apps/pbcs.dll/article?AID=120091004/LOCAL/910040383.

Garcia-Gonzalez, R. (1998). *Teachers' biographies as an influence on beliefs and practices of critical pedagogy: A case study approach.* Unpublished doctoral dissertation, University of San Francisco, San Francisco, CA.

Gerdes, L. (2007, May 11). Undergrads' 25 most wanted employers. *Business Week.* Retrieved from http://www.businessweek.com/print/careers/content /may2007/ca20070514_406243.htm.

Glass, G. V. (May 2008). *Alternative certification of teachers.* Retrieved from http://epicpolicy.org/publication/alternative-certification-ofteachers

Goddard, R. D., Hoy, W. K., & Hoy, A. W. (2004). Collective efficacy beliefs: Theoretical developments, empirical evidence, and future directions. *Educational Researcher, 33*(3), 3-13.

Goodlad, J. I. (1990). *Teachers for our nation's schools.* San Francisco, CA: Jossey-Bass.

Graber, K.C. (2001). Research on teaching in physical education. In V. Richardson (Ed.), *Handbook of research on teaching* (4th ed., pp. 491-519). Washington, DC: American Educational Research Association.

Grimmett, P. P., & MacKinnon, A. M. (1992). Craft knowledge and the education of teachers. In G. Grant (Ed.), *Review of research in education* (pp. 385-456). Washington, DC: American Educational Research Association.

Haberman, M. (1995). Star teachers of children of poverty. In W. Ayers & P. Ford (Eds.), *City kids, city teachers: Reports from the front row* (pp. 118-130). New York, NY: New Press.

Hamilton, M. L. (1993). Think you can: The influence of culture on beliefs. In C. Day, J. Calderhead, & P. Denicolo (Eds.), *Research on teacher thinking: Understanding professional development* (pp. 87-99). London: Falmer.

Hammerness, K., Darling-Hammond, L., & Shulman, L. (2002). Toward expert thinking: How curriculum case writing prompts the development of theory-based professional knowledge in student teachers. [School of Education, The University of Queensland] *Teaching Education, 13*(2), 219-229.

Hanushek, E. A. (1971). Teacher characteristics and gains in student achievement: Estimation using microdata. *American Economic Review, 60*, 280-288.

Hausser, W. (2009, July 24). *Ninth Circuit agrees intern teachers are not "highly qualified."* San Francisco, CA: Public Advocates.

Haycock, K. (2002/2003, December/January). Toward a fair distribution of teacher talent. *Educational Leadership, 60*(4), 16-20.

Haycock, K. (2004). Thinking K-16. *Education Trust, 8*(1), 1-36.

Hilliard, A. (1991). Do we have the will to educate all the children? *Educational Leadership, 49*(1), 31-36.

Honawar, V. (August 23, 2007). *Lawsuit attacks alternative-route "loophole" in NCLB.* Retrieved from http://www.parentadvocates.org/index.cfm?fuseaction=article&articleID=7356

Hoy, W. K., Tarter, C. J., & Hoy, A. W. (2006). Academic optimism of schools: A force for student achievement. *American Educational Research Journal, 43*(3), 425-446.

Johnson, S., & Kardos, S. (2002, March). Keeping new teachers in mind. *Educational Leadership*, 13-16.

Jordan, H. R., Mendro, R. L., & Weerasinghe, D. (1997, July). *Teacher effects on longitudinal student achievement.* Paper presented at the annual meeting of the Consortium for Research on Educational Accountability and Teacher Evaluation, Indianapolis, IN.

Kaplan, R. (Executive Producer). (2009, May 18). *The CBS Evening News with Katie Couric* [Television broadcast]. New York, NY: CBS Broadcasting Company.

Kaplowitz, J. (2003, January 24). My classroom from hell. *The Wall Street Journal*, p. W13.

Kaufmann, D., Johnson, S. M., Kardos, S., Liu, E., & Peske, H. (2002). "Lost at sea": New teachers' experiences with curriculum and assessment. *Teacher College Record, 104*(2), 273-300.

Keller, B. (2007). NCLB rules on "quality" fall short: Teacher mandate even disappoints supporters. *Education Week, 26*(37), 1, 16.

Klima, S. (2003, Summer). Women's studies graduate puts theory into practice in Teach For America. *Women's Studies Newsletter,* 1-2.

Knapp, M. (2001). Policy, poverty, and capable teaching: Assumptions and issues in policy design. In B. Biddle (Ed.), *Social class, poverty, and education* (pp. 175-212). New York, NY: RoutledgeFalmer.

Knaupp, M. (Ed.). (1995). *Teaching for meaning in high poverty classrooms.* New York, NY: Teachers College Press.

Koerner, M., Lynch, D., & Martin, S. (2008, June). Why we partner with Teach For America: Changing the conversation. *Phi Delta Kappan, 89,* 726-730.

Kopp, W. (2003). *One day, all children: The unlikely triumph of Teach For America and what I learned along the way.* New York, NY: Perseus.

Kopp, W. (2008, June). Building the movement to end educational inequity. *Phi Delta Kappan, 89,* 734-737.

Kozol, J. (1991). *Savage inequalities: Children in America's schools.* New York, NY: Crown.

Laczko-Kerr, I., & Berliner, D. C. (2002). The effectiveness of "Teach For America" and other under-certified teachers on student achievement: A case of harmful public policy. *Educational Policy Analysis Archives, 19*(37). Retrieved from http://epaa.asu.edu/epaa/v10n37

Ladson-Billings, G. (1995). Toward a theory of culturally relevant pedagogy. *American Educational Research Journal, 32*(3), 465-491.

Ladson-Billings, G. (2001). *Crossing over to Canaan: The journey of new teachers in diverse classrooms.* San Francisco, CA: Jossey-Bass.

Lankford, H., Loeb, S., & Wycoff, J. (2002, Spring). Teacher sorting and the plight of urban schools: A descriptive analysis. *Educational Evaluation and Policy Analysis, 24*(1), 37-62.

Lewin, T. (2005, October 2). Top graduates line up to teach to the poor. *The New York Times,* p. 1A. Retrieved from http://www.nytimes.com/2005/10/02/education/02teach.html?pagewanted=2&fta=y

Lipka, S. (2007, June 22). Elite company. *Chronicle of Higher Education,* pp. A31-A35.

Lortie, D. (1975). *Schoolteacher: A sociological study.* Chicago, IL: University of Chicago Press.

Lyotard, J. -F. (1984). *The postmodern condition: A report on knowledge. Theory and history of literature* (Vol. 10.). Minneapolis, MN: University of Minnesota Press.

Lyotard. J. -F. (1991). *The inhuman: Reflection on time*. Stanford, CA: Stanford University Press.

Mathews, J. (2009). *Work hard. Be nice: How two inspired teachers created the most promising schools in America*. Chapel Hill, NC: Algonquin Books of Chapel Hill.

McCarthy, C. (1998). *The uses of culture: Education and the limits of ethnic affiliation*. New York, NY: Routledge.

Mercado, C. (2001). The learner: "Race," "ethnicity," and linguistic differences. In V. Richardson (Ed.), *Handbook of research on teaching* (pp. 668-691). Washington, DC: American Educational Research Association.

Meyer, J. (2007, September 13). Recent grads go to head of class. *The Denver Post*, p. B1.

Moir, E. (1999). The stages of a teachers' first year. In M. Scherer (Ed.), *A better beginning: Supporting and mentoring new teachers*. Alexandria, VA: Association for Supervision and Curriculum Development.

Moir, E. (1999). Retrieved from http://www.databdirect.com/Sample /NewTeacherSuccess/p9NewTHandbookA.pdf

Moll, L. (2001). Through the mediation of others: Vygotskian research on teaching. In V. Richardson (Ed.), *Handbook of research on teaching* (pp. 111-129). Washington, DC: American Educational Research Association.

Ness, M. (2004) *Lessons to learn: Voices from the front line of teach for America*. New York, NY: RoutledgeFalmer.

No Child Left Behind Act of 2001, Pub. L. No. 107-110, 115 Stat.1425 (2002).

Ogbu, J. (1990). Cultural models, identity, and literacy. In J. Stigler, R. Shweder, & G. Herdt (Eds.), *Cultural psychology* (pp. 520-541). Cambridge: Cambridge University Press.

Olson, L. (2001). Finding and keeping competent teachers: Education vs. non-education graduates. *Journal of Teacher Education, 36*(5), 56-59.

Pajares, F. (1992). Teacher's beliefs and educational research: Cleaning up a messy construct. *Review of Educational Research, 62*(3), 307-332.

Podgursky, M. (2006, Spring). Is there a "qualified teacher" shortage? *Education Next, 6*(2), 27-32.

Polanyi, M. (1962). *Personal knowledge*. Chicago, IL: University of Chicago Press.

Pope, D. C. (2001). *Doing School: How we are creating a generation of stressed out, materialistic, and mis-educated students*. New Haven, CT: Yale University Press.

Popkewitz. T. (1998). *Struggling for the soul: The politics of schooling and the construction of the teacher.* New York, NY: Teachers College Press.

Pressley-Montes, S. A. (2007, April 23). Education "Peace Corps" expanding area presence. *The Washington Post*, p. B02.

Renee v. (Spelling), U.S. 9th Circuit Court (February, 2009, 08-16661).

Renee v. (Spelling), U.S. 9th Circuit Court (July 23, 2009, 08-16661, D.C. No. 3:07-CV 04299-PJH Opinion).

Reynolds, M. (2004, August). It's time to quit feeling sick and tired. *The Scottsdale Times*, p. 51.

Rice, J. K. (2003). *Teacher quality: Understanding the effectiveness of teacher attributes.* Washington, DC: Economic Policy Institute.

Richardson, V. (1996). The role of attitudes and beliefs in learning to teach. In J. Sikula, T. J. Buttery, & E. Guyton (Eds.), *Handbook of research on teacher education* (2nd ed., pp. 102-119). New York, NY: Simon & Schuster Macmillan.

Rinehart, S. D., Barksdale-Ladd, M. A., & Paterson, J. J. (1994). Story recall through prereading instruction: Use of advance organizers combined with teacher-guided discussion. In E. G. Sturteevant & W. M. Linek (Eds.), *Pathways for literacy: Learners teach and teachers learn* (pp. 237-247). Pittsburg, KS: College Reading Association.

Roehrig, A. D., Pressley, M., & Talotta, D. (2002). *Stories of beginning teachers: First-year challenges and beyond.* Notre Dame, IN: University of Notre Dame.

Rose, L. C., & Gallup, A. M. (2002). How important is it that teachers in the public schools in their community be licensed by the state in the subject areas in which they teach? The 34th annual Phi Delta Kappa/Gallup Poll of the public's attitude toward the public schools. *Phi Delta Kappan, 84*(1), 41-56.

Rose, L. C., & Gallup, A. M. (2006). Why the public believes teachers leave the profession? The 38th annual Phi Delta Kappa/Gallup Poll of the public's attitude toward the public *schools. Phi Delta Kappan, 88*(1), 42-57.

Roza, M. (2009, February 9). $chools in crisis: Projections of state budget shortfall on K-12 public education. *Center on Reinventing Public Education.* Seattle, WA: University of Washington, Bothel.

Rubin, B. (2004, January). Teaching hope. *Good Housekeeping, 238*(1), 84-87.

Saltman, K. J., & Gabbard, D. (2003). *Education as enforcement: The militarization and corporatization of schools.* New York, NY: RoutledgeFalmer.

Sanders, W. L., & Rivers, J. C. (1996). *Cumulative and residual effects of teachers on future student academic achievement.* Knoxville, TN: University of Tennessee Value-Added Research and Assessment Center.

Sawchuck, S. (2009, October 12) *Duncan has harsh words for teacher colleges.* Retrieved from http://blogs.edweek.org/edweek/teacherbeat/2009/10/duncan_has_harsh_words_for_tea.html

Schön, D. (1983). *The reflective practitioner: How professionals think in action.* New York, NY: Basic Books.

Shamma, T. (2009, September 23). Teach For America sees surge in applications. *The Daily Princetonian.* Retrieved from http://www .dailyprincetonian.com/2009/09/23/23870

Shulman, L. S. (1986a). Paradigms and research programs in the study of teaching: A contemporary perspective. In M. C. Wittrock (Ed.), *Handbook of research on teaching* (3rd ed., pp. 3-36). New York, NY: Macmillan.

Shulman, L. S. (1986b). Those who understand: Knowledge growth in teaching. *Educational Review, 57*(1), 1-27.

Shulman, L. S. (1987). Knowledge and teaching: Foundations of the new reform. *Harvard Educational Review, 57,* 1-22.

Shulman, L. S., & Quinlan, K. M. (1996).The comparative psychology of school subjects. In D. C. Berliner & R. C. Calfee (Eds.), *Handbook of Educational Psychology* (pp. 399-422). New York, NY: Simon & Schuster Macmillan.

Sperling, M., & Freedman, S.W. Research on Writing. In V. Richardson (Ed), *Handbook of research on teaching* (pp. 370-389). Washington, DC: American Educational Research Association.

Stover, D. (2007, November). Teacher recruiting especially challenging for urban school boards. *Education Digest, 73*(3), 28-31.

Tajfel, H., & Turner, J. C. (1986). The social identity theory of inter-group behavior. In S.Worchel & L. W. Austin (Eds.), *Psychology of intergroup relations.* Chicago, IL: NelsonHall.

Teach For America. (1997-2005). *Form 990.* U.S. Department of the Treasury. Retrieved May 2, 2008, from http://www.guidestar.org

Teach For America. (2003, September 24). *Internal Revenue Service 501c3 letter.*Cincinnati, OH: U.S. Department of the Treasury.

Teach For America. (2005-2008). *Annual report.* Retrieved from TeachForAmerica.org

Teach For America. (2008, May 16). *The New York Times,* p. 22. Retrieved August 6, 2008, from http://www.nytimes.com/2008/05/16/opinion/ 16fri4.html?_r=1& ref=opinion&oref=slogin

Teach For America. (2007, September 27). *Teach For America launches teach for all to support development of its model in other countries.* Retrieved November 16, 2008, from http://www.teachforamerica.org/newsroom/ documents/092707_ TeachForAll.htm

Teach For America. (2004). *Recruitment manual.* New York, NY: Author.

Teach For America. (n.d.). *Support us.* Retrieved from http://www .teachforamerica.org/support_us.html

Teach For America Act of 2007, H.R. 1971, 110th Cong. (2007).

Teach For America surges on better recruiting, worse economy. (2008, May 14). *USA Today*. Retrieved August 6, 2008, from http://www .usatoday.com/news/education /2008-05-14-teach-for-america_N.htm

Teach For Australia (n.d.). Retrieved on September 8, 2009, from http:// www.teachforaustralia.org

Tkaczyk, C. (2007, May 17). 20 great employers for new grads. *Fortune*. Retrieved June 6, 2007, from http://money.cnn.com/galleries/2007/ fortune/0705/gallery.great_for_new_grads.fortune/7.html

Todd, C. (2004, June 2). Instant teachers proposed: Horne plan would give degree-holders jobs in 30 days. *Scottsdale Tribune*, pp. 1-2.

Toppo, G. (2004, March 16). Highly qualified teacher rules get wiggle room. *USA Today*, p. D9. Retrieved from http://infoweb.newsbank .com/iw-search/we/InfoWeb?-p_action=doc&p_docid=102B98549

United States. (1990). *Individuals with Disabilities Education Act:* Pub. L. no. 105-476. Washington, DC: U.S. G.P.O.

United States. (2009). *Serve America Act*. Washington, DC: U.S. G.P.O. Retrieved from http://purl.access.gpo.gov/GPO/LPS113983

U.S. Congress (1990). *Individuals with Disabilities Education Act*. Pub. L. no. 105-476.

U.S. Congress (2001). *No Child Left Behind Act of 2001*. Pub. L. no. 107-110. Washington, DC: U.S. Government Printing Office.

U.S. Department of Education. (2002). *Strategic plan, 2002-2007*. Washington, DC: Author.

U.S. Department of Education (2008, June 5). *Final audit report letter for Teach For America, Inc. control number ED-OIG/A02H003. The U.S. Department of Education Discretionary grant awards letters*. Office of Inspector General: Audit Services. New York Region.

Veenman, S. (1984). Perceived problems of beginning teachers. *Review of Educational Research, 54*, 143-178.

Viadero, D. (2009, June 1). What does it mean to be experienced at teaching? *Inside School Research*. Retrieved from http://blogs.edweek.org/ insideschoolresearch/2009/06/what_does_it_mean_to_be_...

Vygotsky, L. S. (1978). *Mind in society: The development of higher psychological processes*.Cambridge, MA: Harvard University Press.

Xu, Z., Hannaway, J., & Taylor, C. (2008, March 27,). *Making a difference? The effect of Teach For America on student performance in high school*. Washington, DC: The Urban Institute.

Wachovia advertisement. (2005). *More, 8*(7), 46.

Welch, M. (March, 2008). *A teaching-as-service program's impacts on program participants: A survey of program alumni*. Paper presented at the annual meeting of the American Educational Research Association, New York, NY.

Wirt, F. M., & Kirst, M. (1989). *Schools in conflict: The politics of education.* Berkeley, CA: McCutcheon.

Wolcott, H. F. (2001). Writing up qualitative research (2nd ed.). Thousand Oaks, CA: Sage.

Wolfman, I. (2003, October). Saving America's toughest schools: Class action. *Reader's Digest*, 74-81.

Yaqub, R. (2002, December). To give well, give wisely: As more Americans are bearish about giving, charity is even more needed. *Worth Magazine, 11*(10), 91.

Zeichner, K. M. (2003). The adequacies and inadequacies of three current strategies to recruit, prepare and train the best teachers for all students. *Teacher College Record, 105*(4), 490-519.

Zenilman, A. (2006, September). Now that's classy: How Teach For America turned national service into a status symbol. *The Washington Monthly, 38*(9), 35.

LaVergne, TN USA
08 February 2011
215664LV00002B/5/P